How to build
REALISTIC
Model Railroad
SCENERY

MODEL RAILROAD HANDBOOK NO. 16

BY DAVE FRARY   PHOTOGRAPHY BY THE AUTHOR

Editor: Bob Hayden   Art Director: Lawrence Luser
Copy Editor: George Drury   Assistant Editor: Marcia Stern
Editorial Secretary: Monica Freitag   Artist: Lisa Bergman

KALMBACH K BOOKS

FIRST EDITION, 1982. Second printing, 1982. Third printing, 1983. Fourth printing, 1986.
Fifth printing, 1988. Sixth printing, 1989. SECOND EDITION, 1991. Second printing, 1992

PRODUCTS, MANUFACTURERS, AND SUPPLIES MENTIONED IN THIS BOOK

Hydrocal — correctly called "white Hydrocal gypsum cement," is a product of the Tool and Casting Divison of United States Gypsum Co., 101 S. Wacker Drive, Chicago, IL 60606. Write the manufacturer for the name of your nearest dealer.

Sculptamold — is a white, non-toxic, clay-based sculpting product available in craft and hobby shops. It combines the best features of clay, plaster, and papier-mâché. It is mixed with water and sets in about 30 minutes. It will cling to most surfaces and will not shrink when it hardens. It is made and distributed by American Art Clay Co., 4717 W. Sixteenth Street, Indianapolis, IN 46222.

Flexwax 120 — available from Nasco, listed below, and Edmund Scientific Co., 101 E. Gloucester Pike, Barrington, NJ 08007-1380

Air-Opaque — Badger Air-Brush Co., 9128 W. Belmont Avenue, Franklin Park, IL 60131

Ultraviolet filters — Fluorescent bulb jackets sold by Solar Screen Corp., 53-11 105 Street, Corona, NY 11368, (718) 592-8222. Free price listing.

Rigid Wrap — Activa Products, Inc., P. O. Box 1296, Marshall, TX 75670

Art and craft supplies — Nasco, 901 Janesville Avenue, Fort Atkinson, WI 53538-0901, (414) 563-2446. Free catalog.

Rock and retaining wall molds — Blue Ribbon Models, P. O. Box 333, Swampscott, MA 01945. Send SSAE with two first-class stamps for brochure.

Scenery materials: foam, trees, weeds, etc.
Timber Products, 2029 E. Howe Avenue, Tempe, AZ 85281, (602) 894-1678.

AMSI Scale Model Supplies, 115-B Bellam Boulevard, P. O. Box 3497, San Rafael, CA 94912, (415) 457-6100.

Woodland Scenics, Box 98, Linn Creek, MO 65052

William K. Walthers, P. O. Box 18676, Milwaukee, WI 53218

Library of Congress Cataloging-in-Publication Data

Frary, Dave, 1940-.
    How to build realistic model railroad scenery / Dave Frary. —
Rev. ed.
        p.   cm.
        ISBN 0-89024-124-4
        1. Railroads—Models.   I. Title.
TF197.F68 1991
625.1'9—dc20   91-37623
                 CIP

Acknowledgments

The techniques in this book were gathered and developed over almost 35 years of scenery building. While many of the methods are my own, some were graciously volunteered by other model builders or were developed through the collaborative efforts of many people.

My most sincere thanks go to the following modelers for sharing their ideas and providing assistance: Bob Hayden, Pete Laier, John Olson, Harold Reynolds, and George Sellios.

Dedication

The second edition of this book is dedicated
to the memory of

Allan Hanson

a good friend, neighbor, and pioneer HOn2 modeler, who introduced me to narrow gauge modeling. Allan spent thousands of hours helping me improve my story telling, layout building, and mechanical skills, and he helped me find the true rewards of having lifelong hobbies.

New materials and techniques: the water-soluble scenery method

In a practical sense the only function of model railroad scenery is to provide a realistic setting for the trains to run through, and the better the scenery, the more believable the trains become. The drama of a streamliner rolling across the country at speed or the fascinating deliberation of a peddler freight slowly switching empties on a weed-grown branch cannot be duplicated without scenery, and an accurately detailed train running through convincing scenery makes for an illusion of reality that isn't often achieved in other kinds of modeling.

Scenery does other things for your railroad, too. By covering the necessarily out-of-scale benchwork, scenery keeps viewers from looking below track level to the underpinnings and mechanical details. Scenery brings the viewer's eye to the surface of the layout, where the interest and action are. Scenery also protects your rolling stock by keeping it off the floor. (Until the scenery on my railroad was built, almost every piece of rolling stock ended up on the floor, either from derailments or elbows.)

For many (including me), scenery

INTRODUCTION

For me, the most rewarding aspect of model railroading is scenery building. Here, on my HOn2½ Carrabasset & Dead River Ry., the scenery was intentionally built so that it dwarfs the narrow gauge trains and the tiny backwoods structures.

(Left) Even without scenery, the trains and individual models make every model railroad interesting, but add scenery and your pike becomes a realistic model world.

Measures you'll need: Coffee can, small jar, eyedropper, kitchen spoons, and a tongue depressor with inch marks.

building is the part of model railroading they like best; for others, it's a hobby within the hobby that provides an outlet for their creative talents. However, scenery building need not be an artistic endeavor. If you can paint a boxcar, build a structure kit, or follow an operating schedule, you can build excellent, believable scenery.

A new set of techniques. Build-

ing good scenery is the least expensive part of constructing a model railroad, and the scenery techniques I have developed over the past ten years were made possible by the introduction and popularity of water-base latex paints. For a long time I sought a system that would give realistic results that were quick and easy — scenery techniques that would be predictable and repeatable time after time, on either a large model railroad or a small diorama. Latex paint and other modern water-soluble materials have made such a system possible.

For me, building scenery is a continuous experiment to develop and refine techniques that match my temperament and ability. Those techniques must produce good results with a minimum of talent, because I'm a technician, not an artist. That's why I wanted a systematic approach, one that uses only inexpensive, easy-to-obtain materials. The system I have settled on uses water-soluble materials for scenery construction wherever possible.

Everything dilutes with water: The plaster scenery base materials mix with water, the scenery coloring is water-base latex paint, dyes and stains mix with water, and the adhesives used to hold texture materials in place are water soluble. Cleanup is easy and tools and brushes last almost forever.

Because water is the common denominator, scenery building goes along as fast as you can work, without waiting for one layer or texture to dry before applying the next. You can start an area after dinner and finish the scene before retiring for the night. The next morning everything will be dry and fastened in place, ready for you to touch up the detail and "plant" some weeds. Water-soluble scenery is so fast and easy that I completely scenicked a 4' x 10' railroad in just a week of evenings.

Nothing required for this scenery building method is rare or exotic; you can find all of the supplies you'll need in craft, hobby, art, hardware, or department stores. And, if you take reasonable care in their application, these water-base materials will not damage anything on your railroad except perhaps old-fashioned fiber-tie track. All of the materials are nontoxic, and if used correctly none of them will produce allergic reactions.

How to use this book. Before we get started, I should tell you how this book is set up. First, and foremost, it's a how-to-do-it book; you won't find much here about the history of building model railroad scenery, about geology, or about the theory of color perception. What you will find are methods that have worked for me and for others, and that will work for you.

The chapters that follow cover scenic planning (with a smattering of theory), building scenic forms, adding color and texture, simulating rock and dirt, achieving depth by adding finished textures, making foliage, modeling water, building background and foreground scenery, achieving special scenic effects, refurbishing your old scenery, and modeling the changing seasons. Throughout, I've described methods that work for me rather than surveying all possible methods. For that, I heartily recommend that you obtain two other books: Bill McClanahan's classic SCENERY FOR MODEL RAILROADS, and SCENERY TIPS AND TECHNIQUES FROM MODEL RAILROADER.

Because I hope you'll use this book rather than just read it, I've tried to make the on-the-spot information you will need to refer to again and again as prominent as possible. As you page through the book, you'll find recipe-card boxes that list key ingredients and formulas. Once you've read the whole book and tried most of the techniques, these boxes will serve as your

INTRODUCTION

TOOLS, MATERIALS, AND STANDARD MEASURES

This is a list of basic tools and materials you will need to build scenery as described in this book. Most of these items can be obtained as you need them. If you can't locate some of the tools or materials mentioned, don't be afraid to substitute something similar; it will probably work just as well.

Spring-type clothespins
Scissors
Modeling and mat knives
Steel straightedge
Staple gun
Plastic mixing bowls
Rubber kitchen spatula
Butter knife
Pump-type spray bottles
Paintbrushes from size 00 to 2½" wide
Tweezers
Awl or ice pick
1-cup measuring cup
Teaspoon
Set of kitchen measuring spoons
Eyedropper

I'll mention special modeling and scenery products as we go along, but you can probably find most of these common materials around your house or workshop:

Corrugated cardboard
Scraps of Styrofoam
White glue
Paper towels
Newspaper
Wetting agent or liquid detergent (Kodak Photo-Flo, Joy)
1- and 2-pound coffee cans with plastic lids
Baby food jars or other small jars with lids
Gauze pads or rolls

To obtain repeatable results when you build scenery, you must observe a few simple measuring procedures. When adding ingredients to a measuring cup, make sure there are no air pockets trapped inside the cup and that the ingredients are level with the top. There are several places in this book where I mention using a "heaping cupful." This means you scoop up a full cup of the ingredients, letting the cup hold all it can.

When using a regular spoonful the ingredients in it should be rounded, but a "level teaspoon" means the ingredients are even with the top of the spoon. When using a kitchen measuring spoon, all measurements are with the ingredients level with the top of the spoon.

When using tube-type acrylics, determine the correct amount by measuring the length of paint squeezed from the tube. The best way to do this is to mark the flat side of a tongue depressor with lines 1", 2", and 3" from one end. Squeeze the acrylic onto the flat part of the depressor starting on the correct line. Use the tip of the depressor to separate the paint from the tube spout.

The smallest measurement I use is the drop. Always measure drops with an eyedropper so each is the same size. Eyedroppers are available at all drugstores. Count the drops as they fall, and always wash the eyedropper immediately after use.

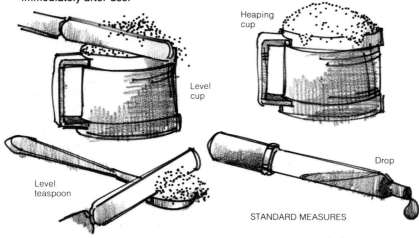

Heaping cup

Level cup

Level teaspoon

Drop

STANDARD MEASURES

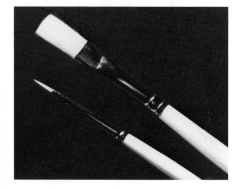

Artist's brushes for scenery. The largest (top) is 1″ wide, the smallest (bottom photo) is No. 00. You'll also need one or two standard 2½″ paintbrushes.

ready reference for repeating previous results. For more general reference, you'll also find an index at the back of the book. Finally, most chapters end with a question-and-answer section that tackles scenic problems fellow modelers have told me about over the years.

Let's get started! I hope by now you're convinced that I've got a new and easy way to build model railroad scenery with common, inexpensive materials, and without vast amounts of time or artistic talent. Now roll up your sleeves and let's begin.

Sculptamold is available in craft stores. To mix and apply it, I use a table knife, palette knives, and a tongue depressor.

INTRODUCTION

This planning model for the HO display railroad shown throughout this book took just two evenings to build. It was a great aid during construction of the actual layout.

Designing scenery with plans and models

No step in building scenery — or in any kind of modeling, for that matter — is as important as planning in advance what you want to build. For me, scenic planning involves three things: an understanding of what model scenery really is, a smattering of research, and a willingness to experiment with dozens of ideas until you find a scheme that you like. Once you've tried it, you'll find that planning scenery is almost as much fun as actually building it.

What model scenery really is. Some modelers select a specific prototype railroad, others base their layouts on track plans published in magazines, and others choose a geographic region such as the Rockies or the eastern coal country and design a free-lance railroad to fit in. No matter which part of the world you choose, it's important to realize that model railroad scenery only represents your impressions of that area. Model scenery can never be a replica of real terrain in the same sense that our locomotives and cars are scale replicas of actual objects, because none of us have enough space for that.

Regardless of how much thought we put into it — and how hard we try — this business of making model railroad scenery is at best a matter of building an effective caricature of real landscape. To some extent every model railroad ends up looking like a Hollywood movie set, that is, the buildings are stylized and the landscape condensed until the scene fits into the available space. If done well, the scene is both convincing and easily recognized as the prototype locale, but in reality it contains only a few key elements — and very little of the vastness — of genuine landscape.

If we tried to build scenery as a scale replica of nature, we'd soon give up in frustration. What we try to build is scenery that is an illusion. The illusion will work as long as the scenery looks good and can be recognized for the area it portrays. The geology and other physical aspects of a prototype locale must be changed to suit the illusion. For example, model river banks must be steeper and the rivers themselves much narrower than the real thing. Even though our mountains and lakes are far too small, they can still convey the look and feel of nature.

Simple geology (or the lack of it). There is no need for model railroaders to know the hows and whys of geological theory. In fact, such knowledge can slow down and confuse a thoughtful modelbuilder, by making him worry about whether his scenery is correct when he should only worry if it is convincing. If you are a good observer and can take notes on the area you are modeling, your scenery will be a good representation of your prototype locale. I can think of only one geologic principle that applies to model scenery: Wind, water, and gravity move everything (land masses, rocks, water, even trees) from high elevations to lower ones. If you keep this in mind, along with the idea that what you are building is really an illusion, your scenery will look natural.

If you are interested in learning about geology and how it applies to model railroading, read the excellent section by Linn Westcott in Bill McClanahan's book, SCENERY FOR MODEL RAILROADS.

Getting the feel of the landscape. To effectively capture the prototype locale you wish to model you must do some research. If you live nearby, all it takes is a weekend family outing with a camera. Take detailed notes: Are the dirt and soil colors the same as those close to home? Are the rocks like the ones you are familiar with — and what colors are they? Are most of the trees coniferous, deciduous, or a mixture of types — and what shades of green are their foliage? Record these facts with your camera, in a notebook, and in your memory so you can refer to them later.

Getting the feel of the area is just as important as gathering lots of facts. First impressions may be fine when dealing with people, but when you are

CHAPTER 1

View blocks around this scene on my railroad screen out other areas that are adjacent to it.

trying to build a convincing model of an area you need lasting impressions.

If you aren't able to visit your prototype area, the information needed to model these places must be obtained secondhand. A good place to start is your public library. Start by leafing through large "coffee table" color picture books, looking for photos that show what you have in mind for your layout. Next try to find photos showing structures or terrain. A good collection of model railroad books and magazines will also provide helpful information.

Developing scenic ideas along with the track plan. It is important to plan scenery at the same time as you plan the track. Concocting a model railroad with long-lasting appeal is similar to designing an amusement park like Disneyland. The route of the railroad, the architecture of the structures, and the locations of connecting railroads, waterways, and controlled viewing angles have to be planned to interrelate with each other to produce a total visual effect.

Once you've selected the theme of your railroad and drawn the track plan, it's time to design the scenery. Most of the time I do this by doodling all my ideas on scraps of paper, then choosing what strikes me as best. The most important concept you should keep in mind while doodling is that your railroad should be divided into scenes, regardless of how small or large it is.

Scenery can greatly "expand" a

small model railroad by dividing the layout into distinct viewing areas. A lot of small layouts have been made to look much larger by carefully planned scenery. If you wonder how this works, just stand outdoors and look around you. Unless you're on top of a mountain or in the middle of a desert, your line of sight will be blocked after a hundred yards or so by natural or man-made barriers.

On the layout, hills, rock cuts, trees, and buildings make effective view blocks. These block areas need only be large (or dense) enough to stop the viewer from looking into adjacent scenes. In stopping to study one scene before moving his attention to the next, the viewer devotes more time to each. Done well, view blocks will leave visitors with the impression that your railroad is much larger than it first appeared to them.

Using theme scenes. Large home or club layouts can be divided into theme scenes to add interest and seemingly expand the space. Each theme scene should have a distinct type of scenery or industry as its center of interest. A mountain theme scene, for example, could be further divided into smaller viewing areas. One viewing area could contain a mine, another a trestle over a ravine, and the next a rough-and-tumble western town clinging to the side of the mountain.

Another example of an overall theme scene might be a railroad connection with the waterfront, divided

into controlled viewing areas such as docks for loading ships, an ore processing plant, and small water-related industries surrounded by city structures. By carefully limiting the visitor's line of vision and making him concentrate on one scene at a time, the visual interest of a larger railroad is expanded to the point where it can't be fully digested or appreciated during one visit.

Developing a scenic plan. To refine your track plan and to make sure the scenery will fit, draw the outlines of the space available for the railroad and the general shape of the benchwork (if you know what it will look like) with a black felt-tip pen, then make several duplicates with a copy machine. Use these sheets to doodle track arrangements and to develop your scenic plans. Note I said "plans," because even after I settle on a track plan I usually work up several scenic treatments, each with its own flavor.

Often, when I'm working up the early treatment for a layout, I draw several track configurations and scenic treatments just for the sake of change. Sometimes this "forced change" will produce new track arrangements and scenes that are far better than the first thing I put down.

Next I transfer the accumulated doodles and sketches onto homemade graph paper. The squares can represent any scale, as long as your whole railroad will fit comfortably on one sheet (for large layouts, tape several sheets together). I draw my plans so

CHAPTER 1

J. C. Myer

Baja Arriba, a Pacific seacoast town on J. C. Myer's layout (above), and the cluttered industrial area at Arcadia on Pete Laier's Arcadia Terminal RR. (below) are good examples of well-thought-out and well-executed theme scenes.

that ½" equals 1'. Make cardstock circles representing each track radius you plan to use to serve as handy templates for drawing accurate track curves. Lightly sketch in all the roads, buildings, rivers, and even rock cuts.

Your final, formal plan will always represent a combination of ideas taken from two or more of your preliminary scenic treatments. Draw this plan carefully, adding as many details and notes as possible to describe the scenic treatment. (Nothing is worse than having a good idea and forgetting it!) Draw track with black felt-tip pen, water in blue, roads and other dirt areas in yellow, buildings in brown, and hills in green. After you complete the plan, put it away for several days and then come back to it, looking for

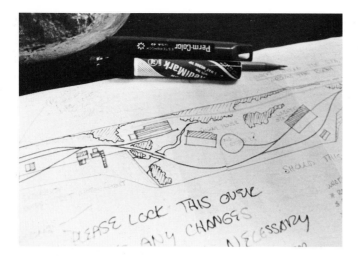

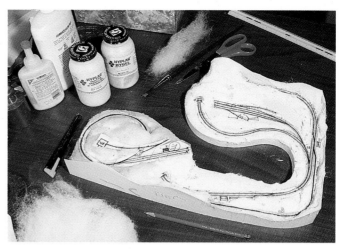

I used this large-scale plan to help design a large section of my layout. At one point, I mailed it to a friend for his comments.

This 1"=1' miniature layout consists of cardboard benchwork and poly fiberfill scenery coated with matte medium.

obvious errors or omissions. Also check to see if the scenery still has the interest and impact that you want.

Remember, it's OK to over plan. Write down everything you can think of to add to the layout. List the different types of industries needed, unique scenic features, types of bridges and culverts wanted, track, scenery and city details, ideas you want to develop further, and major projects in the order they need to be accomplished. The more lists you generate the easier it will be to find small, quick projects on those days when you don't feel like tackling a large one.

Miniature layout models. The ultimate scenery planning aid is a miniature layout model. I often build a model of a proposed layout at a scale of 1"=1' — about the right size to show detail, yet small enough so it takes only a couple of evenings to build. I've also used miniature layouts to study things other than track and scenery: Lighting, benchwork, backgrounds, control areas, and visitor flow are only a few handy uses.

Start by ruling a piece of heavy cardstock or thin plywood with a grid of lines 1" apart. Draw in the area the railroad will occupy and a scale outline of the room, noting doors, windows, and electrical outlets. This is the base that the model will be built on.

The layout plan was drawn to a scale of 1/2"=1', so it has to be enlarged to 1"=1' to fit on the base. My local print shop has a copy machine that will enlarge without distortion and only charges a few dollars for several copies. Glue one of the enlarged copies to stiff cardboard and cut out around the track lines with a sharp knife. (You'll need a second copy of the track plan where tracks cross over each other.) This produces a floppy, cookie-cutter roadbed in 1" scale. Position it on the base and establish the outlines of the benchwork.

Build a 1" scale model of the benchwork to fit under the track plan. Use stripwood, or strips of cardstock cut to scale size with a paper cutter; assemble the parts with white glue. The benchwork model allows me to figure the amount of wood I need, saving on waste later. It also provides the mounting base for the cookie-cutter roadbed. Add small pieces of card-

board for the track risers, just as you will on the full-size benchwork, then add the paper roadbed and photocopied track.

There are several ways to form scenic contours on the layout model. Start by wetting small pieces of paper and cardboard and working them into place as rough contours. My favorite material for forming the final contours is Sculptamold, a commercial scenery product found in art and craft stores. Sculptamold can be applied directly over the wet paper, has good texture, and dries lightweight and hard to the touch. It's also easy to color with water-soluble paints.

On some models I've made the scenery from good old non-drying modeling clay. The clay can be worked indefinitely with any tool that is handy, and after the model has served its purpose, the clay can be stripped off and used again.

I've also tried placing wads of poly fiberfill to rough out the scenery contours, then brushing matte medium over it, pushing and shaping the fiberfill with the point of the brush until I have contours that I like. When the

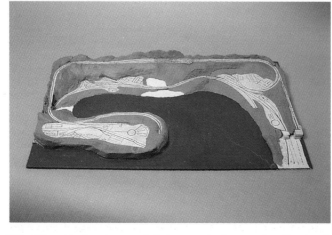

This ¾" = 1' planning model was made by copying the track plan, adding stripwood risers, and building contours from clay.

Small wood blocks representing buildings help you to assess their impact on the scenery and to decide where to put them.

CHAPTER 1

Installing layout lighting before you start construction is not just a good idea, it's a must.

matte medium dries it forms a tough, flexible shell. I troweled acrylic modeling paste in areas to represent rock faces and colored the model with acrylic paints. Coarse foam rubber was sprinkled on the wet paint to represent wooded areas.

When the scenery dries, cut scrap blocks of wood to the sizes and shapes of the buildings on your plan and add them to the model. Move them around until you find pleasing groupings. How detailed you make such a model is up to you. If constructed carefully, it is a valuable construction tool because many measurements can be scaled directly from it. The layout model also makes a great conversation piece and can be referred to until the full-size railroad is well on its way toward completion.

The full-size plan. Now, with a full-color drawing and a model to study, it's time to transfer the complicated parts of the layout to a full-size drawing. Select areas where there's congestion, tight curves or multiple tracks stacked over one another, or where streets interfere with industries. Draw these full size so you can spot errors in planning and correct them now, before construction.

Start with a 4'-wide roll of paper banquet table covering from a paper goods store. (If you don't have a lot of room you can draw the full-size plan in sections and tape the sections together later on top of the benchwork.) Draw grid lines on the paper,

scaling them up from your full-color drawing. Then scale up the track, scenic contours, and buildings just as they appeared on the small finished plan or your model.

Place track sections over the track center lines and draw outlines around them to establish how much room the track will take. Track always takes up more room than expected, and this step eliminates many serious spacing errors. Make paper copies of right- and left-hand turnouts by placing them on a copy machine. Cut these out and tape them to the full-size plan, aligning them with the track outlines. I also make photocopies of all bridge piers to be used. These are taped in place and the bridges, if already built, can be set over these.

In the same vein, place tunnel portals and any built-up structures you have on the full-size plan to see how they will look together. If you haven't built the structures yet but have the kits, make photocopies of the bases to use as positioning aides. I usually don't plan enough room around buildings, and working with them at full size forces me to space them out better before marking final locations. To represent unbuilt structures, I make cardboard-and-tape mock-ups so that height, as well as length and width, can be evaluated.

Important scenic features, such as view blocks, can be simulated on the full-size plan by taping large wads of crumpled newspaper to the drawing.

These mounds of paper help you judge how high a hill or how deep a rock cut should be. The value of the full-size plan is that it gives you a good idea of where everything will be placed and how each major element will look in relation to all the others. You can study the plan for hours and work out all the details before you commit materials or money to the project.

After building benchwork, spread the full-size plan on it and evaluate your planning once again. You'll probably notice one or two areas that require minor changes as you study the plan at benchwork height. This isn't necessarily the last time you'll use the plan; on one small railroad I glued the full-size plan directly to plywood and used it as a pattern for cutting the roadbed, saving hours of redrawing the track outlines.

Planning and installing lighting. One more thing you must consider under the general topic of scenic planning is lighting. Putting lots of light over your layout ensures that visitors will see and appreciate it. I once made the mistake of installing railroad lighting after benchwork construction was well under way. If I'd prepared a simple lighting sketch before I started building, a lot of awkward, backbreaking work could have been avoided.

Regular fluorescent light is good for viewing models because it is soft and diffuse, but fluorescent tubes produce a discontinuous color spectrum — some of the colors of light that

Full-size planning is especially important in yards and industrial areas that will include lots of track and buildings.

should be present are missing. This isn't apparent when you view the layout in person, but if you try to photograph your railroad with color film using only fluorescents for illumination, white subjects will look greenish-blue or reddish-yellow, depending upon the type of tubes you use. (Fluorescents have no effect on black-and-white photos.)

To solve this color balance problem the lights over my railroad are special 5000-degree Kelvin tubes made by GE (lamp No. F40C50 Chroma 50), available through theatrical lighting houses and large electrical supply companies. These tubes are used in store displays and museum dioramas, and for movie and video work where fluorescent lights must be combined with daylight. They cost about $5 each and last about as long as a regular tube. They are a perfect match for daylight film, so no extra lights are needed for photography.

I use 48" fluorescent fixtures that hold two 40-watt tubes for most of my railroad illumination. I space these fixtures about 4' apart and about 2' from walls and corners (for an average ceiling height). The fixtures are inexpensive to purchase and operate, and easy to install; just hang them up and plug them in. Fluorescents give off little heat, and a single 40-watt tube provides the same amount of light as a 150-watt incandescent bulb.

Along with the fluorescent light fixtures my layout has incandescent spotlights along the front edge. These are made from 100-watt bulbs mounted in one-pound coffee cans, and highlight the front of the layout with pools of warmer light. The spots should all point in the same direction to avoid phony-looking double shadows. More information on layout lighting and on building these simple spots can be found in John Armstrong's book, CREATIVE MODEL RAILROAD DESIGN.

One modeler I know placed cool-white fluorescent lamps around the rear edge of his layout, but illuminated the rest of the pike with 100-watt incandescent bulbs. When his layout is viewed from the front the cool-white lamps give the feeling of looking through layers of atmospheric haze into the distance, an excellent and subtle effect.

As important as light is over the railroad, it is even more important over your workbench. Use the same types of lights you have over the layout so you can paint models under the same light they will be viewed under. My workbench lights are about 3' above the work surface, which helps reduce eye fatigue.

Don't rush it! Finally, don't short-change scenic planning because you're in a hurry to start building. Take your time, and give your ideas time to develop. If you've got an itch to start, consider building a diorama or module that can fit into the layout later, but don't rush into building scenery on the layout itself without thinking through what you want and carefully planning the scenes and effects. Sure, planning takes time, but in the end you'll save time, effort, and materials — and more important, planning will help you achieve the results you really want.

CHAPTER 1

Gentle hills or rugged mountains: It's all cardboard web and plaster underneath. This is the scene shown under construction below.

Building scenic forms and shells

Scenery — and for that matter, all modeling — has three general characteristics: form, color, and texture. Just as we must build the basic body of a boxcar model before we can add color and texture to it, the first step in scenery building is to erect a framework and add a shell over it to provide form, or scenic contours.

The scenic support should be easy to build, and it need only be strong enough to support the weight of the scenic shell and perhaps a few structures. I've tried many combinations of support and skin materials over the years, and the one I've settled on as easiest to use is a lattice-like web of corrugated cardboard strips covered by a thin hard shell of plaster-soaked paper towels. With a few exceptions — which we'll get to later in this chapter — this is the system I use for all scenery building.

Cardboard web scenic support. A web of corrugated cardboard is light,

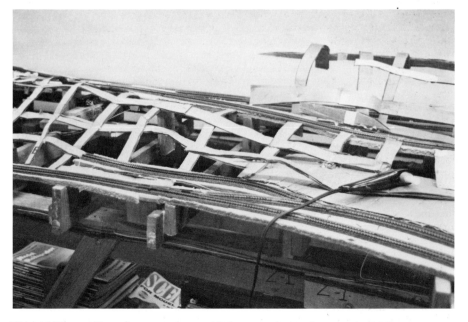

The weblike cardboard scenery support is inexpensive and easy to build. To save time, I used hot-melt glue instead of white glue and clothespins to build this section.

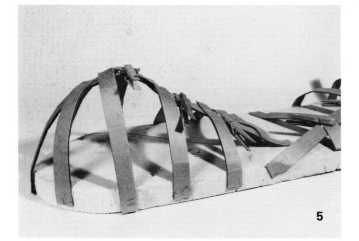

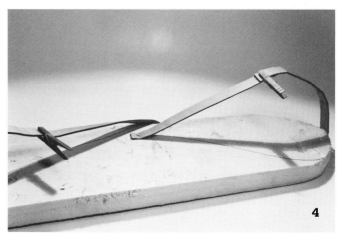

To build the web scenery support (photo 1), cut corrugated cardboard into 1″-wide strips using a straightedge and a sharp mat knife (2). The strips can be any length, and they are easier to form if the corrugations run perpendicular to the long edge. The tools needed to build the web are scissors, staple gun, spring clothespins, and white glue (3). Start by gluing and stapling ridge strips to form hill profiles (4). Use the clothespins to hold sections of cardboard together until the glue dries. Next install vertical strips 4″-6″ apart. Bend and twist them to form the side contours (5). Neatness doesn't count when gluing the strips. Now add horizontal webbing (6). Hold the strips in place, cut to length, then glue and clamp with clothespins. After all strips are added, test the web for strength by pushing gently on it (7). It should be strong and fairly springy. If you want to change the web to make a hill smaller or to push the scenery away from the track for more clearance, just press with the palm of your hand until you crush the web enough to change it. If the web springs back when you let go, add another strip of cardboard and glue it to the crushed area and to the base to hold the web where you want it.

CHAPTER 2

rigid, and surprisingly strong. It holds its shape even when several layers of plaster-soaked paper are laid over it. Corrugated cardboard is usually free for the asking, and you don't need special tools to cut, form, or fasten it to the layout. One big advantage it has over other scenic supports is that the scenery base is hollow, so you can use the area under the scenery to store modeling supplies. The open construction also allows access to switch machines and other mechanical devices that must be located beneath the surface of the railroad.

Before web construction begins I staple clear plastic dropcloth (called "rolled plastic sheeting" at building supply centers) or plastic garbage bags to the underside of the benchwork to catch glue drips, plaster slops, and paint leaks. The plastic can be removed and thrown away after the scenery is built.

Start by cutting corrugated cardboard into 1"-wide strips. The strips will be easier to form if the corrugations, the "grain," run perpendicular to the length of the strip. Use a straightedge and a sharp utility or mat knife (an X-Acto knife will work but the blades dull quickly), and work on a scrap wood surface such as a length of 1 x 4 or a rectangle of plywood. Short strips, up to a foot long, can be cut on a paper cutter, if you have one.

The tools you need to build the webbing are scissors, a staple gun, white glue, and some spring clothespins. A clamp- or pliers-type stapler, while something of a luxury, can replace the clothespins and glue. I also use a hot glue gun for attaching webbing in places where a clothespin or stapler will not work. The hot glue gun allows you to work rapidly, attaching webbing as fast as you can set it in place. Be careful though — I've burned myself badly with hot glue drips; wear heavy cloth gloves and eye protection.

Start by cutting a cardboard profile former for the end of the scenery where it comes to the edge of the layout. Leave a 1$\frac{1}{2}$" tab on the bottom of this end piece so it can be glued and stapled to the benchwork. Then install a ridge strip on the top edge of this end piece. Bend and shape the ridge strip to form the contour of the top of the hill, and leave a 1$\frac{1}{2}$" tab on both ends. Glue one tab to the top of the end piece and use a clothespin to hold it in place while the glue sets.

The next step is to draw a base line, representing the limit beyond which the bottom edge of the hill should not encroach upon track or other features. Now install a vertical webbing strip about every 6", with its bottom just touching the base line. Bend the vertical strips to form them into the rough shape of the hillside,

This old glove with a heavy wrap of duct tape around the index finger is used to soften up cardboard strips for webbing. The stiff cardboard strips are pulled and bent over the taped finger make them more flexible and easier to work with.

Cardboard strips can be added anywhere to make a transition from old scenery to new. Here the strips are glued and stapled in place between an old section of the layout and a slab of Styrofoam that will serve as the base for a new industry.

then staple and glue each to the edge of the roadbed or layout base. Finally, use glue and clothespins to fasten the vertical strips to the ridge strip. Cut the strips to length as you go, either by tearing off the excess or using scissors.

Now install the horizontal strips, also spaced about 6" apart. Glue and staple them where they touch the layout framework or roadbed, and glue and clamp them where they overlap one another. Remove the clothespins as the glue sets, and check the web by gently pushing on it; it should spring back to shape after each push. After you've had a little practice, you'll be able to cut and install cardboard webbing as fast as you can glue the strips.

By the way, on several scenery projects I tried weaving the horizontal strips over and under the verticals.

While this sounds as if it might add strength (like basket weaving), this method took additional time and I didn't notice any extra strength.

Revising the web. This system is flexible. If you don't like the contours of the web, snip away at it with scissors and try again. If an area is too high or wide, crush it down to the desired shape, then either hold the web in that position with masking tape or staple another cardboard strip between the base and the crushed area. After the plaster-soaked paper towel shell is applied these temporary supports may be removed.

Very large sections of webbing may be supported with triangular cardboard "beams." Cut the cardboard to length, then fold and tape it into a triangular cross section, leaving a tab at each end. Staple, glue, or pin the

CHAPTER 2

(Left) Convincing tunnel portal interiors need only be finished as far as the viewer can see. The tunnel walls here are simply black cardboard. (Right) The tunnel interior on this portable layout was closer to the foreground, so I finished it with a pre-cast section of dark-colored rock.

beam in position until the plaster shell sets. If the web section is long, the support should be left under the scenery permanently. On shorter sections the support beam may be removed after the plaster sets.

Tunnel portals and interior walls. Before covering the cardboard web with plaster you must give some thought to areas of the railroad that will become inaccessible. Make sure you have several reach-in areas to clean hidden track and remove derailed cars. Engineer the placement of the cardboard webbing to allow easy access to these areas.

The interiors of tunnels, at least the walls that can be seen when you look into the mountain, should be finished now, before the tunnel is covered with plaster-soaked paper towels.

I like to leave enough room inside the tunnel that I can stick my hand into the tunnel if a train derails. This works out to 4" wide and 4" high in HO scale, oversize by NMRA standards, but just right for the times when I have to extract a boxcar or two. Plan to build the cardboard web opening a little larger than this to allow for the thickness of the plaster-soaked paper towels, interior walls, and tunnel portals.

Tunnel portals should be installed while the cardboard web is being coat-ed with plaster to ensure a correct fit. Portals can be cast from rock molds, built from wood or cardstock, or purchased at the hobby shop. Dozens of styles are available for every era and scale.

To create the illusion of a solid mountain, view blocks are needed inside the tunnel. These keep prying eyes from wandering into the tunnel and seeing the raw plaster and scenic framework. They can be as simple as a piece of black cardboard or printed stone paper glued to a Fome-Cor backing, or as elaborate as a highly detailed rock face with lots of blasting rubble at its base. They should be dark colored and extend far enough into the tunnel so that they block the view from normal viewing angles.

The inner walls of foreground tunnels, where the detail is important, can be made using rubber molds (described in chapter 4). The wall castings can be poured and colored on the workbench and glued in place. Pre-cast plastic foam walls, polyester rocks, or retaining walls available from several manufacturers can be added. A few tunnel portals even come with a matching interior wall. A lightweight inner wall can be made from a crinkled sheet of aluminum foil, held in place with hot glue and colored with dark earth spray paint.

I color tunnel interiors with the basic earth color (Chapter 3) which has about 10 percent black added to it. The color should darken gradually, from the darkened earth color at the tunnel mouth to straight black at the rear edge of the inner wall.

After the inner walls are in place protect them (and the track) from plaster drips with a covering of plastic wrap. This will be removed after the surrounding scenery is completed.

Styrofoam as a scenery base. Flat sheets of Styrofoam, a common extruded rigid plastic foam used for packaging and insulation, makes a lightweight base for layout construction, and it's a reasonable alternative to the cardboard-strip method. As a scenery base Styrofoam can be cut, stacked, and shaped with knives, rasps, and even rotary power tools (Stanley Surform tools work especially well). Because of its expense, I consider this material suitable only for portable layouts and other special applications where its light weight, strength, and resilience are needed. You'll find a complete discussion of the techniques I use to shape and finish Styrofoam scenery in Chapter 10.

The plaster scenery shell. After the scenery base — either cardboard webbing or Styrofoam — is constructed, work can start on the plaster shell,

Add cardboard "wings" around bridges and tunnel portals to provide a surface to which the web strips can be attached.

Instead of adding fancy front paneling, I prefer to bring the scenery down over the front edge of my layout. Support is simple.

CHAPTER 2

To complete the scenery base, hand-size pieces of paper towel are dipped in thin plaster and laid over the web.

or skin. There are many types of plaster, and it is not critical which you choose as long as it sets hard in a reasonable amount of time. It only has to be strong enough to support itself, the textured surface, and an occasional elbow. Although I've used Hydrocal, the alabaster plaster recommended by Linn Westcott for his famous hard shell and zip texturing techniques, with excellent results, here in the Northeast I often have trouble finding it. Instead, I usually use molding plaster (sometimes called casting plaster), a fine grade of plaster with a smooth texture.

In many areas of the country plaster products in bulk are hard to find. Try a masonry contractor or building material supplier; if they don't carry Hydrocal or molding plaster ask about other plaster-based products. One product is floor leveling mix. The brand names change from place to place, but most floor leveling mixes contain Hydrocal and a filler which produces a smooth surface and sets hard in about 20 minutes.

Patching plaster is a coarse grade of molding plaster with a retarder added to slow its setting. I have used it for small scenic jobs with good results. Patching plaster usually comes only in small quantities, so it is quite expensive.

For best results, whatever plaster you use must be as fresh as possible when you buy it. If it has been in a damp warehouse for several months it won't set correctly and won't be as hard as it should be. The best way to tell if plaster is old is to feel it. A fresh bag of plaster will be dusty and will leave a trail of fine powder. Grab a handful; if it feels like cake flour and has a silky texture it is probably fresh. If it feels like sand or is grainy (sometimes it almost has the consistency of oatmeal), it has started to combine with the moisture in the air. Such old plaster will be weak after it sets, if it sets at all. To be assured of a fresh product, always purchase plaster where masonry contractors buy in

large quantities and turn their inventory over often.

I buy plaster in 100-pound bags because it is less expensive than buying smaller quantities. Dry plaster absorbs moisture from the air so it must be stored in an airtight package when not in use. I repackage bulk plaster into 2- or 3-gallon plastic food bags with a twist tie on the top, putting about 5 pounds of plaster in each bag before storing the bags in a tightly covered plastic garbage can. I've had plaster packaged this way stored for more than ten years without deterioration. (Always label the bags so they can't be mistaken for flour!)

How to mix plaster. When plaster is mixed with water the two combine chemically in a process called recrystallization. (During manufacture the water was cooked out.) When recrystallization is complete, the plaster reverts to its original rock-like state. The basic secrets of plaster handling are to mix only the amount of plaster you can use in 3 to 5 minutes, to work fast, and to work the plaster only until it starts to set. When a batch of plaster starts to set, discard what is left in the bucket and mix a fresh batch.

I use a half-gallon plastic ice cream container to mix plaster, and a rubber spatula to stir it. The plastic container allows me to remove leftover plaster after it sets by squeezing and flexing the sides. For small jobs, I line the mixing bowl with a plastic bag, and mix the plaster in the bag. When finished with the job, I throw the plastic bag away along with any leftovers.

Start by pouring one cup of cold tap water into the container. Set it on a level surface and mark the waterline on the outside of the container with a grease pencil; this will be the water mark for future batches. One cup of water plus two cups of plaster makes three cups of mix — enough for 3 to 5 minutes worth of applying paper-towel scenic shell. If you have a helper, mix a larger quantity by doubling the recipe.

Always add plaster to water, never the other way around. While stirring the water, slowly pour in two cups of plaster. Stir the plaster into the water until all lumps are broken up and the mixture reaches the consistency of heavy cream. (If you use a product other than plaster, check the manufacturer's instructions for the correct ratio of dry material to water.)

I use cold water for mixing plaster because it retards setting slightly. (Warm water will speed up setting.) If you find that the plaster sets too fast for you even when using cold tap water, slow it down a little more by adding one tablespoon of vinegar to the water before adding the plaster. This will give you 5 to 10 extra minutes of working time. Refrigerating the water will almost double the working time. There are many variables that affect setting time, including the age of the plaster, the air and water temperatures, and even how hard or soft the water is. If for some reason you want to speed setting time, add a half teaspoon of salt to the water.

By the way, you can't slow down the plaster by using extra water; if you add too much water, the plaster will simply be weak. There is no way to "stretch" plaster; it must be mixed in the correct 2:1 proportion. And, you can't save the semi-set plaster left in the bottom of the bowl by adding water, because once it starts to set the plaster cannot be softened.

Plaster goes through a setting cycle. After it's mixed with water the recrystallization causes it to warm; when the reaction is complete the plaster begins to cool. Most plasters take about 30 minutes to complete their initial set, and until this happens the plaster is weak and cannot be worked. A good way to tell when the plaster is strong enough to begin coloring and texturing is to feel it. If the plaster is cool it is probably strong enough to start painting. Rewetting the plaster after it has set will not harm it. In fact, it may make it stronger by allowing uncombined plaster

---

MIXING PLASTER

Always use the following sequence:
1. Measure 1 cup cold water into a flexible plastic container.
2. Add coloring, if used. Mix thoroughly.
3. Add retarder, if used.*
4. Slowly add in 2 cups plaster.
5. Stir until smooth.

For harder plaster:
1. Measure 1 cup cold water into a flexible plastic container.
2. Add 1/4 cup (or less) white glue to the water and mix thoroughly.
3. Add coloring, if used. Mix thoroughly.
4. Slowly stir in 2 cups plaster.
5. Stir until smooth.

* If plaster sets too fast, add 1 tablespoon vinegar to 2 cups water or use cold (refrigerated) water.

CHAPTER 2

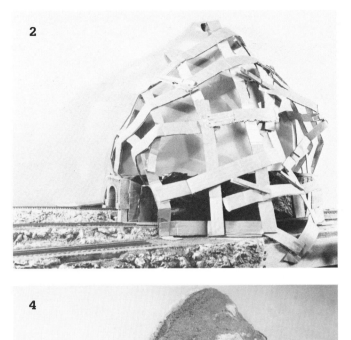

The interiors of the tunnels passing through this mountain were made from crumpled tinfoil painted dark gray (photo 1). After building the cardboard web (2), the covering was applied and brought up to the backdrop to form a gentle fillet (3). The towels are also formed into the tunnel mouth, right up to the tinfoil interior. The finished mountain (4) is ready for final detailing.

molecules to finish recrystallization.

Adding the paper towels. I like plaster-coated paper towels to cover the scenery base. After the plaster is mixed, dip hand-size pieces of paper towel in it and drape them over the cardboard webbing. The paper towels can be either the supermarket roll variety or the institutional type that come as interleaved stacks. The heavier grades — similar to those found in gas stations — work well, and the wet-strength types work best of all, but are quite expensive. All types of paper towels will work as long as they'll hold together long enough to place them over the webbing after they are soaked in the thin plaster. You can substitute brown-paper grocery bags for paper towels; they are strong, stiff, and best of all, free! Prepare the bags or paper towels by tearing or cutting them into hand-size pieces. (When you have a large area to scenic, a paper cutter comes in handy.) I stack the cut pieces in a shoe box for easy handling.

Before mixing the plaster, cover the track with masking tape. For HO track use two 1"-wide strips: The center of each strip covers each rail, and the edges of the tape cover the middle of the track. Protect the floor around

I use molding plaster most often, but plaster of Paris, shown here, also works well. Mix it in a 2-quart plastic container.

Always cover the track with masking tape before applying the plaster-soaked paper towels to the cardboard web.

CHAPTER 2

Small additions, renovations, or repairs can be made easily and neatly with plaster-impregnated gauze. All you need is a regular cardboard-web scenery base, water, and precut strips of Rigid Wrap or Pariscraft (1). Dip each gauze strip in the water and apply it over the web (2). After the gauze shell dries for 10 minutes, it's strong enough to apply a 1/4" layer of Sculptamold (3). Smooth the surface with a large brush dipped in clean water (4). (5) This is how the scenery looks before sprinkling on grass and soil. The pre-painted rock casting was set in place before the Sculptamold was applied. After everything dries it's stronger than a scenic shell built with plaster and paper towels.

the edges of the layout with a drop cloth or newspapers. (You can omit a dropcloth under the layout if you've already stapled plastic to the benchwork.)

If you want a textured surface you could mix a texturing material into the plaster at this point, but I recommend waiting until after the plaster has set and adding the texture to the earth-colored paint. Adding texture now only slows the scenery building process because it makes the plaster lumpy, adds another step to the mixing process, and weakens the scenic skin.

As soon as the plaster is mixed, set the container on the railroad and dip the first piece of paper towel into it. Hold the piece by the top corners, dip it into the plaster, and then lift it out to drain for several seconds. If a

piece balls up or gets wrinkled, gently smooth it out flat. Try to lay the towel so each edge rests on the cardboard web.

It makes little difference whether you start at the top or the bottom, but by starting at the bottom and working toward the top, most plaster drips will fall on areas already covered with toweling. To form a strong shell, overlap each new piece of toweling over the last by a third of its width. (When using plaster-soaked paper towels over Styrofoam, employ the same techniques as on the cardboard web.) As soon as you run out of plaster, wash the container, spatula, and your hands, mix fresh plaster, and continue.

The most efficient way to add paper towels over the cardboard web is to work with another person, one

applying toweling and the other mixing plaster in a second bowl. That way, you can swap the full bowl for the empty one and continue working.

If the towel surface is rough or there are voids or bubbles, take a little plaster on your fingertips and smooth it over the surface, around all overlapping towel edges, and wherever the towels meet the roadbed. To build up an area or fill a hole, dip a piece of towel in plaster, squeeze and roll it into a rope-shaped roll, and use it as a filler. Then drape another swatch of towel over it in the usual manner.

The web technique depends on the strength of the cardboard strips plus the hardness of the plaster to support the scenery. Along the edge of the railroad — or at any other spot where a visitor might place an elbow or reach for support — it's advisable to have a double or triple layer of plaster and towel shell. In other areas, especially those parts of the railroad beyond easy reach, the shell need only support the weight of the scenery itself, and a single layer of plaster and towel is more than adequate.

Plaster-impregnated gauze. For dioramas, modules, and portable layouts you can substitute another material for the plaster-soaked towels: gauze rolls impregnated with Hydrocal. This is the same stuff doctors use to make casts to hold broken bones, but since it doesn't have to be sterile it's a lot cheaper. It's sold in art, craft, and hobby stores under various brand names; Pariscraft and Rigid Wrap are two commonly available ones.

Using this material is simple and tidy: Cut the gauze into hand-size pieces, dip them, one at a time, in a bucket of water, and apply over the Styrofoam or webbing base. The plaster sets fast; it's hard in about 10 minutes. The best part is that this is a one-step process with little mess and almost no cleanup. After pre-cutting the pieces you can apply them as fast as you can move. Because it is more expensive than plaster soaked paper I use plaster-impregnated gauze mostly for repairs, alterations and small additions to existing scenery, and other special jobs.

Two ways to pre-color plaster. On several portable railroads I have used pre-colored plaster for the scenery base, because of the rough handling a portable pike receives. When the color is in the plaster from the beginning, at least when the scenery is chipped or banged the resulting scar will be earth colored. Using pre-colored plaster is also a good way to prevent the white spots that show up when the scenery on a permanent layout is damaged.

My early experiments in coloring plaster met with no success; the coloring agent either weakened the plaster so much that it would not support its own weight, or the color bleached to off-white in a few days. I tried dry artist's pigments, tempera paints, masonry colors, food coloring, latex paint (which slowed the plaster's setting time from minutes to hours), lamp black powder, and even India ink (after 30 minutes, the plaster was still soupy, and I had to throw it away).

The first product I found that worked was tinting colors. These come in plastic tubes, and are meant to be mixed with either latex, acrylic, polyvinyl, or oil-base paints to change their color. They are sold under several brand names; Tints-All, sold in Tru-Value hardware stores, has a large color selection; Tinting Colors, made by Valspar, are available in other hardware and paint stores.

After several tries I came up with a good earth color: 2 teaspoons of Raw Sienna and ½ teaspoon of Lamp Black to one cup of water. Stir this until the colors are mixed, then add two cups of plaster. The tinting colors seem to have little effect on plaster setting times, and the color fades very little.

While experimenting with the tinting colors I also developed a color I call chocolate tan, which can be used to represent rich or moist soil. Add one teaspoon of Burnt Umber, one teaspoon of Raw Sienna, and one teaspoon of Lamp Black to one cup of water. Mix in two cups of plaster. Be careful with the black tinting color — if you use too much the plaster simply turns black and masks out the other colors.

My second plaster pre-coloring

Paint tinting colors, found in most hardware and paint stores, work best for precoloring plaster. They are also used to make some of the colors used to paint rock molds in Chapter 4.

CHAPTER 2

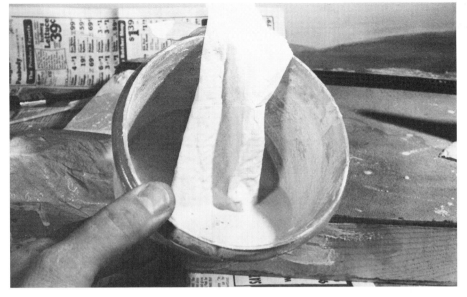

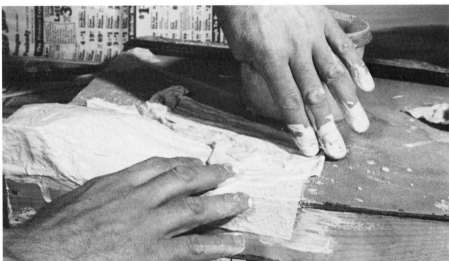

Dip a piece of paper towel into the plaster and lift it out by one corner, allowing it to drain (top). Drape it over the web and smooth with your fingers (middle). The unusual rough texture (bottom) is because this area was to be covered with rock molds.

you have no more than 5 minutes of working time.

Always evaluate the colors after the plaster has dried overnight. These formulas are for light, pastel shades. If the color produced does not look right to you, add more of a darker (or redder) color until you get the desired hue. Mix a sample batch of plaster with the revised formula and allow it to set overnight. Keep careful notes so you can duplicate the colors later.

One more note: If you follow the water-soluble method, the next step after adding plaster-soaked paper towels over the cardboard web is to paint everything with earth-colored latex paint (Chapter 4). By pre-coloring the plaster you do not omit this painting step — everything must still be painted.

Sculptamold for terrain modeling. There are several commercial products sold for terrain modeling, and my favorite by a large margin is Sculptamold. Its manufacturers say it is not plaster, and I believe it includes cellulose fibers, clay, and perhaps a small proportion of a plaster or gypsum binder. It can be mixed with varying quantities of water so it's loose and runny or stiff and clay-like; either way it sets in about 30 minutes and dries hard overnight. Sculptamold doesn't shrink appreciably as it sets, and after it dries it's strong, tough, and lightweight. It takes all kinds of paint well, can be drilled, filed, or carved, and is available at craft and hobby shops.

Three characteristics of Sculptamold make it ideal for diorama and portable railroad scenery. First, it is tidy to use: It doesn't flow all over the place, nor does it stick to the mixing bowl or spatula. On the layout it stays where you put it. Second, it has a natural-looking textured surface, somewhat like rough sandpaper, which provides a good simulation of bare earth or smooth rock. Third, when other materials, including paint, are mixed with it the setting time is only extended a little and the hardness does not change.

I've mixed diluted white glue, sand, plaster bits, ballast, and even sawdust with Sculptamold to achieve different textures. I've even tried Higgins Black Magic India Ink (1/8 teaspoon to a cup of water plus one heaping cup of Sculptamold) to get a dark gray rock shade, which is a good base for roads, parking lots, and the like.

To make a batch of earth-colored Sculptamold, mix 1/4 cup of earth-colored latex paint (the 1:1 dilution, see Chapter 4) with 3/4 cup of water. Using a spatula or table knife, mix a heaping cup (more for a stiffer mix) of Sculptamold with the paint and water. Apply this mix over the scenic base any way you want; when it dries the

technique is even simpler; it's based on Rit fabric dye, and it works every time. The structure of the plaster is not changed much, and the color does not change as the plaster dries. The two dye colors I like best are Dark Brown and Cocoa Brown. Cocoa is lighter and looks a little more like dry

earth. Rit also makes a Tan fabric dye that is a good earth shade.

Mix 1/2 teaspoon of Rit powdered fabric dye to one cup of water, stirring until the dye is completely dissolved. The dye contains salt which does speed setting somewhat, and after adding two cups of plaster and mixing,

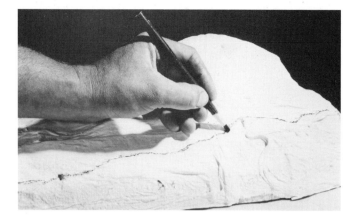

While the scenery base is still damp, mark the locations of rock faces. These should correspond to your planning model.

After covering the web, check clearances with an NMRA standards gauge. In tight spots cut the covering away and reapply.

color will be almost the same as when it was mixed, unlike plaster which usually dries lighter.

As handy as it is, I don't recommend Sculptamold as a substitute for plaster for building the scenery base. It doesn't stick to paper towels well, and is too expensive to use in large quantities. However, for refining terrain contours in small areas, building roads, and otherwise fine-tuning the scenic forms, it's the best product I've ever run across.

Finishing the base. The big advantage of the water-soluble method of scenery construction is that you lose no time waiting for the scenic base to dry before proceeding to the next step. After the plaster-soaked paper towels are in place and the plaster has started to set, mark off the areas where you have planned to install rock faces.

Next, check to make sure there is enough clearance between the scenery shell and the track. I try to leave an inch or two beyond what the NMRA clearance gauge indicates. This extra margin allows for the thickness of rock faces or for trees and shrubs to be placed between the shell and the track.

This also is a good time to look over the scenery to determine if all the contours are correct. If not, cut away and change any unsatisfactory areas. Small holes in the base may either be filled with plaster now or covered with lichen or other scenery material later. The idea is to prepare the shell so that

the next steps — adding color and texture — will go quickly and smoothly.

Questions and answers

Q: I have punched several holes in the hard shell scenery on my layout, and one time my cat put his paw through it. Is there any neat way to fix these holes without making a big mess?
A: Try Pariscraft or Rigid Wrap, the plaster-impregnated gauze material mentioned in this chapter. Soak a small piece in water and drape it over the scenery holes just as you would plaster-soaked paper towels. Smooth it in place with your fingers.
Q: I can get a lot of scrap foam-plastic packaging material where I work. Is this good for scenery building? Can Styrofoam be used on a large model railroad?
A: Any type of rigid plastic foam will work for scenery building. Styrofoam's main disadvantage is cost. Unless you have a free source, Styrofoam scenery is the most expensive you can build, even more expensive than aluminum screen wire and plaster. For most people, this rules out using it on large- or medium-size permanent layouts (where its advantages of light weight and resilience aren't needed anyway).
Q: Can liquid fabric dye be used in place of the powdered kind mentioned?
A: Yes. You'll have to experiment with how much to use, though, because I don't think the powdered and liquid

products are the same strength. Don't forget to write down the formulas you create so they can be repeated.
Q: How can I add extra strength and density to my plaster scenic base?
A: First, use Hydrocal or Ultracal. Both of these gypsum plasters are far stronger than regular molding plaster. You can also thin 1 part white glue (Elmer's) with 4 parts water and use this instead of plain water when mixing the plaster. After the plaster sets the surface will have a hard, marble-like sheen. This mixture is used by museum curators for making copies of sculptures and other works of art. But remember, the plaster is now sealed, and many of the water-soluble painting techniques described in this book will not work properly.
Q. I've had trouble with Sculptamold not sticking to a Styrofoam scenery base. When I trowel it the edges curl, and I have to move the trowel back and forth over and over to get it to stick to the Styrofoam.
A: The simplest solution I've found is to mix Sculptamold with warm water and apply it with your fingers. The warm water reduces the surface tension of Sculptamold and makes it stickier, and your fingers can push it into the various contours you've created. Another option is to mix white or yellow glue with the water before adding the Sculptamold powder. A teaspoon of full-strength glue to a cup of water helps Sculptamold stick to a variety of nonporous surfaces.

CHAPTER 2

Note how the basic tan latex Earth color shows up in the soil, rock, and even the ballast in this scene, blending all the elements.

Basic colors and textures

We covered how to build the scenic base in the last chapter, and the next steps are to add color and texture. Here, I'll talk about how basic colors and textures are used to rough-finish the scenic shell, and in later chapters we'll cover refinements and special situations. With the water-soluble system, color and texture are applied in the same step, but we'll take them one at a time.

The basic coloring agent: latex paint. The basic coloring in water-soluble scenery construction is flat latex wall paint. Although commonplace in house painting, latex paint has only found its way into hobbies and crafts in the last ten years. I use earth-colored latex paint as the base color for all scenery; when brushed over damp plaster it works into all surface irregularities, forming a sturdy, flexible film. Even when thinned it has enough body to hold sawdust, ground foam, and other textures sprinkled on its wet surface, and once dry, the paint's adhesive properties hold the textures as if they were glued.

Latex paint can be thinned and used as a wash around tracks and buildings, simulating the effects of dust and dirt. It can even be mixed with white glue and sawdust to form a

 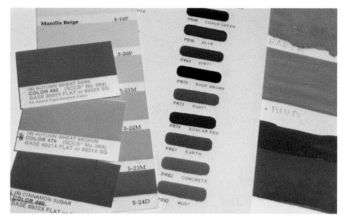

(Left) When comparing paint swatches to dry soil in the field to choose a basic earth color, evaluate only the color of the paint, **not whether it is lighter or darker than the soil. Document the color with a sample (right) so you can duplicate it later.**

textured scenery putty. I use this to build small contours and to refine areas around structures, sandpiles, and stream beds.

The paint is made from a water-base vehicle with pigments to provide color and durability. When the paint is spread, the water evaporates and the acrylic resin particles in the vehicle polymerize, or lock together. As the paint dries, the simple acrylic molecules transform into a tough, flexible film, and after the film dries completely it is impervious to water.

A simple approach to color. The colors that you select for your scenery are more important than any other consideration. The right colors will establish and reinforce the illusion of realism, while the wrong colors can destroy that illusion altogether. To build scenery, you don't need to know about primary, secondary, or complementary colors, and you don't have to know

what makes colors look colorful or how they are compounded. All you have to do is go outdoors and look at the colors around you. These are the colors of the real world, the ones you will have to duplicate to build realistic scenery.

For this reason, it's important that you use reference materials and other memory aids to ensure that your scenery is very close to natural colors. The two most valuable general lessons about scenic colors that I've learned over the years are that earth colors tend to be lighter than I remember them, and rock colors tend to be darker. But that's not good enough; we need a way of finding the specific colors that will make our scenery resemble the real thing.

Finding the right earth color. You may remember that in Chapter 1 we discussed how to get the feel of the area you want to model. An important aspect of this is recording specific colors. Without a doubt the most important color to match is that of dry earth. Earth colors range from light brown through the reds to grayish-cream, and rock colors go from light blue-gray and medium brown-green through the pinkish-reds of granite and sandstone, to chalk white.

I first experimented with latex paints when I wanted to find an economical alternative to using hobby paints for scenery. I started by buying several shades of flat latex interior wall paint, looking for an earth color to match the hobby paint I had been using. This worked so well that I then went to the paint store, where they have a machine that will mix thousands of colors. I found a close match to Polly S Earth: Tru-Test Dusty Sage, flat latex color No. C220. This worked fine, and I've since used several other latex earth colors from other manufacturers, all close matches to earth. The recipe box lists several earth colors that produce excellent results.

If the earth color for the region you are modeling differs substantially from those listed, obtain a dry earth

LATEX EARTH AND MUD COLORS

Earth:
Tru Value Hardware Tru-Test No. C220 Dusty Sage or No. C216 Antelope.

Pittsburgh Paints: No. 3491 Franciscan Gold, No. 3610 Poplar, or No. 4489 Tulip Wood.

Sears: Easy Living No. 600 Autumn Wheat Dark, No. 589 Sage, No. 574 Parisienne Beige (satin finish only — this is OK because after thinning the paint loses its shine), or No. 068 Sand (a good light earth color).

California Paints: No. 35C-3D Boca Raton or No. 35B-3D Cameron (a little on the red side but good for rich farmland).

(Sherwin-Williams Fringed Jacket is an earth color that I haven't tried.)

Mud:
Tru Value Hardware: Tru-Test No. C214 Sugarloaf.

Pittsburgh Paints: No. 4491 Leather Vest, No. 7483 Earthenware, or No. 4606 Yorktown Brown (reddish).

Sears: Easy Living No. 585 Guernsey Beige.

California Paints: No. 35C-4A Oakheart or No. 36C-3D Cassel Brown.

Color names and numbers change with home decorating styles. Most stores have a cross-reference book to match old names and numbers to their replacements. Ask the store clerk. If you still cannot find the exact colors mentioned above use your color chip to select something close.

These colors are only starting points. Your own taste or the prototype you're modeling may differ, so feel free to substitute colors **you** like!

Also buy a quart of flat white for lightening and for use with tinting colors. If the earth or mud seems too dark, add flat white before diluting the paint.

CHAPTER 3

sample or color photos from the area. Bring the sample with you to the paint store and look through the color charts until you find a close match. It's important that you bring the sample or soil photo to the paint store, as store lighting will fool you. Our memories just don't work well when it comes to colors; colors that look good in the store may be much too blue or pink under your layout lighting. If the paint sample on the color card is close to the soil shade, or a bit lighter, it's probably as close as you can get and will look OK on the layout.

I like to choose at least two latex earth colors for every project: the closest match to dry earth, and a darker, browner shade of the same color to simulate rich, damp earth. Many of the colors I have used for moist soil are close matches to Polly S Sand Yellow (79), No. PCG708.

After I find a color match, I record the number in my notebook along with a rough estimate of how much white paint should be added to the standard color to make it light enough for model use. (Lightening the earth colors compensates for the difference between strong sunlight and our weak indoor layout lighting.)

Lighter shades. By my own definition, one shade lighter is the color that results when I add 10 percent white to an existing color. A color two shades lighter would have 20 percent white added. An easy way to mix shades is to add nine parts paint to one part white for a 10 percent mix, eight parts paint to two parts white for a 20 percent mix (two shades lighter), and so forth.

Rock colors are handled the same way. I favor model rocks that are neutral gray with only a little of the actual rock color added. Rocks in nature are always much too dark to look good on the layout. When selecting rock colors, always go two or three shades lighter than what you see outdoors.

While you're researching earth colors for your railroad, you should also find matches for foliage colors. Glue half a dozen shades of green scenic foam or dyed sawdust on a piece of cardboard, hold the cardboard up at arm's length, and compare the colors to the grass and trees several hundred yards away or in the photos. Take notes, and if two shades are equally close to matching Mother Nature, always select the lighter of the two.

Other coloring agents. Although latex paint is the most important coloring agent in the water-soluble scenery system, several other types of colors are useful for specific jobs. Tube-type artist's acrylic paints have a chemical base similar to latex paint and can be thinned with water. With them, you can alter the basic earth shades or tint flat white latex paint for

Look closely at the variety of textures used in this small scene. Included are ground foam, sawdust, sifted dirt, commercial ballast, small pebbles, and lichen scraps.

special applications. These high-quality paints are used by artists, either straight from the tube or mixed with an acrylic gel or medium to change their working and drying characteristics. As scenery builders the only time we will mix tube acrylics with a medium is to build water, Chapter 7.

Acrylic tube paints are expensive, but they go a long way and with proper storage they will last a long time. The most useful colors are listed in the recipe box. Purchase these colors to start, and other colors as you find a need for them. I have used the AquaTec, Grumbacher Hyplar, and Utrecht Linens brands of acrylics because they are available in my local art supply and hobby shops; any available brand should work just fine. Instead of buying white tube acrylic, buy a quart of flat white latex interior wall paint. Use this to lighten all scenery colors.

If you are an active modelbuilder,

you are familiar with the Polly S line of water-base hobby paints. These are compatible with all the water-soluble scenery materials in this book. Polly S paints are available in most craft and hobby shops, and the line includes a wide variety of railroad, military, and craft colors. I use Polly S straight from the bottle to color detail parts and for dry-brushing, and dilute it with water to make thin washes for weathering. Like latex paint, after drying Polly S forms a tough film that is not affected by water- or oil-base paints. Start with the Polly S Weathering Kit, which contains one small bottle each of Grimy Black, Oily Black, Mud, Rust, Dust, and Dirt. Also purchase one bottle each of Concrete, Grass Green, and Sea Blue.

Tinting Colors are described in the section on precoloring plaster in Chapter 3. These can be mixed with water, rubbing alcohol, glue, paint thinner, and almost any other medi-

ARTIST'S ACRYLIC TUBE COLORS

The acrylic colors I recommend purchasing first are:

- Cobalt Blue (or Ultramarine Blue)
- Raw Umber
- Burnt Sienna
- Mars Black
- Raw Sienna
- Oxide of Chromium Opaque (green)
- Green Gold
- Yellow

Purchase additional colors only as you need them.

Polly S hobby paints are water soluble, so they work perfectly with all our other water-soluble scenery materials and coloring agents. These colors plus this weathering set provide a good starter assortment.

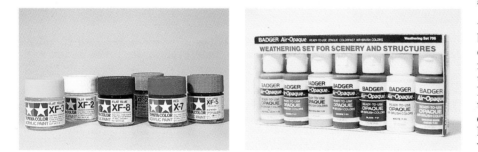

Tamiya Color acrylic paints are new and compatible with the water-soluble method of scenery construction. Badger Air-Opaque paints are formulated for airbrush application but can be thinned with water and brushed onto rocks and earth.

um. They can also be sprayed or brushed, with properties similar to artist's gouache (a favorite of airbrush artists).

New to the hobby industry are Pactra and Tamiya acrylic paints. Pactra thins with tap water, but Tamiya paints should be cut with their own thinner or automobile windshield-washer solvent. Brushes can be cleaned with tap water. Both brands are available in hobby shops in a wide variety of colors.

Another basic coloring agent I use is India ink. One brand is Higgins Black Magic India Ink, which is sold in stationery and art-supply stores.

Texture — the key to realism. One of the great model railroaders, the late Frank Ellison, liked to describe a model railroad as the stage on which the actors, trains in this case, performed. To make the scenery on this stage setting believable we have to stand back and observe what really happens in nature. To me, the

texture of the scenery is the key to realism. In this discussion we are not concerned with the actual texture of the ground covers, rocks, and trees. These are important later, during construction, but let's set them aside for the time being so we can concentrate on the overall impression of texture.

If you have been lucky enough to have flown over the United States during the clear summer months you know that from two or three miles up everything looks smooth and the colors are muted pastels. Even rugged mountain country is reduced to gentle undulations with the contours of water flow patterns predominating, and the deep forest appears as a faded green mat with a pebbled surface. Buildings and other man-made features look like small geometric shapes with the bland character of Monopoly-game props.

As we fly closer to the ground certain details begin to appear, colors become brighter, and textures appear coarser. We see that the smooth-looking field of wheat that seemed to undulate as a single unit is really millions of individual plants all standing two or three feet from the ground. The clipped fairway of the golf course looked as smooth as suede when viewed from a distance, but up close it is rough looking, perhaps with bare areas where the soil shows through.

To effectively use textures on the layout we have to keep in mind how things look from a distance. Most of the textures we will use will be quite fine. Let's take a look at some of them.

Types of texture material. Dozens of things can be used to add texture and simulate vegetation in model railroad scenery, but the four most useful are ground foam rubber, dyed sawdust, crushed gravel, and real earth. You can purchase the first three of these in a wide selection of colors and grades at your hobby shop. The real earth can be gathered, for free, from your backyard. No one texture is best;

Woodland Scenics offers a broad line of texture materials intended especially for model railroads and dioramas, including these ground foam colors.

Decomposed granite is a favorite rock texture material of western modelers. You can find it at garden centers or home-supply stores, where it's sold as a base for driveways and paths.

CHAPTER 3

Powdered fabric dyes are used to color ground foam, sawdust, lichen, and other homemade scenic textures and growths.

in fact, you'll need to use all of them to achieve the variety that is an important aspect of the realism we're after.

Without a doubt the best way to obtain the textures you'll need is to buy them at a hobby shop, and I recommend that you do so. However, because on several occasions I needed special colors not then available, and because you might want to try it just once, here's how to make your own sawdust and ground foam.

Making dyed sawdust. Several weeks before "D" day (dyeing day), I make the rounds of the local lumberyards, looking for clean sawdust. Try to obtain sawdust free of Masonite or particle board chips; these don't absorb dye, and always look like raw wood. Gather about twice the amount of sawdust you think you'll need, because fully half gets thrown away.

The tools and materials needed are one or more 5-gallon metal pails, newspapers, a 2'-long stick, rubber gloves, a large window screen, and an assortment of colorfast fabric dyes. I have used Rit and Tintex fabric dyes with good results. Purchase a packet each of the medium leaf-colored greens, from Forest Green through Medium Green to light Yellow-Green. It's hard to say how much dye to buy; I'd suggest buying more than you think you'll need. Any dye that is left over can be used for other pickling and coloring projects. Do not buy bright yellow, and stay away from really dark colors.

The best place to dye sawdust is outdoors, on a sunny, calm day. You can work in a cellar or garage, but I like the great out of doors because cleanup is fast and easy. Start by heating about 2 gallons of water almost to boiling (a camp stove works fine, and keeps you out of the kitchen). Pour the water into the 5-gallon pail, and add one packet of your lightest green dye. Stir the dye until it dissolves completely.

Now add the sawdust, a handful at a time, and stir. Keep adding sawdust until all the liquid is absorbed, then set the pail aside and let it cool. While you're waiting, start heating another 2 gallons of water for the second batch.

After 15 or 20 minutes the sawdust in the first batch will be cool enough to handle. Put on the gloves, grab a handful of wet sawdust, and squeeze as much water as possible out of it and back into the pail. Spread the sawdust on several thicknesses of newspapers arranged on the ground. To speed drying, use lots of newspapers and spread the sawdust as thinly as possible.

Now start another batch. Add enough new hot water to the pail to make 2 gallons (there will be about half a gallon of green water remaining from the first batch), and stir in a packet of the next darker shade of dye. Repeat the process, and keep going until you run out of dye or sawdust.

Keep the different colors of sawdust separate while they dry, and turn the sawdust every two or three hours to allow for air circulation and even drying. Move the damp sawdust indoors to a basement or garage overnight. Under normal conditions it takes about two days for the sawdust to dry completely.

After the sawdust is dry, sift it through the window screen to break up the lumps and remove the larger pieces. Throw away any large chips and splinters that will not pass through the screen. This will be about half the volume of the dyed sawdust, but don't try to sift the sawdust first and then dye it; it will be too fine and hard to remove from the water, and will dry in hard lumps.

Place the screened sawdust in plastic food storage bags labeled with the dye color and manufacturer so you can duplicate a particular color later.

Grinding foam rubber. Coloring foam rubber involves the same steps as sawdust, except that you have to grind the foam beforehand. Grinding foam is hard work, and I recommend it only if you need a very large quantity or a special color that is not available commercially.

The first step is to find a source for foam rubber; I usually obtain scraps from upholstery shops. The best foam for grinding and dyeing is genuine latex foam rubber. I haven't had much success with pre-shredded pillow stuffing or any other type of plastic foam. The rubber foam absorbs dye and retains color better than the plastic substitutes.

To grind the foam you'll need a crank-type meat grinder, the kind made for making sausage meat. The cutting blade should be fine enough to grind the foam very small. Most grinders come with several blades, so you can grind the foam to several grades to represent different types of vegetation.

Fasten the grinder to a solid surface. I clamp it to the edge of a heavy wooden picnic table, which provides firm support and keeps the mess outside. Place a pan under the grinder to catch the foam as it falls from the blades.

Dyed sawdust was one of the first scenery texture materials. A thick layer, applied over dilute matte medium or thinned white glue, looks like long grass.

CHAPTER 3

COLORFAST DYE COLORS FOR SAWDUST OR FOAM

Start with the following colors:

- Dark Green
- Forest Green
- Jade Green
- Kelly Green
- Light Green

Purchase additional colors only if you want to experiment or want to match a specific vegetation color. Olive Green is a good choice if you simply want to try something different. Powdered fabric dyes are made by Rit, Tintex, and others.

Rit has discontinued Forest, Jade, and Light Green. To make these colors using available Rit dyes use the following formulas (provided by Rit):

Forest green:
    1 1\frac{1}{8}-oz. package Dark Green
    1/2 package Kelly Green

Light green:
    2 teaspoons Kelly Green
    1/2 teaspoon Yellow

Jade green:
    1 1\frac{1}{8}-oz. package Kelly Green
    1 1\frac{1}{8}-oz. package Yellow
    1/2 package Dark Green

Store mixed dye in a labeled glass jar with a tight-fitting lid.

All you need to grind foam rubber is a crank-type meat grinder and lots of elbow grease. Make a cardboard hopper to feed chunks of rubber into the grinder.

Start by ripping or cutting the foam into pieces about 2" square. This is only a rough size and you may have to change it depending upon the grinder you have. Place a few chunks at a time in the grinder's hopper (you may want to add a cardboard extension to the hopper if it will hold only one or two chunks of foam).

Now start turning the crank. Use an old ruler or stick to coax the foam chunks into the feed auger. If you add too much foam the handle will be hard to turn, but once you get the hang of it you can grind quite a bit of foam in an hour or two. You'll usually obtain several different grades of foam from the grinder; even with a fine blade some larger chunks will manage to squeeze through. These can be used as is or sifted out and ground again. By the way, if you have an arthritic shoulder or a bad heart grinding foam is not the job for you; turning that crank is hard, tiring work.

Coloring ground foam. After the foam is ground you can dye it anytime. I like to color sawdust and foam at the same time so there is only one mess to clean up. All the dyeing steps are the same, except you should use a little less water: 1\frac{1}{2} gallons of water to one packet of dye is about right. This yields a higher concentration of dye, which is needed to color the less-porous foam.

To dry the foam place it on several thicknesses of newspapers or on a simple frame made by stapling an old bedsheet over the window screen. Raise the frame off the ground so air can circulate underneath. Always label the colors so you can repeat the results later.

Finishing the scenic base. Now, with several colors of foam and sawdust (or other textures) at hand it's time to apply them over wet latex

Dyed sawdust is excellent for the initial texture coat that is applied over wet latex Earth paint. I use a homemade shaker jar.

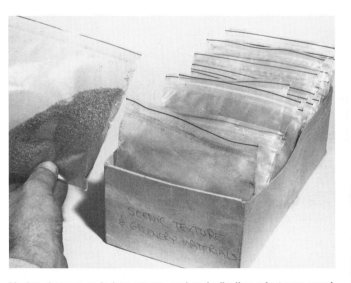

Variety in texture is important, and so is finding what you need. I store scenic material in plastic bags in an old shoe box.

CHAPTER 3

Brush on earth paint, diluted 1:1, using a wide brush. Apply plenty of paint so that the texture will have something to hold it in place. Cover a section of scenery about 18" square.

Apply texture material right over the wet paint. The first texture, in this case ground foam, provides a base for subsequent finish texture applications.

paint. The best way is with a shaker bottle. I use a screw-top food jar with holes punched in the lid (the more holes the better). Punch the holes with a 10-penny nail or an awl. A large spice container (I like oregano) with the holes already formed in the plastic top works well, or you can go first class and buy your foam shaker bottles at a hobby shop. To cover large areas, I also use a flour sifter. You can apply texture using any device you want as long as the texture is evenly distributed over the wet paint.

Choose one or two greens, either sawdust or foam, for the first texture. I like to use a medium-green sawdust. I fill the shaker jar with sawdust and set it and the plastic bag holding the reserve supply of sawdust near the area I intend to color and texture.

Dilute the basic earth latex paint 1:1 with water and place the thinned paint in a one- or two-pound coffee can. Brush this paint onto the scenery base with a 2½" brush, covering all the nooks and crannies of the scenic shell. Be generous and don't brush the paint out too much. Work in small areas, about 18" square.

As soon as the paint is applied, sprinkle on a heavy coat of texture material. Where the scenery is steeply inclined, place texture on the palm of your hand or in an empty white glue bottle and either blow or squeeze it onto the wet paint. The idea is to cover all the scenery areas that have not been marked off for rock faces with earth paint and a basic coating of texture.

This step in scenery building goes fast, and a large area can be completed in a short time. Work along until all scenery is covered with texture. The earth latex paint and texture give the scenery an instant "finished" look, even though real scenic finishing has just begun.

If the plaster scenic base has set and dried by the time you get there

with the latex paint, rewet it. I use a pump-type spray bottle filled with water and several drops of detergent. Spray water until the scenery base is soaked, because latex paint that is applied over a dry plaster base will have most of its water absorbed into the base the moment it is applied, leaving little moisture to grab and hold the texture.

Now let the scenery dry. The next day the textures will be firmly stuck to the base. Remove all texture that fell on unpainted areas or did not stick by gently brushing with a wide, soft brush. Return the excess texture to the proper plastic bag for use later on. Vacuum up any texture that got into the trackwork. Don't worry about small bare spots, because most of the basic texture will be covered with other, finer textures. The real job of this initial texture coat is to provide "tooth" to hold "detail" textures later on.

Water-soluble adhesives. Before we discuss rocks, dirt, and detail textures, I should mention the adhesives we'll use to glue them down. The first, and by far the most important, is acrylic matte medium, a milky acrylic polymer which dries to a flat, clear film. It is a strong, tough, flexible adhesive, and modelers have been using it for years for ballasting track. Diluted with water, I spray it over loose texture material, and after drying it bonds the material to the base without buildup or objectionable shine.

White glue came to the market about the same time as acrylic paints; you probably use it already for benchwork and wood kit construction. I use white glue diluted 1:1 with water as an adhesive to hold texture in place, but only under the texture, because it sometimes leaves an unwanted shine, and it can be re-softened by repeated application of water. Thinned glue is brushed on the scenery base and tex-

White glue and acrylic matte medium are the two most important scenery adhesives in the water-soluble method.

tures are sprinkled over it. This method is good for holding heavy textures, such as sand or gravel, on slopes or hillsides. I also dip pieces of foliage and metal detail parts into this 1:1 white glue solution and place them directly on the scenery.

Questions and answers

Q: I built my layout several years ago when the "zip-texturing" method was popular. The scenery now shows the effects of age and dust and generally needs to be spruced up. I wonder if I can use water-soluble scenery techniques over what I already have?

A: Sure you can, and it's easier than you might think. Just use the standard water-soluble materials — earth latex paint and texture materials — right over the existing scenery. Start by vacuuming up any loose plaster and dry color, and if the scenery is

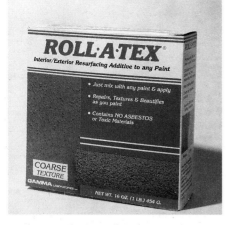

Roll-A-Tex and similar materials are mixed with latex paint and used to add rough texture to ceilings. This sand cut was "painted" over the scenic base using a thick mixture of Roll-A-Tex and earth-colored latex paint.

crumbly, wet it with a "wet-water" spray and seal it with a generous squirt of dilute acrylic matte medium. Be sure to protect the track and remove structures and details wherever possible before applying paint. The matte medium and the latex paint will bond all the zip-texture pigment and plaster in place, eliminating the powdery surface that is often a problem with zip-textured scenery.

Q: I bought several packages of surplus dye at a store closeout. After dyeing, my sawdust came out much too dark. Is there any way to salvage it?

A: You could mix the sawdust with lighter green colors and try to lighten it that way, but I've had little success blending light-colored sawdust with darker shades: The results usually look like salt and pepper. You could try re-coloring it in a bucket of dilute green latex paint just as you would if you were dying it.

I've lightened scenic foam by diluting 1/4 cup liquid bleach in one gallon of water. Toss the foam in the water and let it soak. Watch it — remove it when it reaches the shade you want, squeeze the water out, and let it dry on newspaper.

As a last resort you could reserve this too-dark sawdust to mix with plaster, Sculptamold, or latex paint for added texture. If all else fails, throw

the sawdust away, buy the correct dyes, and start again.

Q: Can I substitute any other kind of paint for the tube-type acrylics?

A: Not really. I've experimented with several other types of paint, and perhaps the closest to acrylic is tube-type watercolor. The big disadvantage of inexpensive watercolors is they are not permanent; the colors fade in time. They do thin with water, are easy to mix, and give good results. I like them best for weathering plastic structures. Another type of paint I tried was tempera. I did not like its working characteristics after thinning it with water, and it, too, seemed to fade after several months on the layout.

Q: I have a hard time matching the rock colors on my layout with those on my prototype. I even took a piece of rock home and matched my rock color to it but it was too dark.

A: A good way to accurately judge the color of rocks and earth outdoors is to stand at least 50 to 100 yards away from them. It is what you see at these distances that must be transferred in miniature to your model scene. Hold color samples at arm's length and look for a match to the rock color. When viewing scenery outdoors try to always do it at the same time of day and under the same lighting conditions.

Q: Would it be possible to color and texture scenery at the same time by adding texture material to the paint?

A: Yes and no. No, because usually we want the texture to be a slightly different color than the basic earth or mud color beneath it; yes, because in some special cases this approach will work.

The photos show one example that worked: I mixed a lightweight paint texturing product called Roll-A-Tex with earth-colored paint and used it to model a sandy cut. The effect was instant, and when the paint dried, the sand looked realistic.

Q: Have you even had the problem of flat paints drying glossy on scenery?

A: Every so often you'll apply one of the latex or Polly S paints over a smooth plaster or Hydrocal surface and even though the paint is billed as flat it will dry with more sheen than you'd like. To further dull the paint try mixing talcum powder with it. You'll have to experiment with the exact proportions for your conditions. I pour several teaspoons of paint into a shallow dish and mix in about 1/2 teaspoon talcum powder. If the paint thickens add several drops of water and mix. The talc may change the color of the paint slightly, so try it out on a piece of scrap wood or plaster before using it on your scenery.

CHAPTER 3

This rugged molded-plaster rock face was cast in place from molds taken from two separate pieces of real rock.

Modeling rock and rubble

I'm often amazed at the lengths to which some modelers will go to build "geologically perfect" model rocks. I've seen heavy pieces of actual stone built into model railroads (which looked like real rock and did not blend with the rest of the scenery), and I've seen meticulously hand-carved rock faces that looked as if a sculptor had copied in plaster the bare stone walls of a nearby quarry. All this work just isn't necessary; you don't have to copy rocks exactly as they appear in nature. Like all other aspects of scenery, effective model rocks need only be caricatures of the real thing.

The fastest and easiest way to make rocks is to mold them in plaster, using flexible rubber molds made from finely detailed real rocks. Model railroaders have used this method for at least 20 years, so in this chapter I'll discuss rock molding and coloring not as a new technique but as an integral part of the water-soluble method.

Excellent rock molds are now available commercially, so you don't have to produce your own to be able to use this technique. However, because mold-making is easy — and fun — I'll describe the steps. The first is to find an appropriate chunk of real rock, one that has several small faces, each with many cracks and crevices. Whenever possible, bring the rock home to make the molds, because out in the field you are at the mercy of the weather, not to mention unsympathetic landowners and insects.

Making rock molds. Next, gather tools and materials. Most important, you'll need liquid latex molding rubber, an air-curing rubber that dries strong and flexible. It is sold in craft and hobby shops. Purchase a couple of rolls of 1"-wide surgical gauze at a pharmacy, and while you're there, pick up a small can of talcum powder. For tools you'll need several inexpensive, disposable No. 6 or No. 7 paintbrushes, a stiff 2" brush, and scissors.

Place several thicknesses of news-paper on your workbench and set the rock on them. Using the stiff-bristled brush, scrub the rock to remove all loose dirt, crumbled rock, and vegetation. Then wet the brush with warm tap water and repeat the process. It is important to remove as much foreign matter as possible, because anything on the rock face will be embedded in the face of the mold and will shorten its useful life.

After cleaning the rock, check the face where you will make the mold for fossils, small shells, or any other out-of-scale elements. Chip these off with a hammer and an old chisel (or a large nail).

Next, add several drops of liquid detergent to a can of water and work this solution into the rock face with one of the small brushes. The detergent helps the water flow into all the small nooks and crannies, and in turn, the water thins the first coat of rubber slightly and lets it flow into all surface irregularities. The detergent also acts as a mold release and helps in removing the finished mold from the rock.

Now carefully apply the first coat of molding rubber with one of the small brushes. Spread the first coat thin, and make sure that no air bubbles are trapped in the crevices. Remove bubbles by pricking them with a pin or toothpick. This first coat must be as perfect as possible, because this is the part of the mold that will make contact with the plaster. Brush the first coat over the entire rock face, letting the rubber extend beyond the edge of the face from ½" to 1". We'll trim away excess rubber after the mold is complete.

How big should the molds be? Well, first and foremost, don't try to make a mold for a specific situation on your railroad, because it's unnecessary, and the idea is to use the same mold over and over in different places. Small molds are hard to use because you have to fill and apply them over and over again, and large molds are tricky to handle when they are full of plaster. I make all my molds a little larger than the size of my open hand, a size that can be used in almost any situation.

When the first coat of molding rubber dries, it will turn from milky white to transparent yellow (some molding rubber is red; it turns from pink to bright red when dry), and will be slightly tacky. Now apply a full-strength coat of rubber and allow it to dry overnight.

Reinforcing the mold. Keep the brush you are using for the rubber in the can of water between coats to keep it soft. After the mold is complete the brush will be clogged with rubber and not worth keeping; throw it away.

During the next week, apply five more coats of rubber. Allow each coat to dry overnight before applying the next. Complete drying is important, because any uncured rubber trapped between coats will remain soft for weeks or months, weakening the mold.

While the sixth coat of rubber is drying, cut the surgical gauze into strips a little longer than the mold is wide. Cut enough strips to cover the mold twice. Now brush on a thick coat of rubber and push the gauze into it with the brush, coaxing the gauze into all the mold contours. Each gauze strip should overlap the next, forming a web. Add another thick coat of rubber over the gauze, again prodding it into the contours of the mold. This coat of rubber locks the gauze in place.

The mold should now dry for two or three days before any further handling. To remove the mold from the rock, start at one corner and gently

pull the edges. Work around the perimeter until all edges are free, then work toward the center, pulling and prying until the mold comes free. The mold must be removed gently and must not be allowed to touch itself as it will stick together. As soon as it comes free, dust the mold with talcum powder inside and out, and trim the ragged edges with scissors.

Molds can be ruined by carelessly throwing them into a box or bag and allowing them to be folded and distorted. I store rock molds in a large cardboard box filled with Styrofoam "peanuts" packaging material. Place the molds in the box and pour the pea-

Scrub the surface of the rock with a stiff-bristled brush, detergent, and water. Besides cleaning the rock, the detergent acts

as a release agent to help peel the mold off after it is completed. Apply the first coat of latex to the rock while it is damp.

　　　　CHAPTER 4

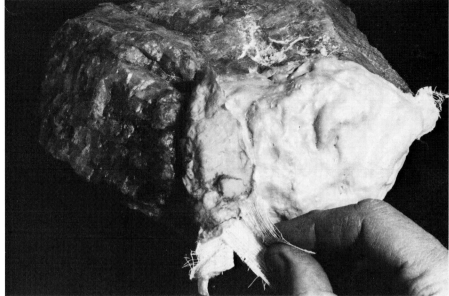

When the final coat of rubber is thoroughly dry, remove the mold from the rock with a gentle, even pull. Small bits of rubber may remain in some of the deeper cracks on the rock, but this will not lower the quality of the plaster castings made from the mold.

(Left) Extreme lighting shows off the detail of this finished rock face. Several castings had to be overlapped and blended together to make this scene.

nuts over them so they retain their shapes and do not touch each other.

Casting rock faces in place. There are several ways to use rock molds. Some modelers precast sections of rock, color them, and glue them to the scenery, others cast rock faces first and build the adjacent scenery around them. I mold the rocks directly in place, which leaves no gaps or edges to cover up and allows me to paint the rocks at the same time as the rest of the scenery. This way, the rock faces conform to the contours of the established scenic base, and add less than an inch to the total thickness of the scenery.

Start by pre-wetting all the molds

you expect to use during the casting session. Hold the inner surface of the mold under the warm water faucet until it is thoroughly soaked. Wetting the mold surface helps the plaster flow into all the surface irregularities in the mold, which makes a sharper casting. Spray the inside of the mold with wet water (water with a few drops of detergent added) and shake off any excess.

Use the standard plaster mixing formula for rock molds: Pour one cup of water into the mixing bowl and stir in two cups of plaster. This yields three cups of plaster, enough to fill two hand-size molds.

When mixing plaster for rock molds try not to include air bubbles. Stir the plaster slowly and gently until it starts to thicken (about 2 minutes).

Support each mold by wadding up an old towel underneath it to keep the plaster from running out, and pour the plaster into the molds until they are almost full. Shake and bump the molds to eliminate air bubbles clinging to the inner surface. (If you're making castings to be placed in the scenery later, stop here and allow the plaster to set until the mold is warm and the plaster hard. Gently peel the mold away from the casting and proceed to painting.)

Before placing the plaster-filled molds on the scenery base, rewet the area. Using a pump-type sprayer bottle, spray on water until the surface is thoroughly soaked. (If the base were left dry, it would absorb most of the water from the rock casting, causing it to dry rather than set, and leaving

Each coat of rubber must dry completely before applying the next. After the sixth coat, press strips of gauze into the wet rub-

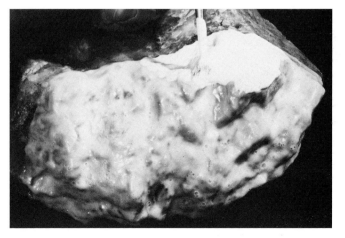

ber and cover them with another coat. This final coat will be thicker than the preceding ones and will take longer to dry.

CHAPTER 4

(Left) This completed rock mold is just about the right size, a little larger than my hand. (Above) The first step in making a rock casting is to pour the plaster mix into the mold. This plaster has been pre-colored brown with Rit fabric dye.

ROCK COLORING FORMULAS

Where earth is called for, use the same earth latex paint you have selected for the rest of the layout, scene, or diorama.

Black relief wash:
    1/2 teaspoon India ink
    1 quart water
    4 drops detergent

Basic rock color:
    12 ounces (1 1/2 cups) of 3:1 earth latex paint (3 parts water, to 1 part paint)
    20 ounces (2 1/2 cups) water

Any quantity of basic rock color can be mixed — use one part 3:1 earth latex paint mixed with two parts water.

Blue rock:
    12 ounces 3:1 earth latex paint
    20 ounces water plus 1" Cobalt Blue tube acrylic

Red rock:
    12 ounces 3:1 earth latex paint
    20 ounces water plus 1" red oxide tinting color or tube acrylic color

If the blue or red rock color dries too dark either add more water or use less tube color.

us with weak, powdery molded rocks.)

Watch the plaster as it starts to set. The mold should be placed on the scenic base just as the plaster loses its soupiness, but before it becomes inflexible. Pick up the mold, hold it in the palm of your hand (one reason for those hand-size molds), and push it onto the scenery base. Run a finger along the edge of the mold to make sure the outer edges are in contact with the base. Don't worry if excess plaster is forced out at the edges; this is easy to remove after the plaster starts to set. Hold the mold in place for several minutes until it becomes warm, indicating that the plaster is setting.

You can vary the shape of rock faces by pressing and distorting the molds. If you have an odd-shaped area or need to bring the rock face up to the edge of a bridge abutment, wall, or backdrop, trim the edge of the mold with scissors. If you need smaller rock castings, fill only half or a third of the mold with plaster or cut the mold to a different size or shape.

Removing the mold. Leave the mold in place until the plaster gets

This large rock promontory was temporarily covered with sawdust grass. The first rock mold is ready and the grass area has been soaked with wet water. The molds are applied overlapping one another. When building a large rock face the work goes faster with two people, one person holding the mold in place until the plaster sets and the other person preparing and filling the next mold.

CHAPTER 4

Trowel plaster into the edges of the mold just before applying it to the scenery.

warm. (If the scenic base contours are irregular, you may have to hold the mold in place longer.) After about 10 minutes peel back one corner of the mold to see if the plaster has set. Check the mold surface — if no plaster clings to it the mold can be removed. Although the plaster is still weak at this point, the mold should be removed to avoid damaging it. As the plaster hardens further its surface crevices will trap the mold, and the rubber will rip when the mold is removed. The best way to strip the mold from the plaster is to start at one corner and pull toward the opposite corner.

As soon as the mold is removed use a modeling knife, palette knife, or butter knife to chip away excess plaster around the edges of the rock face to fit the scenery contour. Slice and scrape the edges of the casting, but be gentle — you don't want to damage it or crack the scenery base. Use the tip of a hobby knife to finish the edges. Fill holes or gaps in the casting with leftover plaster from the next mold you fill. Add more castings to build a large rock face; where castings meet or overlap, disguise the seam by scraping and chipping, using a jabbing and twisting motion until the seam blends into the rest of the rock face.

Remove plaster chips with a stiff paintbrush and save the scraps for making loose rocks and rubble.

I work with four molds, two at a time; while I wait for the plaster to set in the first two, I mix plaster to fill the second pair, and so on. After a rock casting session is over, wash the molds in warm water to which several drops of detergent have been added, and pick out any bits of plaster stuck to the inside surfaces. Dry the molds, dust with talcum powder, and store.

Urethane foam for rock castings. Realistic and extremely durable rock

After building up most of the rock face and spraying it with the India ink wash, I decided to add another casting. The brush helps blend it into the surrounding surfaces.

As the plaster starts to set the mold will become warm. A minute or two later, gently peel the mold away from the casting.

This rock face is ready for coloring. You can proceed while the castings are still damp, or perform the coloring steps later.

After applying a thin black India ink relief wash over the entire rock surface, the next step is to spray on the rock color. The center section of this face was colored with the basic rock color, while the sections to the left and right show the blue variation. Now is the time to paint the shadows under the rock overhangs. I used the rock shadow color and a small brush to "jab" the paint into the casting.

castings can be made by substituting two-part polyurethane foam for plaster. One brand is Mountains in Minutes Polyfoam. This makes a lightweight, dense, resilient rock, good for portable layouts and modules. Polyfoam is expensive, there's lots of waste, and you don't have nearly the control that you have with plaster. But, if weight and durability are the most important considerations, urethane rocks are for you. Complete instructions are provided by the manufacturer. Be sure to use a release agent; if you don't, your molds will be ruined. You'll find more information on

urethane rocks and other lightweight scenery techniques in Chapter 10 of this book.

Considerations in rock coloring. The most important consideration in choosing rock colors is that they should not be radically different from your earth color. The soil in most parts of the world is largely decayed rock anyway: Decomposing granite usually produces tan-gray soil; volcanic rocks break down into a dark, almost black soil; and sandstone or iron-bearing rocks form reddish soils.

A second consideration is whether the rock faces are old or new. Old rock

that has long been subjected to the weather is relatively dark and dull; new rock, recently exposed by blasting, construction, or rushing water, has brighter colors. Whatever type of rock face you model, the colors should be light, almost transparent, because model rocks look darker than they are when viewed under average layout lighting. We'll keep the coloring light by using thin color washes to tint the wet plaster and slightly darker washes to bring out surface texture.

Remember, too, that coloring only suggests a specific type of rock, not duplicates it. Even if the rock colors you choose are only close to those of the rocks you want to simulate, they will work fine.

The four-step rock coloring sequence. The basic coloring sequence goes like this: As soon as the rock mold is removed, spray the casting with a thin, dark wash to tone down the white plaster and to give some relief to all the crevices on the rock face. Next, spray on the rock color. This is a thinned-down earth color, sometimes tinted. Next, brush a darker earth color into the natural shadow areas of the rock, to make the rock texture show up under regular layout lighting. To finish, dry-brush the highlights with a lightened earth color.

Mixing rock colors. I mix all the required rock colors ahead of time and store them in jars or coffee cans. For application I decant each color into a labeled pump-type spray bottle. You'll find the formulas for my favorites in the recipe box.

Many variations of these three basic rock colors can be made by adding small amounts of other tube acrylic colors. Start with one part 3:1 earth mix, add two parts water, then add the acrylic color a little at a time. Always try the new color on a piece of wet scrap casting and let it dry overnight before using it on the layout.

Coloring the castings. Because the coloring agents we use are water soluble, rock castings can be colored as soon as the molds are removed. This way, the castings are still full of water and the plaster absorbs a minimum of color. Dry plaster absorbs far too much paint, producing dark, unrealistic rocks, so if you have put off coloring until after the plaster has set and dried, start by soaking the castings with wet water spray until it will absorb no more. Incidentally, the coloring sequence can be stopped at any point and continued later; just be sure you rewet the plaster thoroughly before continuing.

Start by spraying the entire wet rock face with black relief wash. Spray a little extra under overhangs and in other areas that would normally be in shadow. The black wash will tone down the white plaster and add relief so you can see what you're doing. Spray on black wash until some runs off. If the castings absorb a lot of the wash or look too black, then they weren't wet enough. Rewet and try again.

Next, spray on one of the rock colors. Cover the entire rock face. Don't be alarmed if the black wash loses some of its intensity; the casting will look different after all the water dries out of it, and if it's too light you can add more black wash. If it looks like you've applied too much color or you want an area to be lighter, hit it with your wet water spray. Hold the sprayer close to the casting and wash away some of the color. This technique also works well for lightening the tops of protruding rock faces.

Painting shadows. Now paint in shadow areas. Many people balk at this, thinking you have to be an artist to use a paintbrush. Just try painting shadows and see how easy it is — and how much more realistic the rocks become. Mix the shadow color by combining 2¼ cups of the rock color with ½ teaspoon of India ink. Store this mixture in a screw-top jar.

Turn on all your regular layout lighting and turn off any special work lights. If you're building a portable pike, work under average room lighting. Note where shadows are cast

under rock overhangs and on the lower surfaces of the castings and, using a soft brush, apply the shadow color in these shadow areas. Use the tip of the brush to dot small shadows with color.

Apply the shadow color to half of a rock face, then step back to view the difference it makes. The shadowed rock seems to have more detail and texture. Where the shadows are deep, you may not be able to see exactly where the coloring is going, so shine a flashlight directly onto the rock face to see if you missed any spots. The shadow color may also be stippled onto a smooth rock surface to give it added texture.

Now it's time to let the rocks dry, at least overnight, before adding highlights. Don't try to judge the color at this point; the rocks will become lighter and duller as they dry.

Dry-brushing highlights. Dry-brushing has much the same effect as painting in the shadows: It gives the castings additional texture and character. To mix the highlight color add 1 teaspoon of flat white latex paint to ¾ cup of the basic rock color. Apply this color only to the upper surfaces of the castings, places where noon sunlight would strike the rock. As with the shadow color, highlights should be applied under normal layout lighting.

Pick up a small amount of paint on a ¾" brush and wipe off most of the color on a rag or paper towel. Pat it on the highlights. The patting action tends not to leave brush marks, and if

I spray extra black relief wash under overhangs and into any other places where natural shadows would occur.

Dry-brushing rock faces adds highlights, lightens the upper surfaces, and brings out the fine texture and detail in the castings.

To add interest to this rock face I painted several areas to look as though another type of rock bubbled up through the molten lava. Here I used a mixture made from one part burnt umber acrylic color and three parts water.

The brush handle is pointing out the finished dry-brushing on the rock highlights. Trees, vegetation, weeds, and man-made details will complete the scene.

CHAPTER 4

These expanded-foam rocks were painted too dark. The first step in saving them was to prime with flat white latex paint.

Then, after brushing on a coat of 1:1 Earth, I sprayed them with black relief wash which washed away some of the Earth color.

the brush is held at a slight angle, it touches only the high points of the rock. Keep adding paint to the brush, wiping most of it away and dry-brushing the rock surfaces until all the highlights are accented. As the brush becomes drier it can be drawn across some of the vertical surfaces of the rock face to bring out texture and relief. You may want to go one step further and dry-brush pure white onto the very tips of the rock profile, but be careful not to add too much white — you don't want your rock faces to look frosted.

Adjusting the color. If the colors seem too light as the rocks dry, you can darken them slightly without changing their basic color. Thoroughly wet the castings and carefully mist on more black relief wash, starting at the bottom and working up the face. If the rocks are still too light after the casting dries, repeat the process, only this time do not wet the plaster as much, so it will absorb more color.

Castings that turn out too dark can be lightened by rewetting and respraying them with the basic rock color to mask some of the black wash. If the highlights disappear when you do this, add a little more white to the highlight, mix, and reapply.

Pre-coloring rock castings. Pre-colored plaster can be used to make rock castings. Use the formulas in Chapter 2 (page 20). Colored plaster may take longer to set because of the coloring agent, and sometimes it will not set as hard as plain plaster, but neither is a problem in rock casting.

To complete the coloring sequence when pre-colored plaster is used, spray the black relief wash on the damp casting, and after it has dried, dry-brush the highlights with a color a little lighter than the casting. Washes and tints like those used to color the white plaster castings can be flowed over the surface to modify the cast-in color slightly, and other tints can be made from acrylic artist's colors and universal tinting colors. Dilute the

tube colors with lots of water to make a very thin wash. Remember that the casting will always turn lighter as the plaster dries.

Saving improperly colored rock castings. If you make a mistake while coloring rock castings or you don't like the results, all is not lost. Carefully paint the casting with flat white latex paint, and let it dry overnight. This acts as a primer, and seals the surface so you can repaint the casting with a new rock color. The trick is to make the color look thin and transparent, to match other rocks on your layout.

Start with the basic 1:1 dilution of earth latex paint, the same mix we used to color the scenic base (Chapter 3). Apply this to the rock casting with a 1" brush. Then gently spray black relief wash onto the wet latex paint. Some of the earth latex will wash away, leaving highlight areas, and the black wash will mix with the earth color and settle into cracks and fissures. Use rags, sponges, paper towels, and newspaper to sop up excess water, and let the casting dry overnight.

The rock now has its basic color. The white paint exposed when the earth color washed away serves as the highlight, and the black wash fills the cracks and grays the earth color.

To finish recoloring the rock, make a shadow color by mixing several brush loads of 1:1 earth latex paint with full-strength black India ink, a drop at a time, until the earth is several shades darker. Two or three drops of ink are usually enough. Now wet the rock face again with black relief wash. Because the white latex paint primer coat has sealed the casting, most of the wash will run off, leaving the surface wet.

Pick up some of the shadow color with a small brush, and paint in the shadows as before. Because the surface is wet the shadow color will flow into areas where the brush cannot reach. The water will also cause some of the shadow color to flow onto flat

These rubble stones are scrap plaster that was crushed with a hammer and colored with the basic rock colors.

surfaces, bringing out the rock texture. If the shadow looks too dark or is in the wrong place, wash it away with wet water. Now let the surface dry.

Thin tints and washes can be applied to alter the color of the castings. If the rock still lacks punch, dry-brushing highlights will add sparkle.

Making rubble. As you make rock castings, save all plaster scraps in a heavy paper bag. When the bag is a third full, place it on its side, hold the top shut, and break the plaster into small pieces with a hammer. Remove any large chunks of plaster and pour the contents of the bag into a 2-pound coffee can.

Color this rubble with the same paints used on the rock castings. First moisten the plaster pieces with water, then pour dilute rock color into the can and snap on the lid. Tip and swirl the can until all the pieces are coated with paint, then pour the remaining paint back into its jar. Dump the wet rubble onto several thicknesses of newspaper, spreading the pieces out as thin as possible. Allow them to dry for several days, turning occasionally.

After the rubble dries the pieces will be lighter and will look dull and flat. Use the black relief wash to bring out their surface relief and color them to match the rock faces. First wet the

Grass was sprinkled on the rocks and bonded with dilute matte medium. While the matte medium was still wet a brush was used to push rocks and rubble that have fallen out onto the water surface back into the pile.

stones with water so they won't absorb too much black, then spray with the wash. Because the plaster absorbs the water unevenly the ink wash also is absorbed unevenly, making the stones realistically streaked and speckled.

Leave the rubble on the newspaper for several days to dry completely, then sift the stones through a piece of window screen to separate the medium-size particles from the coarse ones. Use a tea strainer to sift fine particles into a third pile, and store all three grades in boxes, ready for use.

Building rubble piles. Use your homemade plaster stones at the base of the rock faces to represent fallen rock and construction rubble. Start with a pinch of the larger rocks, dropping them along the base of a rock face. A small brush helps to push the rubble close to the casting. Add a pinch of smaller rocks over the first layer, and work them into position. These small rocks should fall in between and around the larger ones. Next, sprinkle some of the finest rubble over the pile. These fine tailings will fill in between the larger rocks, creating a natural look.

Now mist the rubble pile with wet water. The spray will wash some of the finer particles into the cracks, so fill the holes with another sprinkling of fine or medium-size rubble. Then soak the pile with a spray of one part acrylic matte medium diluted with three parts water, with a few drops of detergent added to make it flow. Apply plenty of matte medium — some should run out of the rock pile and soak into the surrounding texture. This ensures that the larger pieces will be bonded in place. Let the pile dry overnight.

The final step is to dry-brush the top surfaces of the rock pile. Mix 1/2 cup latex earth color with 1/2 teaspoon of flat white latex paint. Choose a short-bristled, stiff brush, dip the very end in the paint, then scrub most of the paint off the brush onto a rag or paper towel. There is just enough

paint on the brush if only a trace of paint comes off when you stroke the bristles over the back of your finger.

Gently dry-brush the upper surfaces of the rock pile, working from top to bottom. The brush should leave light highlights on the stones; if the effect comes out right, only the top surfaces will be lighter, and absolute-ly no brush marks should be visible.

Vegetation. After dry-brushing, tear small bits of lichen, dip them in white glue, and jam them into the larger cracks between rocks. Do the same with weeds, sticks, and twigs. A thin green wash can be flowed on the "north" sides of the rocks to represent moss. To finish the pile, sprinkle a lit-

ACRYLIC MATTE MEDIUM BONDING SPRAY

Acrylic matte medium varies in consistency: some brands are as thick as catsup, others as thin as cream. The formula below will always work, but if you purchase a heavy brand of matte medium, try increasing the proportion of water in the solution up to as high as 6:1.

Combine:
      1 cup acrylic matte medium
      3 cups water
      4 drops wetting agent

IMPORTANT NOTE — Some brands of matte medium use silica or talc as a filler. When the diluted medium dries it leaves behind a white powder residue. The residue can be eliminated by:
● Painting over the white powder residue with the basic earth color.
● Adding texture over the white residue.
● Diluting the matte medium, letting the white filler sink to the bottom of the bottle, and decanting the clear fluid from the top.
● Changing brands of matte medium.

WHITE GLUE BONDING SPRAY

Combine:
      1 cup white glue (Elmer's)
      3 cups water
      4 drops wetting agent

Different brands of white glue dissolve differently. If the glue seems reluc-tant to dissolve try mixing it with warm water. Also, white glue may soften when re-wet, but will harden again after drying.

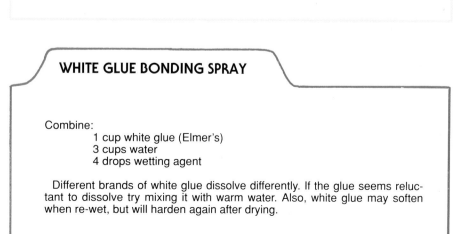

CHAPTER 4

This home-cast retaining wall was colored using the four-step coloring sequence. After the paint dried the wall was lightly weathered with pastel chalks and small bits of foliage added.

RETAINING WALL COLORS

"New" wall color:
        8 ounces (1 cup) 3:1 earth latex paint
        1/2" Raw Sienna acrylic color
        1 quart (4 cups) water

"Old" wall color:
        8 ounces 3:1 earth latex paint
        1/2" Burnt Umber acrylic color
        1 quart water

Basic brick wall:
        2 teaspoons Polly S Boxcar Red
        Several drops of Polly S Roof Brown
        4 drops liquid detergent
        6 ounces of water in spray bottle (Vary water to change intensity)

Concrete wall No. 1:
        1" Medium Gray acrylic color
        1/2" Raw Sienna acrylic color or 2 teaspoons Polly S Reefer Gray
        1/2 teaspoon Polly S Earth
        4 drops liquid detergent
        8 ounces of water in spray bottle

Concrete wall color No. 2:
        8 ounces 3:1 earth latex paint
        1" Medium Gray acrylic or 1/2 teaspoon Polly S Reefer Gray
        1 quart water

Granite wall color:
        8 ounces 3:1 earth latex paint
        1" Red Oxide acrylic color
        1 quart water

Red granite wall:
        1/2 teaspoon Polly S Rust
        6 ounces basic brick wall color

Always experiment with new colors on a scrap wall casting before using them on your layout.

tle brown ground foam to look like dried leaves and some fine green foam for grass. Using a soft brush, push the foam under the edges of the pile so it looks like nature put it there. A gentle mist of wet water followed by a soaking with matte medium spray will bond everything in place.

Casting retaining walls. Rock faces aren't the only scenery elements you can cast. I've applied the technique to retaining walls, which can be installed and painted along with the rest of the scenery. I produce my own masters and make molds from them.

As with rock castings, you have the option of either casting retaining walls on the workbench and installing them later, or casting them directly into the scenery base. I prefer the latter. Either way, the shapes of the walls can be altered or you can fill imperfections by mixing a little soupy plaster and applying it with a toothpick before painting.

I color wall castings right after the plaster sets, while it is still damp. First spray the casting with the black wash — use enough that the excess runs off. The second color should be the basic rock color; several choices are listed in the recipe box. Always experiment with new colors on a piece of scrap wall casting before using them on your layout, and always evaluate colors after the plaster has dried.

The next step is to paint some of the individual stones a slightly different color. In a shallow dish, mix several tablespoons of the basic wall color. Open several bottles of Polly S colors that are darker than the stones in the wall, plus a bottle of Reefer White.

CHAPTER 4

Three different types of retaining walls, all painted using the four-step procedure. The top two walls are metal castings, the third is embossed paper.

A single rock mold was used to build this face, but the mold was oriented every which way to give the finished rock castings some variety.

Work under your normal railroad room lights. Dab a brush full of Polly S paint from one of the jars, mix it with some of the wall color, and pat this onto the surface of a stone. Evaluate the color. If it looks good, continue painting individual stones at random. Wash the brush in water and try another color. Paint some of the stones a lighter color by mixing the Reefer White with the rock color. Continue until about half the wall has different-colored stones. Let the paint dry completely.

The last step is to dry-brush the stones to emphasize surface detail. Weather your wall casting with thin acrylic washes and powered pastel chalks exactly as you would a structure. Detail the wall with bits of lichen, scenic foam, or other texture material.

Questions and answers

Q: There's a lot of water involved in your rock-coloring techniques. Won't this damage the track on my layout? I have hand-laid Code 70 rail.
A: Not if you take two easy precau-

tions. First, tape the track to keep plaster out of it, as you would during any scenery work. Second, blot up excess water with rags or sponges as you go. As you gain experience with the sprayer bottles, you'll find you can control the volume of water quite easily. I've used the water-soluble system on a railroad with hand-laid track, with no problems. The only thing I noticed was that some of the spikes rusted, which improved their holding power.

Q: I've read about using crinkled aluminum foil to make rock castings. Will foil work as well as rubber molds?
A: Yes and no. These "molds" are crumpled, hand-size pieces of heavy-duty foil that are filled with plaster and set in place just like rubber molds. They are easy to make and use, but their big disadvantage is that the rock face is not predictable and certainly not repeatable. Too often the resulting rock faces look exactly like what they are made from, crumpled aluminum foil.

Q: I tried rock castings a few years back, and had poor results. The plaster took a long time to dry, and its surface has always been powdery. The problem was old plaster. Is there any way to save this situation, short of ripping out the rock faces and rebuilding them?
A: Try this: Spray the rock faces with the standard acrylic matte medium bonding solution used throughout this book. When the rocks dry, paint them as explained in the section on recoloring rocks. The combination of the matte medium spray and the flat white latex paint should bond the surface of the weak plaster and cure the powdering problem. If not, you'll have to blast — figuratively, of course.

Q: The area between rock castings, where the two molds are blended together, is shiny and does not take paint. What's the problem?
A: The surface of some plasters loses its porousness if it is worked. The more you trowel or shape it, the denser it becomes. Always use only a quick picking, chipping, and twisting motion to remove excess plaster. Never trowel or smooth the area between castings if you want them to take color the same as cast rock. To treat your existing shiny spots so they will take paint evenly, seal all the surfaces with white latex paint before coloring.

Adding texture over texture gives scenery depth and life, and ensures that the ground-cover materials look loose and natural.

CHAPTER 5

Scenic finishing: texture over texture

One of the keys to realism in model scenery is varied texture. When you look at effective scenery, you know that the large, flat, green areas aren't filled with scaled-down blades of grass, but the texture can convince your mind that the scene is right anyway. Without carefully modeled textures, nothing in a model scene will look real. In this chapter I'll assume that you have built the scenic base, added rock faces, and applied coloring and an initial texture coat of sawdust or ground foam. Now we come to the part of the scenery that the viewer sees, the topmost layer. We'll build depth and life in the scenery by applying texture over texture. This final texture coat also covers minor construction errors and little spots that need to be touched up here and there.

A variety of textures. Start by gathering as many kinds and colors of texture material as you can find. A good starting selection is at least three shades of fine green sawdust or foam, one medium-fine brown foam or sawdust, one light tan foam, one yellow-green foam, and several colors of scale ballast and gravel, including coal, sandstone, and medium gray. I keep these basic textures in a multi-compartment texture tray made from old kit boxes.

The basic colors in the texture tray provide the scenery with its finished color, so it is important that you choose them carefully. These basic textures should be materials you can duplicate easily, either by purchasing more at the hobby shop or by making more yourself, so you can touch up the scenery later and match the original colors. The box on this page lists miscellaneous useful textures, and the more types you keep on hand, the faster you can finish a given area of scenery.

Arranging texture materials. I like the surface of the finished scenery to look loose and natural, and my method for adding finish texture makes that result easy to achieve. You can work over the just-completed latex paint and first texture coat, or let it dry and come back later to finish the texturing. If the scenery base is dry, spray on enough water to make it damp. After deciding where roads, paths, and other flat dirt areas will be, fill a shaker jar with basic dirt texture from the tray, usually light tan ground foam. Sprinkle on the dirt texture, and

don't worry if some strays outside of where you planned it, because grass texture will cover the dirt edges later.

Next apply grass textures. Load another shaker jar with a basic green texture and sprinkle it on. Use your fingers to add pinches of the other basic green textures here and there, working directly from the texture tray. Try to vary the greens as much as possible, but avoid a salt-and-pepper effect. Use light greens and yellow-greens on steep hills and along

roadways, and darker greens in low areas and on flat meadows and lawns.

Next, pile coal, gravel, and ballast wherever they will look natural. If heavy textures such as coal or ballast will not cling to steep slopes, rewet the surface with wet water. Add logs, sticks, old weathered wood, and small rocks with tweezers.

Now put brown or tan foam or sawdust in another shaker and sprinkle it lightly over the grass to represent thin spots. If you know where

My texture trays are made by stapling old kit boxes together. Each compartment holds a different type or color, and the tray makes the materials easy to find and handle.

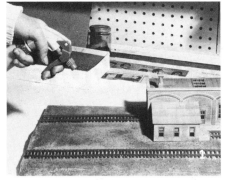

An example of texture over texture. After pre-wetting the surface (1), fine dirt is sifted through a tea strainer onto the base to make a road (2). Pinches of grass texture are sprinkled along the edges of the road (3). Larger areas are covered with texture from a shaker bottle (4). I work with several shakers, each containing a slightly different grass color. A soft brush is handy for manipulating texture into the joint between the building and the base (5). A little ballast is piled on the roadside (6), and some crushed plaster stones are sprinkled in a low area (7). More grass texture will be added later.

some of your trees will be placed, the brown texture can be sprinkled over the grass to represent fallen leaves.

To simulate coarse low bushes or the lush growth in the bottom of a drainage ditch, layer the textures. Start with finely chopped lichen scraps, and sprinkle green and yellow foam over the lichen. Then add dirt or a little ballast, and drop in sticks, stones, and larger pieces of lichen until you like the effect. Coarse ground foam, available commercially, is useful for modeling small shrubs. Drop a small pinch of foam onto the scenery and push it around with a small brush to separate it into single bushes.

Bonding texture in place. So far, all the texture has been manipulated dry, which means that if something falls where you don't want it, it can be moved with a brush, or even vacuumed up altogether. Now look over the sce-

nery to make sure there are no pieces of foam, sawdust, or gravel where you don't want them. Check all the track for obstructions, and make sure there is no texture material around switch machine linkages. Also check along roads and around buildings. Use tweezers and a small soft brush to remove or rearrange the offending pieces. It is important to remove the texture now before the bonding step; after the acrylic matte medium bonding spray dries, anything you don't like will have to be scraped away.

Now pre-wet the texture with wet water. Spray the water gently, because the texture must not be blown around by the force of the spray. With a little practice you'll find the correct spraying force. Keep the sprayer nozzle 12 to 18 inches from the surface of the scenery. The wet water will hold the texture in place, and help the matte

medium flow through all the texture layers.

In many cases it's the little things, almost unseen, that make for successful scenery. As I mentioned above, everything must look loose, and there cannot be a trace of glue. Dilute acrylic matte medium applied with a spray bottle is my favorite bonding agent, because it dries flat and colorless and leaves no residue. See the box on page 31 for the formula for matte medium spray.

Spray on the dilute matte medium, thoroughly soaking the texture. Hold the spray bottle far enough away that the mist loses most of its force by the time it reaches the scenery. Keep spraying until the textures are milky white, almost until they will not absorb any more liquid. The texture acts as a wick, drawing the bonding solution down toward the scenic base. If

CHAPTER 5

A brush is used to sweep away unwanted texture (8). After spraying the stones with matte medium (9), more ground foam is sprinkled over some of them (10). After all textures are in place the area is pre-wet again and soaked with matte medium spray (11).

you wet only the surface texture, the bonding solution will form a crust on top of the scenery, leaving the textures underneath loose. The first time the crust is broken the loose material will be spread all over the railroad. If a puddle of matte medium forms it can be sopped up by sprinkling on a little more foam or sawdust.

After you're through with the matte medium spray, remove the pump and nozzle from the bottle and run warm water through them until it comes out clear. Do this every time you use the sprayer, and it will always be ready for use next time. If the nozzle becomes clogged, take it apart and run a fine wire through the small hole in the tip. Bits of dried matte medium can be picked off the outside of the nozzle with a model knife. Keep the pump and nozzle clean and you'll get years of use out of a sprayer; neglect to rinse it

thoroughly even once and you can plan on throwing it away!

After soaking the texture with bonding solution, you can let the scenery dry or you can use white glue diluted 1:1 with water to glue down barrels, boxes, tires, and scrap lumber. Sticks, logs, small bushes, weeds, and even trees can be installed now. Or, you can leave the detailing for the time being and come back later to add more.

Ballasting track. I ballast track after final scenery texturing is complete, so the ballast texture will overlap the dirt and grass along the track. To model weed-grown track that sees little care, all you have to do is work some grass or dirt texture up and over the edges of the ballast.

The color and size of the ballast are important. I use medium gray and light gray N scale ballast on my HO

railroad, because the stones are equivalent to about two inches in HO scale, a good size. I mix the two colors and keep the mixture in one of the compartments in my texture tray. Mixing two or three close shades of the same color makes the ballast look as if it has been subjected to the effects of sun, weather, and engine splatters for years. However, do not mix light colors with dark colors or the result will look

Details like this twig are glued to the scenery with white glue diluted 1:1 with water. Small bits of lichen are dipped in dilute

glue and set on the scenery to represent bushes and scrub growth. This can all be done while the texture is still wet.

I use a folded 3 x 5 card to deposit ballast along the track, and a stiff-bristled brush to spread it around the ties (top photos). Then I spray the track with wet water, and soak with matte medium. Adjust the spray so that it covers only the roadbed.

A small cluster of clutter adds detail and interest to the end of this platform. The pieces were pushed into the texture while it was was still wet from the matte medium spray.

like salt and pepper instead of ballast.

Use a folded 3 x 5 file card to distribute ballast along the sides of and in between the rails, then spread it with a 1½"-wide stiff-bristled brush. Run the brush down the track so the bristles sweep away the ballast down to the level of the tie tops. Do not spread any ballast around the moving parts of turnouts; the stones will act like a wick and draw the adhesive into the linkage.

Push and spread the dry ballast until it is even with the tops of the ties and there is a natural slope leading away from the tie edge. Carefully check the track to make sure all flangeways are clear and that there are no thin spots needing more ballast. When everything is where you want it, mist the ballast with wet water, working in 2- or 3-foot sections. It is important to soak the ballast so a crust will not form.

Now apply the matte medium bonding solution. There are two ways to do this, depending on where the track is. If the track runs through open scenery where there are only a few turnouts, use the sprayer bottle, keeping the spray to the width of the ballast. If there are buildings or other features, protect them against matte medium overspray by holding a scrap square of corrugated cardboard in front of them. Move the cardboard along with the spray bottle.

Matte medium cannot be sprayed where the track is close to many buildings or includes many turnouts, because there is danger of getting the adhesive into areas where it is not wanted. Here, pour dilute matte medium into a small dish or jar, and use an eyedropper to deposit the solution between the rails. The solution will soak into the ballast; use enough that some runs out into the surrounding textures. If the matte medium gets into any moving parts, blot it up with a Q-tip.

After ballasting, but before the bonding solution has dried, carefully wipe the railheads with a damp cloth.

Toning down new ballast. After the ballast has dried overnight it may look a little bright, especially if you are modeling a branchline railroad. To tone it down, mix some of the 2:1 Earth latex paint used for basic scenery coloring with 5 parts water and flow it between the rails. This thin wash will spread out into the ballast, and when dry, the ballast will take on a dusty appearance. (Use this same wash on grass texture to simulate dead grass.) Always wipe the railheads with a damp cloth to remove any traces of paint.

Clusters of clutter. A trick that will fool viewers into thinking there is a great deal of detail in a model scene is using clusters of clutter. Save all

CHAPTER 5

The finished scene. Note how the clutter clusters on either side of the open dirt space help frame the area.

scraps from your modeling projects, such as bits of wood, metal, and leftover plastic parts. When you have a handful of such items, paint and weather them and place in clusters on the railroad. A typical cluster includes several rocks, a few weeds, a board, and an old tire. Another might have a pile of old weathered boards and a few cement blocks. The larger items are placed first, and the small pieces added around them. Glue large parts with the 50/50 glue-water solution, but just set the smaller items in place and soak them with matte medium as you would other scenic texture.

I use clutter to break up large or medium-size expanses of scenery into smaller, more defined scenes, because small areas make the railroad look larger than it is. Clutter also can be used to lead the viewer's eye into a scene and toward or away from certain features. The important thing to remember is that the clusters should be small groups of different things, not just large detail parts that call attention to themselves. In this sense, clutter is a scenic texture instead of detail, and if you think of it and use it that way, you can achieve a detailed look for your railroad without spending vast sums on commercial detail parts.

Using real dirt as scenic texture. Bare soil is a fairly difficult texture to model convincingly, especially when the bare soil is to represent a dirt road.

My favorite material for representing bare soil is dried and sifted dirt. The color of real dirt is usually appropriate, and in most areas, dirt is free. Dirt cheap, you might say.

Using real soil does have one or two disadvantages. Many soils include small flintlike particles that glitter and sparkle after the dirt is applied. Painting will eliminate some of the sparkle, but paint gives scenic texture a dead look. George Sellios of Fine Scale Miniatures discovered the best type of soil for scenery: the clay-like dirt from a baseball diamond. This is very fine, light earth tan, and includes little foreign matter. Best of all, baseball diamond dirt has no sparkle.

Soil, sand, or baseball diamond dirt must be dried before sifting. I spread it on newspaper and let it dry on my cellar floor, but if you're in a hurry, place the soil on a baking sheet and put it in a warm oven (250 degrees). Stir it to expose all surfaces to the heat, then turn off the heat and leave the dirt overnight with the oven door ajar. Sift the dirt through a food strainer or an old window screen. Discard any dirt that does not fall through the screen.

Now divide the sifted soil into two piles. Half the dirt can be used as is, for modeling gravel piles, abandoned quarry operations, stream beds carrying fast-moving water, or around rub-

A coffee can with a hole cut in the lid and a piece of nylon stocking stretched over the top makes a great dirt sifter.

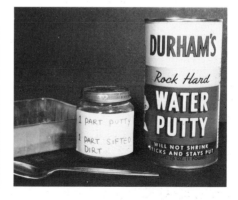

If the sifted dirt you have is too dark, try mixing it with an equal part of Durham's Water Putty to lighten it.

I textured the steep banks in this sandpit by blowing or "whisking" fine sifted sand onto white glue.

ble piles and construction sites. Sift the second pile again, this time through a tea strainer or nylon stocking material. This second sifting should produce two fine grades of dirt: the coarser will have stones 4″ to 6″ across in HO scale, the finer grade is almost dust. The fine grade is good for roads or well-trodden backyard dirt, and it makes great sandpiles.

If the dirt is too dark to match the earth color on your railroad, lighten it by adding Durham's Water Putty (available in hardware stores). Start with equal parts of sifted soil and putty, mixed together dry, and make further color adjustments after some of the mix is applied and allowed to dry. Because the Water Putty is off-white and has a fine texture it can be added to soil without changing the soil's realistic look.

Apply the sifted soil using a tea strainer, gently tapping the sides of the strainer to lay down an even layer of dirt. If you don't have a tea strainer, a nylon stocking stretched over the end of a cardboard tube will do. Sprinkle the dirt onto the wet latex paint first, before other textures are added. To add a slightly different texture, try sprinkling one of the coarser grades of earth over the fine soil. Moisten the dirt area with wet water and bond the dirt in place with matte medium spray. Dirt driveways, backyards, and paths can be made by sprinkling the soil over the existing scenery, wetting it, and spraying with matte medium. Use a soft brush to push the soil into areas where it belongs before spraying with water.

Whisking. To apply fine powdered dirt to a steep bank or to almost vertical surfaces, such as in a sandpit, I use a technique called "whisking." This involves holding the dirt in a folded 3 x 5 file card and blowing the dirt against

The "loose" gravel around this station is builder's sand sifted through a kitchen strainer. The dirt road at right is Durham's

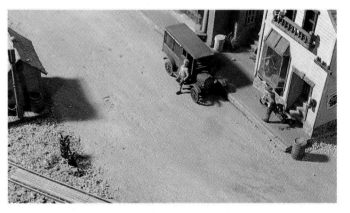

Water Putty, smoothed with wet fingers. After setting it was colored with latex paint and weathered with dilute India ink.

CHAPTER 5

To build a road over the scenery, work out the location with cardboard strips (1). Glue the strips down with white glue (2), weighting them to conform to the contours. Make shoulders with Sculptamold (3), and fill seams between the sections. Rub Sculptamold over the surface (4). At first it will not stick, but continue rubbing until a thin, textured layer coats the road.

the freshly painted surface with a stream of air from a drinking straw. If the powdered dirt does not stick to the paint because the slope is too steep, brush the area with diluted white glue or matte medium. Several applications may be needed to achieve the proper loose-looking texture. Try to find a little darker-colored dirt to whisk up and under overhangs to strengthen the shadows.

One word of caution: Some soil contains tiny magnetic particles that can work loose and cling to locomotive motors and bearing surfaces, ruining moving parts. I vacuum areas where I have applied soil several times to make sure all loose material is removed.

Building dirt roads. There are two ways to build roads: as part of the scenery base, or on top of it. If you know where the roads will go before you build the scenery base, glue cardboard strips 10 to 25 scale feet wide on top of the cardboard web with white glue. Then lay plaster-soaked paper towels over the road when you cover the rest of the scenery base. The only difference in rough texturing is that after applying the latex Earth paint the road gets a sprinkling of fine soil while the rest of the scenery base gets a coating of foam or sawdust.

To add a road after the scenic base is built, again cut road strips from corrugated cardboard. Glue these strips to the scenery base with white glue, letting the road find its own contour and elevation, but smoothing out unrealistic dips or sags. Use weights to hold the road strips until the glue dries. I like to install all the strips for a road in one session, so I can see the total impact and make any changes before adding texture.

When the glue dries mix a batch of Sculptamold and use it to blend the road into the surrounding scenery. This is also the time to add ditches, gravel piles, or embankments. To add surface texture to the road, spread Sculptamold over the surface of the cardboard with your fingers. Rub it back and forth in the direction of travel, smoothing it level. The more you rub the Sculptamold, the stickier it becomes and the thinner it can be applied. If the Sculptamold starts to stick to your fingers, dip them into a glass of water and continue rubbing. Add potholes and wheel ruts with the wooden end of a small paintbrush or a piece of scrap wood. After you get the hang of making this type of road by applying the Sculptamold with your fingers, you'll never go back to using a putty knife or trowel.

As soon as the top is finished, paint the whole road with latex Earth paint. Brushing the paint on the road surface will further smooth it. Sprinkle enough sifted dirt to cover all of the paint. Sprinkle green foam or sawdust along the sides of the road where it meets the scenic base, and add stones, dirt piles, or other coarse textures. If the middle of the road needs grass or other texture, drop it in place with your fingers, coax it into position with a brush, and mist it with matte medium.

Footprints and tire tracks can be modeled in the earth texture while it is wet. I put several sizes of wheels on a toothpick or dowel and roll them over the terrain. For footprints, use an old figure and push the feet lightly into the soil. Don't forget to flow a little black wash into the footprints and tire tracks to make them stand out.

It's best not to try to correct minor errors in the road surface while the matte medium is wet, because you'll usually end up with a bigger mess than when you started. After the surface dries it can be filled or changed.

To build a road over existing scenery, clear a path through the texture, removing lichen, stones, trees, and anything else in the way. Then glue cardboard strips over the scenic base, cutting away any base that interferes. To help the Sculptamold stick better, wet the existing scenery

CHAPTER 5

(Left) After painting the road with Earth latex paint, fine sifted sand is sprinkled over the wet surface. (Right) This backwoods road includes detail in the middle. Fine sawdust, green foam, and small rocks were sprinkled in place, moved to exact position with a brush, and then soaked with matte medium spray. Ruts and potholes were formed with the handle of the brush.

before applying it. The rest of the steps are the same as those described above.

Road texture tips. Virtually any material compatible with the water-soluble scenery method is a candidate for making roads. I even tried cat litter, but it was too coarse. I reduced it to scale size by putting a handful in a paper sack and beating it with a hammer. If you want the crushed litter to have a uniform size run it through a window screen. Put the lumps that do not pass through the screen back into the bag and whack them again.

Very fine, powdery dirt can be hard to control. Try applying it using an empty white glue bottle that has had the nozzle opening trimmed to 1/4" in diameter. Fill the bottle halfway with dirt, aim at the scenery, and squeeze. With a little practice you can get the dirt to puff where you want it.

Working with acrylic spackle. Since this book was first introduced, several new acrylic-based materials have been introduced to the home-repair market. They thin with water, will not shrink, are easy to work with, and dry overnight to a hard, yet flexible surface. Check in a large hardware store for the different brands and formulas available.

One product that works well for roads (and for patching small areas of existing scenery) is acrylic spackle. It's sold under a variety of trade names for many different uses. The one I like best is sold to be used as mortar for attaching tile and decorative half-bricks to kitchen walls. While not inexpensive, a little goes a long way.

The fine sand that has been added to the acrylic to simulate mortar adds nice texture to the surface. The acrylic spackle can be spread over the scenery base with a trowel or thinned with water and applied with a wide brush. I've tried it over Styrofoam, plaster-soaked paper towels, burlap, and Rigid Wrap. It can even be thinned to the consistency of paint and

All of the roads on George Sellios' HO Franklin & South Manchester railroad are highly detailed. Here Durham's Water Putty was troweled in place, worked with the tip of a hobby knife, then sanded smooth. A black wash made from rubbing alcohol and India ink was flowed onto the road surface to bring out the texture.

To simulate a dirt road here I applied plaster with a butter knife. After it started to set, I smoothed it with my fingers. It was colored with earth latex paint while it was still wet.

CHAPTER 5

The texture here was bonded in place with a liberal application of dilute matte medium. It looks white now, but the next morning the matte medium was dry, and invisible, and none of the texture was loose.

applied over wood retaining walls to simulate rough concrete.

Acrylic spackle is available in several standard colors, including white, black, and gray, but you can change the tint by mixing it with acrylic colors straight from the tube. It can be painted and colored using any method. It's just one more handy gadget in our water-soluble scenery toolbox.

Questions and answers

Q: I've had trouble with texture material not adhering properly to the layout. Even after the matte medium is thoroughly dry, the texture comes loose if I touch it.
A: There are two possibilities here: Either you've diluted the matte medium too much, or you haven't applied enough of it to properly bond the texture. Usually, it's the second problem. Many modelers are hesitant to soak the texture, fearing that the moisture will damage the track or layout. But the trick is to apply the bonding spray until the texture turns white and will absorb no more.
Q: I'm modeling a railroad that runs through areas of dusty, dry, bare ground. You mention adding green texture over the latex paint, but this is not suitable for bare ground modeling. How would you model bare ground using the water-soluble method?
A: Start by building the scenic shell or base to the point of covering the web with plaster-soaked paper towels. While the plaster is still damp apply another thin coating of plaster or Sculptamold. This coat is used to smooth out irregularities of the scenery base and to give you a surface for texturing. The texturing can be applied by stippling the wet plaster with a brush or by pressing rolled-up tinfoil into the surface. After the plaster starts to set, apply latex earth paint, then sprinkle sifted dirt onto the wet paint instead of grass-colored foam or sawdust.

After the paint dries, color the earth surface using the same techniques as are used to color rocks. To alter the color, try dusting the dried dirt with powdered pastel chalks. After the chalk powder is in place, a light spray of clear flat fixative such as Testor's Dullcote will seal and hold it.

Q: I've had a problem with latex earth paint cracking after it dries. It looks like an antique oil painting. What is the cause of this problem and how can it be eliminated?
A: I've never encountered this in over 15 years of building scenery. There are several possible causes. First, cracking could be caused by using latex paint that was not diluted to the proper consistency. Thicker paint seems to shrink more while drying.

Another cause may be allowing the painted plaster scenery base to dry for several weeks before applying texture, wet water, and matte medium. Perhaps the re-wetting may cause the plaster base or the latex paint on top of it to expand and contract. I'd suggest applying a second coat of thinned earth paint and proceeding from there with more texture and matte medium.
Q: What do I do when the matte medium spray balls up and doesn't penetrate the texture material? This seems to happen a lot with N scale ballast and other fine mineral textures.
A: Some types of texture are reluctant to absorb even our "wet" water — it beads up on the surface and runs off, leaving unwanted rivulets. With such materials I use a half and half (1:1) mixture of rubbing (isopropyl) alcohol and water, applied either with a spray bottle or an eyedropper. The alcohol has low surface tension, and will soak the area without disturbing the surface. Follow it with matte medium spray. Be sure your work area is well-ventilated.
Q: I want to add new water-soluble texture to several areas of my layout, which is almost complete. How can I protect my finished track and scratch-built structures from the wet water and matte medium sprays?
A: Track, buildings, and backdrops can be masked from unwanted spray by holding a sheet-cardboard shield in front of them while spraying. Work dry texture right up to the foundations of buildings with a brush, then wet and bond with an eyedropper to control the flow of the fluids.

Here are two ways to model bare soil. (Left) The exposed earth on this diorama is a combination of sifted decomposed granite and finely ground vermiculite, a soil conditioner available at garden stores. (Right) The bare ground of this contractor's yard was made from finely sifted sand held in place with matte medium and colored with diluted earth-color paint. Before the matte medium set, all out-of-scale stones in the scene were removed with tweezers.

Trees, stumps, weeds, and vines

(Left and above) No single tree or bush in this scene is a striking model in its own right, but, taken together, the effect is convincing.

Growing things are an important part of the great outdoors, and in this chapter we'll discuss methods for simulating foliage on your layout. As with texture, the key concept in using foliage to best effect is the idea of variety; that is, of using as many different materials as possible.

Making deciduous forests, a tree a minute. Trees are the most conspicuous growing things in our scenery, and the first important thing to remember about trees is that you need lots of them, even for a small layout or module. Because of this, if you want a forested look on your railroad you'll have to abandon the idea of building trees as individual models — even if you're modeling the sparsely treed West.

Diorama builders lavish hours constructing a single tree, but that's out of the question when you need 600 of them. Many manufacturers offer ready-made trees, most of which look good in clumps but only fair when standing alone. What we need is a shape and texture that can be mass-

produced and that shouts "I'm a tree!"

My technique for mass-producing convincing deciduous trees is nothing new or revolutionary; in fact, it's based on techniques that have been described many times in model railroad magazines and that are used in some commercial tree kits. I merely substitute materials that I have on hand and rely heavily on water-soluble adhesives and coloring agents. I use twigs and sticks instead of commercial cast metal trunk armatures, and I use both stretched poly fiber fill and scrap lichen for branch or foliage material. I cover the foliage material with ground foam or sawdust "leaves," and use matte medium spray to hold the texture material in place. I call the method "a tree a minute," but some do take a little longer to produce.

Mass-producing trees is repetitious work, and a good way to combat boredom is to watch television while you do it. (Tree building uses about half of your mental faculties, and most TV programs use less than half of what's left.) A pleasant evening of TV

will produce several dozen fine trees, more if you can persuade others in your family to help!

Coloring tree trunks. The "tree-a-minute" technique works just as well for commercial tree kits as for scratch-built, so if you have kits on hand you can follow along as I describe the method. Tree kits usually feature trunk armatures made from plastic or soft metal. To save time, I bend and form several of these at once, and I also gather natural armatures such as sticks, twigs, and dried weeds.

For Woodland Scenics tree kits, I clip the stubby mounting pin from the bottom of the trunk and file the bottom flat. Drill a No. 62 hole in the base of the trunk and use 5-minute epoxy to glue in a $1\frac{1}{2}$" piece of $\frac{1}{32}$" brass wire. This longer, thiner pin serves as a handle for the tree, makes it easy to poke the tree into a Styrofoam block, holds the top-heavy tree upright while the glue dries, and simplifies installing the tree on the layout.

After bending and twisting the

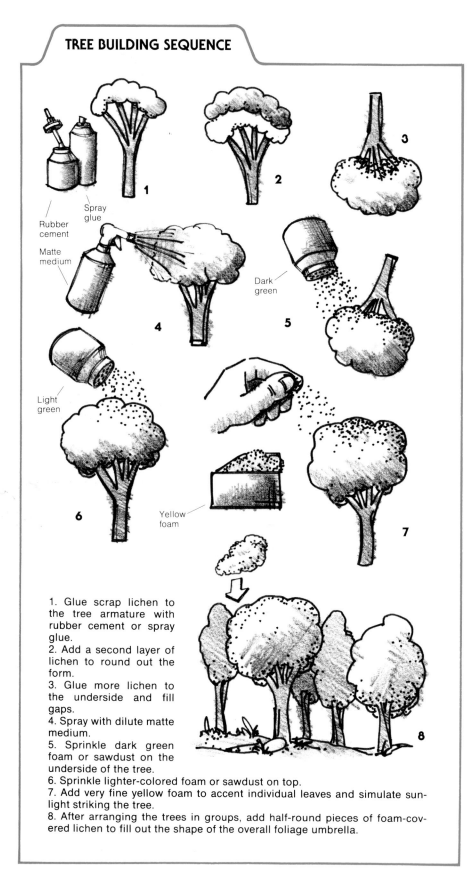

TREE BUILDING SEQUENCE

1 — Rubber cement / Spray glue / Matte medium

2

3 — Dark green

4

5

6 — Light green

7 — Yellow foam

8

1. Glue scrap lichen to the tree armature with rubber cement or spray glue.
2. Add a second layer of lichen to round out the form.
3. Glue more lichen to the underside and fill gaps.
4. Spray with dilute matte medium.
5. Sprinkle dark green foam or sawdust on the underside of the tree.
6. Sprinkle lighter-colored foam or sawdust on top.
7. Add very fine yellow foam to accent individual leaves and simulate sunlight striking the tree.
8. After arranging the trees in groups, add half-round pieces of foam-covered lichen to fill out the shape of the overall foliage umbrella.

After soaking these plastic Christmas decorations in warm water and detergent to remove the glitter, I used them to make tree armatures and dead trees.

them to length just before planting.

Separate the armatures and weeds into piles, each of which will have its trunks painted a slightly different color. I color one pile medium gray to represent willow, elm, or cypress, and make another dark brown to represent wild cherry, maple, or walnut. Yet another pile will be colored white and light gray to simulate birch or aspen. Except for the birches, paint all trunks with a brownish earth-colored latex primer coat (the birches get a grayish-white primer).

There are two ways to color large quantities of trunk armatures: Either spray them with a bark-colored base coat, or dip them in the same earth-colored latex paint used for scenery building. Spray painting is okay, as you can find realistic flat colors in spray cans. Work with spray paint in a well-ventilated area, and be aware that a lot of paint is wasted in overspray.

Dipping the armatures is by far the easiest and quickest way to color them. Fill a two-pound coffee can one-quarter of the way with earth latex paint, diluted 1:1 with water. Add two inches each of raw umber and burnt sienna tube acrylic colors and mix. This will give you a light gray-brown. Place all the armatures except those for birches into the can, snap on the lid, and gently swirl the can until everything is coated with paint. Remove the trunks one by one, drain, and arrange them on newspaper to dry, turning them several times to avoid sticking. The colors will darken

commercial armatures into three-dimensional forms, wash them in warm, soapy water and stick them in Styrofoam blocks to dry overnight. Trim the tops of weed stems with a large pair of scissors, removing flowers, most seed pods, and irregular branches. Some natural growths like

sumac tips look better if the seed pods are left intact; these weeds are usually already tree-shaped and as long as the seed pods are not dry and falling off, they look good covered with foam. If the pods are loose or crumbly, they must be trimmed. Leave the stems long enough for easy handling; trim

CHAPTER 6

Yarrow, a common weed (top left), makes good mass-produced trees. Trim the flowers and seed pods with scissors (bottom left), paint the armature, and add scrap lichen foliage support (above). Apply ground foam or sawdust leaves as shown on page 54.

as they dry. Other bark color formulas can be found in the box on page 55.

Color birch trunks the same way. A quick way to make the dark scars on the birch tree trunk is with a fine-tipped black marking pen.

Bark relief washes. When the armatures have dried overnight, the next step is to color them further with relief washes. Make the wash by adding 2 teaspoons of India ink, 1/4 teaspoon burnt umber, and 1/4 teaspoon raw sienna tinting color to a quart of rubbing alcohol (this is also a good weathering mixture for everything from barrels to buildings).

This dark wash looks best over the light latex base colors. The wash will run into the cracks and crevices in the trunks, adding natural shadows and highlighting the bark texture cast into commercial armatures.

Pour a cup of the wash into a two-pound coffee can, place a handful of armatures in the can, swirl them around, and spread them on newspapers to dry. If the relief color is too light after the alcohol stain dries, add more burnt umber and raw sienna tinting color to the wash and dip the armatures again. The birch trunks should be dipped in a black-only alcohol wash.

After the armatures have dried, dry-brush the bases of the trunks with Polly S Reefer White. Stick the finished trunks in Styrofoam blocks for foliage application.

Adding branches and foliage. I use coarse scrap lichen as a branch structure for trees because I make my

TREE TRUNK COLORS

BASE COLORS:

Gray-brown (most trees):
        2 cups 1:1 Earth latex paint
        2" Raw Umber acrylic tube color
        2" Burnt Sienna acrylic tube color
        3 to 5 drops detergent

Red-brown (western pine):
        2 cups 1:1 Earth latex paint
        2" Burnt Umber acrylic tube color
        1" Red Oxide acrylic tube color
        3 to 5 drops detergent

Light gray (birch and aspen):
        2 cups 1:1 flat white latex paint
        2" Mars Black acrylic tube color
        3 to 5 drops detergent

BARK RELIEF WASHES:

Medium dark:
        2 teaspoons India ink
        1/4 teaspoon Burnt Umber
        1/4 teaspoon Raw Sienna
        1 quart rubbing alcohol

Black wash:
        2 teaspoons India ink
        1 quart rubbing alcohol

own and have a lot of it on hand. You can substitute any of the newer synthetic materials, like poly fiber fill or horsehair scouring pads.

Lichen has one disadvantage: It's heavier than the commercial poly fiber material, so large trees may be top-heavy. Fasten the lichen or poly fiber to the armature with rubber cement, white glue, or spray glue. Cut large pieces in half with shears, and place these flat side down on the branch tops to make pleasing, rounded shapes. Add pieces of lichen until the tree looks like a tree, but allow the glue to dry on each layer of lichen before adding more. When you are satisfied with the shape and all the glue has dried,

J. C. Myer

These realistic tall pines on J. C. Myer's layout were made by inserting individual branches in tapered dowel trunks.

CHAPTER 6

(Top left) After gluing a second layer of scrap lichen to the tree armature, let the glue dry thoroughly so that the matte medium spray used to adhere the leaves will not alter the tree shape **(bottom left)**. When you install the tree on the layout **(above)**, take pains to make sure it is vertical. Even though crooked trees exist in nature, crooked model trees usually look phony.

spray the treetops with matte medium bonding spray, and shake off excess liquid.

Next, either put the trees in a plastic bag with green foam or sawdust and shake it, or sprinkle on green foam or sawdust using a shaker bottle. When using the shaker bottle, turn the trees over and shake dark green texture on the underside and lighter green on the top, to reinforce the illusion of light and shadow. The illusion can be enhanced by sprinkling a few flecks of yellow foam on the tops of the trees to represent sun-drenched leaves. Always build trees over several sheets of newspaper so you can recover surplus leaf texture for reuse.

If you choose the plastic bag "shake and bake" method, gently shake the trees in the bag with the foam or sawdust until all branch surfaces are covered. Shake excess texture back into the bag, and remove foam from the trunks with a soft paintbrush. Stick the trunk into a Styrofoam block until the matte medium dries.

Make small trees the same way, rolling each in different textures from your multi-compartment texture tray (Chapter 5). Very small trees are easy to build; just dip twigs in a small jar of matte medium bonding solution, shake off the excess, and roll the branches in sawdust or foam. Even all-plastic trees become presentable when covered with texture.

Using poly fiber fill. A modern replacement for lichen in making the branch structure for trees is poly fiber fill, a cotton-like synthetic material used to stuff pillows and craft projects. Craft and fabric stores usually carry white poly fiber, and some have it in charcoal and dark green, which is ideal for tree making. Occasionally you'll find the dark green variety in hobby shops, specifically packaged for tree making.

Use the fiber by gently stretching, pulling, and tearing it into filmy, see-through pieces, then glue the pieces to the tree armatures as you would lichen. Follow with a spray of matte medium and ground-foam foliage. With practice you can make excellent trees that will be suitable for use in

Group homemade and commercial trees together for the best overall effect. Here an AHM birch tree is alongside two homemade deciduous trees and one homemade pine.

Commercial tree kits are available in a wide range of styles. (Above) this is a typical kit from Woodland Scenics, with a cast-metal trunk and fiber-and-foam foliage. (Left) At the other end of the spectrum are these kit-built plastic palms.

Sagebrush twigs, like many other natural growths, make good-looking trees either used "as is" or when covered with poly fiber fill branches and foam leaves.

Sumac tips are one of the best natural growths to model small deciduous trees. Their height varies from 4" to 7". Covered with foam, sumac tips make quick and easy trees that look good when placed in clusters.

the foreground areas of your layout.

Using dried florist's materials. A friend gave me several catalogs from companies specializing in dried flowers, weeds, and other decorative materials. There are dozens of dried weeds (called "fillers" because they are used to fill out floral arrangements) perfect for model trees, weeds, and other scenery applications. Most come in several shades of green and about every other color under the sun.

Several dried weeds can be used without a lot of modification. I like wild oregano, broom, many varieties of gypsophila, densiflora, star flowers, and stirlingia. The best place to find these products is in the craft section of department or variety stores; you may also be able to buy them from florists, garden centers, or gift shops. Don't be put off by the wild colors; all can be recolored with spray paint.

Convincing deciduous trees can be built from wild oregano. Gather five or six stems in your hand and turn them

so the seed heads point outward. Bind the sprigs together tightly with thread, and insert a 1½" piece of glue-coated wire into the base of the stem. After the glue dries, spray the seed pods with acrylic or enamel paint to produce realistic foliage.

When the paint dries, build up a realistic trunk by coating the plant stems with a stiff mixture of Durham's Water Putty. Scribe in bark texture while the putty is soft, then stand the tree in a piece of Styrofoam until the putty dries. Then paint and dry-brush the trunk using the methods described above.

To the forest! As you plant trees on the railroad, try to group them in clumps of not less than three. The more variation you can put into the groups the better they will look. Make a small hole in the scenery with an awl or drill, add a drop of white glue, and insert the tree. Crooked trees only look good in nature, so it's worth going to great lengths to make sure the tree stands straight while the glue dries. I use paint bottles, weights, and anything else that will hold the tree upright and straight.

Group homemade and commercial trees together, making sure there are several varieties in each group. If, after planting, a group of trees does not look full enough, try gluing a foam-covered piece of scrap lichen or poly fiber on top of the cluster to round it out.

As you build and plant whole forests, you'll find that relatively few trees need to have "classic" shapes. When used in groups, individual trees need only look vaguely like real trees to be convincing, and the only trees you should bother to paint and shape carefully are those that will stand near the front of your layout.

Modeling evergreen trees. There must be as many methods for modeling pine trees as there are modelers building them. My construction methods for evergreens are traditional, similar to

CHAPTER 6

Molded plastic trees can be saved: Coat them with foam to hide the shine and bright colors, then group them with other types to disguise their regular shapes.

This weed (1) is Astilbe A. arendsii, also called false spirea, a widespread perennial. After trimming (2), spray with dilute matte medium (3), and coat with fine green foam (4). The finished trees (5) are most convincing in small groups (right).

This large pine tree trunk was painted using the "western pine" color. After the color dried a black shadow wash was flowed on and allowed to dry overnight. The trunk was dry-brushed with Polly S Reefer White.

those found in commercial pine tree kits.

Start by carving and sanding a 3/8"-square balsa stick into a dowel. Continue sanding to make a long, pointed trunk. Add bark texture by running a coarse file up and down the trunk, dig knotholes with the tip of a modeling knife, then color the trunk using the methods described above. Pine tree bark is usually coarser than deciduous trees, so don't be afraid to exaggerate the texture and dry-brush the highlights with Polly S White.

Realistic bark for big foreground pines can also be created by wrapping a tapered dowel with textured paper, such as crepe paper. Attach it with white glue or Pliobond contact cement.

For branches, you can use any of

several foliage materials. Caspia is a useful natural growth, as is the "old man's beard" mentioned as a weed material later in this chapter. Dip or spray the branches green, mist with matte medium, and sprinkle with dark blue-green ground foam. Drill small holes in the trunk and insert the branches, starting with the largest ones at the bottom and adding progressively smaller branches as you go up. I use these hand-built trees only in the foreground where the effort in making them can be appreciated.

Stiff nylon scouring pads (one brand is Brillo Nylon Scrubber, sold in supermarkets) are another source of evergreen branch structures. Rip the pad apart into irregular wafers, then impale them on the trunk, leaving

space between. Fasten the wafers to the trunk with a drop of white glue, then coat the branches with spray glue or matte medium. Sprinkle on dark green foam to complete the tree.

To mass-produce small pines for the background of your layout glue bits of coarse, dark-green foam to painted toothpick trunks; make others by impaling small pieces of scouring pads on toothpicks, then spraying with Floquil Forest Green and sprinkling with dark foam.

Most commercial evergreens, even the shiny cast-plastic ones, are vastly improved if you spray them with matte medium bonding solution and sprinkle on a little blue-green foam, sawdust, or flock.

Bumpy chenille pines. Craft and

This plastic holiday decoration includes several components that will make interesting trees. After separating the individual parts and discarding the useless items, spray the tree-shaped pieces with matte medium and sprinkle on sawdust or foam. (Right) One section of the decoration and a little blue-green foam yielded several small pine-like trees.

One of the oldest ways to build pine trees is from tapered wooden dowels drilled to hold air fern branches. The tree shown here was built from a Campbell kit.

Miniature pine trees are easily made from colored toothpicks with bits of foam or nylon scrubbing pads glued to them. Groups of these trees look great in the middle distance and on background hills.

From left to right, the pine tree is made from a carved wood trunk and shredded nylon scrubbing pads covered with foam for the branches, and the tall pine tree armature is a natural growth sold by Sweetwater Scenery Co.

variety stores carry a colorful selection of a product called bumpy chenille. I don't know what it's intended to be used for, but it's inexpensive and it makes convincing small evergreens. Out of the package it looks like 12"-long pipe cleaners that are alternately fat and thin along their length. Each 12" piece will make 8 small (1¼") or 4 large (2") trees, or any combination in between.

Bumpy chenille can be used, as is, by cutting individual trees from the pipe cleaner with a pair of wire cutters. If the color isn't to your liking, spray the chenille stems first with flat enamel. Change the shapes of a few trees by rotating them over a candle to burn off the fuzz around the base of the wire trunk.

Dip the bases of the trees in white glue and plant them in small holes punched in the scenery base, or simply push them into your lichen or poly fiber background treetops. For variety, spray a few bumpy chenille trees with matte medium or spray glue and then sprinkle on fine, dark-green foam.

Stumps by the dozen. Building a railroad through wooded country means cutting down lots of trees, and that leaves stumps behind. Excellent plastic and metal tree stumps are available commercially, but I need so many stumps that my favorite method of making them is to carve masters from modeling clay, make molds from liquid latex rubber (the same rubber used to make rock molds, Chapter 4), and make dozens of plaster duplicates.

The first step is to carve the master stumps. Use regular non-hardening modeling clay, starting with a cube about 1" square. For HO scale, cut this into eight smaller cubes and place them on a slab of flat plastic sheet, leaving enough space around each so you can carve it.

The carving is easy and does not require artistic talent. I use an old dental pick, but you can make a similar tool by forcing a large sewing needle into the end of a dowel. Roughly shape the clay into a cylinder, adding small pieces at the base for roots.

Next run the tool up and down the sides of the stump to form rough, irregular bark channels. Follow the vertical contours of the stump and extend the bark along the root sections. Add saw marks to the top of the stump, and model the undercut used to fell the tree. Use the tip of the tool to draw concentric growth rings and to add a ragged edge to the saw cut. When the stump is finished, gently press the clay to smooth out unnatural sharp edges. Coat the stumps with a light spray of Pledge furniture polish to prevent the mold rubber from sticking to the clay.

Making a stump mold. Now coat the clay stumps with molding rubber. Brush on a very thin coat of rubber. Check the stumps for trapped air bubbles and puncture them, being careful not to damage the clay underneath. Let the first coat dry overnight, then apply five more coats, allowing each to dry completely. With the fifth coat, add strips of surgical gauze to reinforce the mold. Add a final heavy coat of latex over the gauze and let the mold dry thoroughly, usually two or three days.

Carefully peel the mold off the plastic base, pry the clay masters out of the mold, and pick out any remaining bits of clay. Trim the edges of the mold with scissors, and dust it lightly with talcum powder to keep it from sticking to itself.

Make a plaster backing block to hold the mold flat and level when pouring castings. Place the mold face down on a slab of plastic, construct a cardboard-and-masking-tape box around it, and spray the box and mold with furniture polish. Fill the box with thick molding plaster or Hydrocal. When the plaster starts to set, run a straightedge along the top of the cardboard sides to level it. After the plaster sets, remove the sides and gently peel the mold away from the plaster block.

Molding plaster stumps. To use the mold, spray with wet water and leave wet. Mix two heaping teaspoons of Durham's Water Putty, molding plaster, or Hydrocal with three to four teaspoons of lukewarm water. You want the consistency of heavy cream — add more water if the mixture is thick. Stir slowly (to keep bubbles from forming) for about one minute (the longer you stir, the faster the plaster will set). Spoon the mixture into each stump cavity, trying not to trap air bubbles. After filling, tap the mold sides with a pencil to release air bubbles and place the filled mold on a level surface.

Allow the plaster to set completely. Thirty minutes to an hour is usually enough for fresh plaster; overnight for water putty. After the plaster sets, remove the mold from the backing block and gently flex it to pop out the

(Above, top) Bumpy chenille, a craft material, makes excellent small evergreen trees. The trees can stand alone (middle), or they can be used to lend variety to massive background forests of lichen (bottom).

To make a modeling clay stump-mold master, start by shaping the clay into a squat cylinder. Slice away excess material with a dental tool, and form the remaining clay into an irregular stump

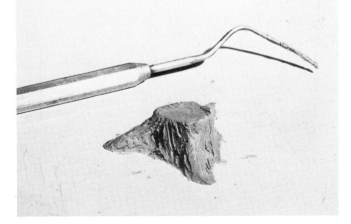

shape. Use the excess clay to form roots. Scribe in heavy bark detail, brush away unwanted scraps of clay, and use the tip of the dental tool to model saw marks on top of the stump.

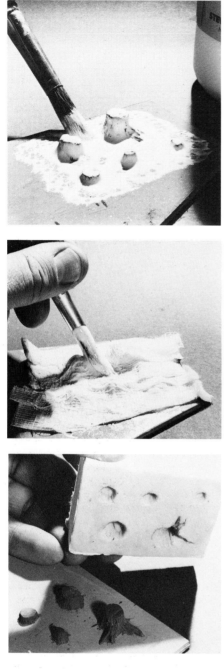

Brush liquid latex over the stump patterns, gently prodding out bubbles (top). After six coats, brush on more latex and cover with gauze strips (middle). Add a final coat, then wait several days before removing the finished mold (above).

These home-cast plaster stumps add interest along the side of this one-stall enginehouse. The scraggly vine growing up the enginehouse wall was made using the technique illustrated in the box on page 64.

For painting, stretch a strip of masking tape, sticky side up, on a piece of scrap cardboard, then stick the stumps to it.

stumps. Examine each under a strong light and remove bubble holes with the tip of a hobby knife. Put the stumps in a warm place to dry, and rinse the mold in warm water to remove plaster residue.

Making stumps requires minute amounts of plaster, so I always fill the mold when I do other scenery-building chores that require mixing plaster. I keep the stumps in a box until there are enough to paint.

With a couple of simple tricks you can achieve a lot of variety with a single stump mold. Try filling the molds only half to three-quarters full to make mini-stumps. Model overturned stumps by scooping cavities out of the stump mold while the plaster is wet, then add exposed roots with glue-soaked string or yarn. Use stumps that have air holes or bubbles to model overgrown stumps — and cover the defects with foam, sawdust, or lichen.

Before painting, sand the bottom of each stump so it will sit level on the railroad. The sandpaper will clog rapidly, but a 4" x 5" sheet will handle about 30 stumps.

Stump painting. After sanding, place the stumps on a square of cardboard with several lengths of masking tape, sticky side up, on it. This makes it easy to handle the stumps during painting.

The bark color of a stump is not the same as a living tree; stumps are much grayer, sometimes almost silver. Bark colors range from light reddish gray, through brown, to dark silver-gray.

I paint stumps with Polly S colors; the recipe box on page 63 lists the formulas. You'll need a soft No. 7 round paintbrush and a No. 6 tapered flat brush. You'll also need two shot glasses or small cups, one for water and the

other to use for mixing the colors.

After applying the base color, add a relief wash while the paint is still damp. If the stumps start to dry out, moisten with water. The relief wash is 2 teaspoons India ink in a quart of rubbing alcohol. Flow this wash over the stumps with a soft brush, completely covering the tops and sides. Let it dry overnight.

To highlight the bark texture, put a brush load of Polly S Reefer White on a scrap of plastic and mix in a speck of Polly S Roof Brown to tone it down. Dry-brush the raised portions of the bark. This technique is the same as the one used for rock molds, but only a light white highlight should be left on the stump tops and the bark.

Add a green "moss" effect on a few stumps. Mix Polly S Depot Olive or Dark Green with several brush loads of water and flow it on one face; this becomes the "north" side. Don't overdo the green or the stumps will be lost in the surrounding foliage.

Adding stumps to the scenery. When they're dry, gently remove the painted stumps from the masking tape and dab a large drop of white glue on the base of each. Push the stump into place on the scenery, covering any glue that squeezes out with texture material. Fill gaps between the scenery and the stump with a drop or two of glue and a little grass texture. Add more detail after the glue sets. Make vines by painting dilute white glue up the bark and over the tops of the stumps, then dust with green foam or sawdust and blow away the excess. Stumps look best when placed in groups of three to five. Vary the position and sizes used in each group.

In cutover logging areas stumps should be placed in a random fashion and some should be grouped in twos

CHAPTER 6

In these paint formulas I use the term "brushload." A brushload is a No. 7 brush dipped 3/4 of the way up the bristles into well-mixed Polly S paint.

Add extra water to the paint so it will flow onto the dry plaster stump castings without being absorbed immediately. I use a shot glass full of water with a drop or two of detergent in it to thin the paint and also to clean my brush as I go.

If you model an area where tree bark is a distinctive color, add a little of that color to the basic formula. For example, in the Pacific Northwest bark is redder, so add a drop or two of Tuscan or Caboose Red to one of the basic formulas; if you're modeling aspen stumps, add white to lighten the basic color.

All colors are Polly S.

New, raw wood:
>1/4 teaspoon water
>1/4 brushload Polly S Reefer Yellow
>1 brushload Polly S White

Using the brush, mix the paints on a piece of scrap plastic. Flow the color onto the raw wood areas of the stumps. Try not to get any paint on the bark.

New bark:
>1/2 teaspoon water
>1/8 brushload Reefer Gray
>1/4 brushload Roof Brown

Make this thin enough so that a fully loaded brush will color one stump.

Weathered wood:
>1/4 teaspoon water
>1/4 brushload Reefer Gray
>1/8 brushload Reefer Yellow

Weathered bark:
>1/2 teaspoon water
>1/4 brushload Reefer Gray
>1/8 brushload Roof Brown

The black wash is optional. It works best on stumps that are saturated with water. Dip the stumps in a shallow tray of water until they won't absorb any more. (The colors will darken as the stump absorbs water; they will lighten as they dry). Place the stumps on a double layer of paper towels to drain off excess water. Now, flow on the black wash. Apply more on the bark than on the tops, and fill all the depressions. Follow with dry-brushed highlights.

Black wash:
>1/2 teaspoon water
>1/4 brushload Flat Black

Dry-brushed highlights:
>1 brushload Reefer White
>1/4 brushload Roof Brown

Don't add any water; the paint should be on the sticky side for dry-brushing. Pick up a little paint on a No. 6 flat, stiff-bristled brush and brush it on a paper towel until only a slight trace of white remains on the bristles. Stroke the brush gently up and down over the bark texture, touching only the raised detail.

and threes for the best effect. Add small pieces of lichen and bits of twigs to the newest stumps to simulate attempts at second growth. Other appropriate details around the stumps are 4' to 6' lengths of cut wood and small piles of brush. Finally, don't forget the friendly beaver: Carve a few stumps with pointed tops and place them near a pond or waterway.

Growing your own vines. Vines are handy devices to use on model buildings. They provide a visual transition that helps tie the buildings into their surroundings, and they also can be used to hide construction errors such as an imperfect corner joint or a roof that doesn't quite fit. Vines can be used to break up large, flat areas on factory walls and retaining walls, and if only one side of a building is vine-covered, it can look like two different buildings.

To make vines you'll need white glue diluted 1:1 with water, the miscellaneous textures in your texture tray, an assortment of small sticks and twigs, and green, yellow, and brown Polly S paints. Start by spreading a newspaper over the workbench to catch surplus texture.

Brush diluted white glue onto the surface where you want the vines, starting at the bottom and working up. Using a small brush, draw the branches into fine tips. As soon as you've brushed out the glue, sprinkle on green texture and press it into the glue with your finger. After the glue dries brush away excess texture with a soft brush. If some areas look bare, add more glue and texture.

On foreground buildings the vines will look better if you add individual stems and branches. Place small pieces of twigs on the bottom parts of the vines, working the texture material over and around them. Vary the color of the vegetation using thinned Polly S colors — one part paint mixed with two parts water is about right. Touch a brush load of thinned green paint to the texture and capillary action will draw the color along the vine. After the green dries, dry-brush yellow highlights and dab splotches of brown here and there to simulate dead leaves.

Using lichen effectively. Lichen has been a popular tree and shrubbery material for as long as model railroaders have been building scenery. Years ago, store-bought lichen was coarse, brightly colored stuff that didn't look realistic, and this gave lichen a bad name. Today's commercial lichen is considerably finer, and the colors better.

Using lichen to best advantage involves no special skills — all you have to remember is that the lichen should look like natural vegetation. Clumps of lichen look better than individual pieces, and masses of lichen look like distant forests.

To make the massive lichen cover that forms the forest background on my layout, I work from front to rear, placing fine lichen tufts close together so they look like the tops of trees. Dip each tuft into 1:1 diluted white glue so the glue just covers the bottom, and place the tuft on the scenery base standing upright. If a tuft won't stand on its own, spear it in place with a nail until the glue dries.

To make lichen bushes, tear fine-textured tips from a clump of lichen, hold them with tweezers, dip in dilute white glue, and place them on top of the textured scenery. Wedge small lichen tufts into cracks and crevices, and keep in mind that bushes, like trees, look best when several are placed together in a small group.

To use leftover lichen scraps, cover them with "leaves" of foam, sawdust, or other fine texture material. If the lichen is too bright or too dark, the leaves will disguise the color. To texture small tufts, soak them in matte

CHAPTER 6

Vines add age and "respectability" to model structures, cover imperfect joints (left), or break up large, flat, uninteresting areas with texture. (Above) The shrub-like vine on the corner of this foreground building includes the extra detail of a small twig that simulates a trunk-like stem.

medium bonding solution, squeeze out most of the liquid, and roll them in the texture tray. Gently shake off excess texture and set the lichen tufts aside to dry, then use them on the railroad just as you would fine-textured lichen. Larger pieces are treated the same as "shake and bake" trees: Spray with matte medium bonding solution and shake in a plastic bag filled with texture.

Chopped scrap lichen is a useful addition to the texture tray. Use scissors to snip coarse lichen scraps into pieces 1/2" across or smaller. I use this material to represent low swamp growth and thickets. To make dense undergrowth, arrange chopped lichen in a gully or ditch, soak with matte medium bonding spray, and sprinkle on texture.

Lichen is also useful for covering gaps in the scenery. Tufts of lichen forced into cracks or positioned in front of gaps can hide minor defects.

Modeling tall grass. Materials to model tall grass are varied. Hobby shops carry several brands of grass mats that consist of rolled paper with green flocking attached. Fake fur, an inexpensive synthetic fur bonded to a fabric backing, is available in fabric stores. The nap is about 1/2" high and the fur comes in several colors. Texture papers sold by Faller, Life-Like, Noch, and others are good for background areas of your layout, and the techniques for installing and coloring are the same as for taller grass.

Any scenery base can be used for mounting grass mats, including bare screen wire, hard shell, and old, dusty scenery in need of rejuvenation.

ADDING VINES TO BUILDINGS

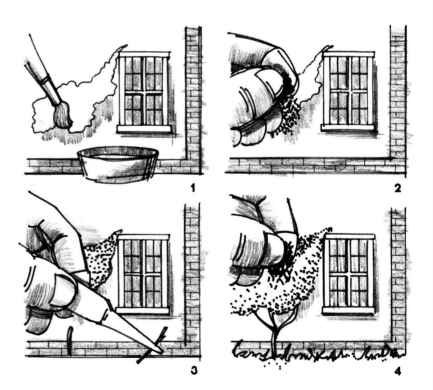

1. Use a small brush to coat the area to be covered with a 1:1 mix of white glue and water.
2. Sprinkle green texture material on the side of the building. I like to add vines at the workbench, working over a tray or old kit box to catch excess texture material.
3. Glue a small piece of twig on the side of the building to represent the vine's stem.
4. To add a little three-dimensional texture to some of the vines, recoat with white glue and add another layer of sawdust or foam.

CHAPTER 6

Lichen looks like this in its natural state. It is usually found growing on rocks in dense forests. Lichen is soft after a rain (wet weather is the best time to pick it), but it becomes hard and brittle during dry weather.

After the lichen is removed from the processing solution (top), it must be drained and squeezed to remove most of the liquid. Then it can be spread out on newspaper to dry (bottom). It's a messy job.

On untextured scenery, fit the grass mat by setting it in place and trimming it to size with scissors. Remove the mat and coat the bare plaster with full-strength white glue ("see-through" grass mats should be glued over an earth-colored scenery base). Prod the fabric into place and weight the edges until the glue dries. To make grass mats adhere to irregular scenic contours I hold them down with small plastic bags of pebbles or ballast.

To use fake fur, look for earth-colored material with a fairly stiff, short — 1/2" or less — pile. Trim the fibers with scissors (I use an old dog trimmer) to vary the length, and comb out all loose hairs with a stiff wire brush. Vacuum the fur to keep it from shedding further.

Because it's made from synthetic fiber, fake fur resists water-soluble coloring methods. The products that will

PROCESSING YOUR OWN LICHEN

Few modelers elect to pick and process their own lichen, but for those hardy few, here's how to do it. The first step is to find a source of natural lichen, which grows in wet, wooded areas all over North America, from Central Florida to the Arctic Circle.

Gather several large plastic bags of lichen from the forest and take it home. The next step, and the most time-consuming part of the process, is picking through the lichen to remove pine needles, sticks, bits of leaves, rabbit pellets, and the unusable coarse portions of the lichen itself. You'll throw away two-thirds of what you brought home (it's great garden mulch), but if you've found a good stand in the forest, what remains for processing will be much finer than anything you'll find in a hobby shop.

Unprocessed lichen will not keep. It will either dry out, get brittle, and handling will reduce it to powder or, if left damp, will get moldy. So plan to process the lichen as soon as possible after it's removed from the woods.

Always process the lichen outdoors to keep the heat and mess out of the house. You'll need a picnic table and a camp stove, and on the stove you'll need the biggest tub or pot you have, one that holds at least five gallons. On one lichen-picking trip I brought the processing equipment with me and spent the best part of a week's vacation camping and preserving lichen.

BASIC LICHEN PRESERVING SOLUTION

      3 gallons water
      1 gallon commercial-grade glycerin*

*Buy the cheapest commercial-grade glycerin you can find; it will still be expensive. Check your Yellow Pages for a local chemical supplier.

Dissolve 1 1/2 packets of green powdered fabric dye such as Rit or Tintex in the basic preserving solution. To give your lichen realistic variety, buy all the green dye colors that look like foliage, plus several shades of yellow. Start with the lightest colors, and every time you dye a batch of lichen replenish the glycerin and add a darker dye.

Heat the glycerin, water, and dye solution almost to its boiling point. The ideal temperature is about 230 degrees Fahrenheit — close to a simmer. Stuff as much lichen into the pot as the solution will hold, continue heating to return the solution to a simmer, and simmer for 5 minutes. Remove the pot from the stove and set it aside to cool. When the solution has cooled enough that you can stick your hand into the liquid, remove the lichen. Wearing heavy rubber gloves, grab a big handful and squeeze out all the liquid you can.

Reheat the glycerin solution to process the second batch, replenishing it with the following:

REPLENISHING SOLUTION FOR A 4-GALLON BATCH

      1 1/2 pints fresh glycerin
      1 packet dye

Use a packet of the next darker shade of dye. I usually pick so much lichen that processing it takes an entire day. The last batch should be the darkest, almost blue-green.

As you remove each batch from the pickling solution, spread the lichen on newspaper to dry, turning it frequently. I like to do this outdoors, in the sun, but even so, the processed lichen often takes two or three days to dry. At night, stuff the lichen into plastic bags and bring it indoors. When the processed lichen no longer leaves visible moisture or green color on your fingers when you squeeze a piece, store it permanently in the same plastic bags.

color it are Floquil's model railroad colors and Pactra paints. I've used both thinned with equal parts of their thinner (Dio-Sol and mineral spirits, respectively).

To paint the fur, pour a little green paint in a shallow dish and add enough Dio-Sol or mineral spirits to make a thin wash. Pick up some of the wash on a large brush and scrub it onto a 6"-square area of the fur. If the

color looks too dark pick up a brush full of clean thinner and scrub into the painted area. For variety dapple in other earth and grass colors. Allow the paint to dry thoroughly, then fluff the fur with a comb.

If you're starting from scratch there's no need to build a plaster-covered scenery base. A framework of contoured screen wire is enough. Cut the fur to size and glue it in place with

Tufts of fine-textured lichen simulate tree-covered hills in the background scenery on my layout.

This overgrown lineside ditch was made with finely chopped lichen. After sprinkling the lichen with sawdust and ground foam, I soaked it with matte medium bonding solution.

Excellent shrubs, bushes, and small trees can be made by covering poor-quality lichen with green texture. Simply spray the lichen with matte medium bonding solution and roll it in texture material.

Woodland Scenics Field Grass can be used to make nice-looking, realistic weeds when it is applied in small clusters.

acrylic varnish, latex molding rubber, or full-strength acrylic matte medium. Weight the corners until the glue sets. If your scenic shell is already built just glue the fake fur to the base.

Fake fur works well for long grass; for a shorter look, sprinkle on fine sand after painting and work it into the fur, then bond with matte medium spray. Hide the grass mat or fake fur edges by sprinkling on earth, ground foam, or other texture. Bond this in place with wet water followed by matte medium. If the grass mat abuts a waterway, pour the epoxy or resin water before the fur is firmly attached to the banks. After the water hardens, glue the edge of the fur up to the water.

A friend showed me his upside down technique for using fake fur to add grass between the rails of his narrow gauge logging layout. He starts by coloring a large swatch of fake fur with several shades of Floquil green thinned with equal parts Dio-Sol. After the paint dries he brushes the fur so it stands up straight.

Prepare the area to be grassed by painting and texturing as you would normally. Be sure to use matte medium as the adhesive because we're going to paint white glue over the texture layer, and the matte medium will resist softening by the white glue. Allow the texture to dry overnight.

Now paint the area with a heavy coat of white glue. Paint it everywhere you want grass, even between the rails (stay away from switches and switch machines). Cut a section of pre-colored fur large enough to cover the glued area, and press it, fur side down, into the glue. Don't press so hard that the nap is flattened. The fur should stand about 1/4" off the scenery. Allow the glue to dry overnight.

The next day remove the backing material. Use a single-edge razor blade or long, sharp, fish-fillet knife in a sawing motion, cutting the fur as close to the backing as possible, like skinning a fish. Work from the corners toward the middle, and don't pull on the backing material while cutting or you'll tear the fur fibers out of the scenery. Remove the backing and fluff the grass with your fingers.

Add more texture around the tall fur fibers. When you finish you'll have great-looking grass growing in places you never thought possible.

Weed materials. I've already mentioned many of the things that pass for weeds on my layout: bits of chopped or foam-covered lichen, tiny twigs, and clumps of dried flower material. Here again, variety is the key to realism, and I'm constantly on the lookout for new materials to use as nondescript growth.

One of the best places to look for weed materials is at a florist shop. Flo-

CHAPTER 6

Many types of grassland texture material and texture paper are available at the hobby shop or from a fabric store. Some come pre-colored and only have to be cut to shape and glued in place. Others, like the white "fake fur," need to be combed and colored first. Fake fur makes realistic long grass. Fine sand was sprinkled on the grass and combed in to represent bare ground areas in the grass.

ral materials vary from coast to coast so I cannot recommend specific types, but a trip to a large florist supply house is worthwhile just to see what is available.

Short pieces of brush bristles, green carpet, and small lengths of yarn and rope also make good weeds, but coloring them, especially those made from synthetic fibers, can be difficult. For absorbent materials such as cotton yarn and string, start with one of the recipes in the box on page 68. Mix the coloring recipe in a mayonnaise jar, add 6" to 8" lengths of the material to be colored, cover the jar, and shake. Dry the weeds on paper towels, then cut to length and store in a bag. (By the way, I once tried thinning the Polly S weed colors with matte medium, hoping the dried weeds would have more body, but it just made them stick to the paper towels and each other.)

Brown jute twine has stiff, coarse fibers perfect for weeds. One ball of wrapping string will make enough weeds for several dozen large layouts. Cut the string in 18" lengths, and soften them by boiling in a quart of water for several minutes to remove the sizing. Turn the heat off and add two teaspoons of brown or green fabric dye. After the string has absorbed the color, remove it from the dye and hang it up to dry. Weight the lower end of each length with a clothespin so the string will dry straight.

Once dry, cut short lengths and insert in holes drilled in the scenery. Use white glue to hold them in place. Fluff out the weed tops after the glue dries. Cattails and flowering weeds can be modeled by gluing ground foam to the tops of the string weeds. The tips of fiber weeds can be colored with yellow, green, and brown felt-tip markers.

Dark green indoor-outdoor carpeting makes convincing weeds. Clip individual fiber clumps from the carpet backing with side-cutting pliers, dip them in glue, and place them in holes in the scenery. These weeds look better

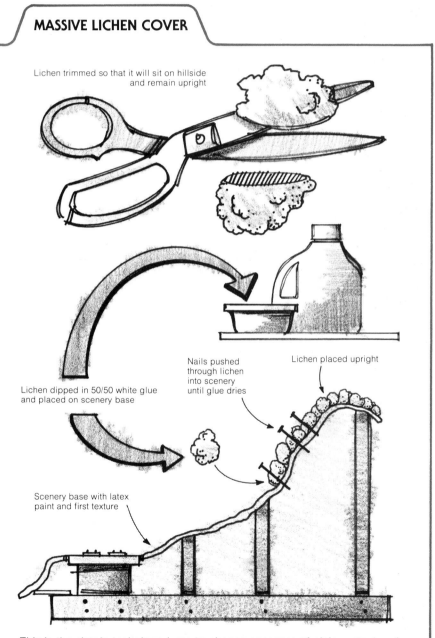

MASSIVE LICHEN COVER

Lichen trimmed so that it will sit on hillside and remain upright

Lichen dipped in 50/50 white glue and placed on scenery base

Nails pushed through lichen into scenery until glue dries

Lichen placed upright

Scenery base with latex paint and first texture

This is the simple technique I use to change expanses of plain, untextured scenic base into forest land. Trimmed lichen tufts are dipped in white glue, then placed upright on the painted base. Texture and detail on the base are not important wherever it is to be covered with lichen.

CHAPTER 6

(Top) These weed-like growths came from a florist's shop. The one on the left is air fern. (Above) One of my favorite natural weed materials was this product, called Tom Thumb Trees. No longer sold, I believe it was a type of barley grass. The fronds could be used intact as trees, or pieces broken off to make individual weeds. (Right) All these weeds were made from natural materials.

Coarse hemp string can be dyed at home to make a wide variety of weed colors. This piece is enough for dozens of weeds.

if you vary their color, so I dry-brush them to add highlights and make the tips look dried out. The carpeting is easy to dry-brush while the tufts are still on the backing. Use straight Polly S Earth on a stiff-bristled brush and run the brush over the tips of the carpet fibers, depositing paint with a scrubbing motion. Brushing a few tips with white glue and sprinkling on colored foam makes a good approximation of wildflowers.

Pickling natural growths. Besides being generally beneficial, an afternoon walk in the fields and woods is a good way to gather many kinds of miniature vegetation. Look for small, gnarled sticks and twigs that have good bark texture, and collect mosses, lichen-like growths, dried-out weed tops (for trees), and interesting seed pods. Bring along a small plastic bag and a pair of sharp pruning cutters.

If properly preserved, most mosses and lichens can be used for scenery. The greatest danger to these fragile plants is drying out; when dry, they become brittle and fall apart. I particularly like a tree growth called "old man's beard," a stringy, Spanish moss-like growth found on oak trees from Cape Cod south along the East Coast. When properly preserved and colored it's excellent for several types of foliage, including the most convincing

scale briar patches I've ever seen.

To prepare natural materials, make the preserving "pickle" recipe on page 69 and store it in a screw-top mayonnaise jar. Rinse dirt and debris from the natural growths and place them in the jar. In the solution, some of the water in the cellular structure of the weeds is replaced by glycerin and green dye. The longer you leave the vegetation in the pickle the longer it will last on the layout; one week is the minimum soaking time, but two or three weeks is better.

Remove the pickled material and spread it on newspapers to dry. After drying, separate the growth into small pieces and store them in plastic bags. The lifespan of these materials on the layout varies, but it takes about four years for most to dry out completely, and even then they will be all right if left untouched. This can be extended by heating the pickling solution as is done with lichen, but some of the delicate growths are destroyed by the heat.

Planting weeds. After gathering and preparing a good selection of weed materials, cut or tear each into working pieces and store them in one compartment of your texture tray. Random placement is a key to realistic weeds, and I like to plant as many different types together as possible. Place them

This green carpet material yields fine individual weeds. I also used it to make the rows of garden plants shown in the photo on page 53. Clip off clumps of fibers with cutting pliers, working close to the rubber backing of the carpet.

COLORS FOR WEED MATERIALS

All colors are Polly S.

Yellow-green dip for synthetic fiber materials:
    Dark Green ¼" deep in small jar
    4 drops Mud
    4 drops Reefer Yellow
    Equal part water

Straw brown dip:
    4 parts Earth
    1 part Roof Brown
    2 parts water

CHAPTER 6

(Top left) This little forest plant is found throughout the northern U. S. The color ranges from dark to light green. (Bottom left) A park ranger identified this fungus growth that lives on oak trees in the eastern United States as "old man's beard." (Above) The tangled thicket by the railroad crossing sign is a ball of old man's beard.

in small groups along with other scenery detail items, including clutter clusters. Just like trees, it is important that weeds stand up straight. Don't bother to place weeds under trees or behind other objects where they won't be seen.

I add weeds after most other scenery-building operations are completed, because many weed materials are easily damaged; they don't look like weeds after being squashed by a misplaced elbow or bent over flat by setting a bottle of glue on them. Two or three modelers working together can completely "plant" an average 4' x 8' railroad in two or three evenings.

Make a hole in the scenery base for each weed clump, using an awl or a No. 60 drill in a motor tool. Drill only five or six holes at a time, counting as you go so you won't miss half the holes. To plant, grab a weed with tweezers, dip the bottom into 1:1 diluted white glue, and stick it in the hole. Take pains to ensure that each weed stands perfectly upright.

Questions and answers

Q: I dyed my own lichen following your instructions and the last batch ended up very dark green. I don't want to throw this lichen away; is there any way to save it?
A: Don't throw out the dark lichen! It makes great trees and foliage when

PRESERVING "PICKLE" FOR NATURAL GROWTHS

2 cups rubbing alcohol
1 cup glycerin*
1/2 tablespoon yellow-green fabric dye

*Small quantities of glycerin are available at drugstores.

covered with light green foam. The dark interior looks like branches in shade. I once dyed a batch of forest green lichen specifically for use in the background. I covered it with two light shades of green foam.
Q: Why do you use rubber cement to hold the foliage material in place for tree building? Why not white glue or some other water-soluble adhesive?
A: With white glue you must wait three to six hours for it to dry hard. It's true that rubber cement doesn't stand up as well under handling, but it dries in 30 to 40 minutes and remains flexible. Also, the water in the matte medium bonding spray can soften white glue, causing the foliage to fall off the armature.
Q: I have sedum, yarrow, and other plants that dry out in the fall and make good trunk armatures, and I've made some nice trees with them. But on the layout the trunks dry out completely, and if I accidentally brush against them while cleaning the track, they break. Is there any way to make

these homemade trees more resilient?
A: First, when you use a dried natural growth (in contrast to a pickled growth, like lichen), it should be put somewhere out of harm's way, where it won't be hit when cleaning track, rerailing cars, or just leaning on the edge of the railroad. On most layouts that still leaves plenty of areas where you can use brittle, natural-weed trees. Use trees with plastic or metal trunks near the track.

Nothing I've found makes dried weeds truly resilient, but here's a procedure that will at least make them more durable. Harvest the stalks or branches in the fall or winter, after they have dried thoroughly. I wrap a rubber band around the bottom of a bunch of stalks and hang them upside down in a cool, dry place, such as my garage or cellar.

Trim off the flower clusters and unwanted branches or stems. Mix a solution of equal parts water and matte medium in a two-pound coffee can, and soak each stalk in it at least

CHAPTER 6

(Left) Use a sharp awl to punch a small hole in the scenery for each weed. Don't press too hard or the awl will make a hole larger than the base of the weed. (Right) Hold the weed material with tweezers, dip it in glue, and tuck it in the hole.

overnight. Stuff as many stalks as possible into the can without crushing them.

After soaking them, remove the stalks and stick each in a Styrofoam block to dry. When dry, dip each stalk into full-strength latex earth paint, shake off the excess, and return the stalk to the Styrofoam block. In two or three days the trunks will be ready for a relief wash and tree building, but they should still be placed out of harm's way.

Q: What is the best height for weeds?
A: I like weeds that are tall enough so they can be seen but not so tall as to dwarf a scale figure. The tallest should stand roughly between a scale figure's waist and shoulders. Make background weeds shorter than those in the foreground.

Q. I have a lot of scrap grass matting left over from a large scenery project.

Is there any way to use these pieces?
A. Cut them into 1/2" and 1" strips to represent crops in a farm or garden scene. Spray paint each strip a different shade of green and top them with colored ground foam to represent corn, wheat, tomatoes, and other garden plants.

Q: I've had bad luck with hobby-shop trees and tree kits. You say they can be used to good effect. How?
A: Never dismiss commercial trees — especially at a bargain price — as too brightly colored or misshapen to be useful. Some will benefit from a coating of ground foam, others can be made more realistic by cutting them apart and reshaping the pieces. Still others merely need the color toned down with an airbrush or spray cans. When your layout needs 2,000 trees, consider everything you can get your hands on!

Two simple planting tricks for

commercial trees can go a long way toward adding variety and realism to your forests. First, if the trees come with relatively long trunks, shorten some of them so the trees will vary in height. Second, one large tree can provide the materials for two or three smaller ones, or dozens of bushes.

Campbell, Color-Rite, and others offer pine tree kits which provide air fern for the foliage. This dried sea weed is sold as "forever plants" in dime stores and the material will stay pliable for years. There are a couple of things you can do to vary its texture and coloring.

First, try lightly airbrushing the branches with Floquil RR81 Earth to dull the green color and accentuate the fine detail. Or mist the branches with dilute matte medium and sprinkle on green and yellow flocking (often sold as "static grass") to make needles.

Commercial pine trees look good when they are mixed together on the layout or are placed in clusters. These trees (left) were sprayed with matte medium and then sprinkled with dark green scenic foam. Inexpensive manufactured trees (above) look better when they are covered with an extra layer of scenic foam and grouped in a scene with other similar trees.

CHAPTER 6

The rippled water in this scene is a thick coat of acrylic gloss medium, an easy-to-apply water-soluble material.

Modeling water

Waterways are important features of every kind of scenery, and they are doubly important to model railroaders because surveyors often routed real railroads along watercourses to take advantage of existing terrain contours. Modeling water always presents a challenge, but the results are always well worth the effort. It's extremely gratifying to watch a visitor gingerly reach out to touch the water on your railroad to make sure it isn't wet, even if you do have to go back later and wipe away the fingerprint!

When planning scenery you must decide what type of waterways fit into the scheme of your layout. Modeling each has its own unique problems and solutions. The only geologic principles you must bear in mind are that water always flows downhill, and that calm water is perfectly flat.

Flat bases for water. The easiest type of water to build is flat, relatively calm water such as is found in ponds, lakes, oceans, or broad, slow-moving rivers. The most obvious way to make a base for flat water is to build a piece of plywood or Masonite into the rail-

road where the lake or pond will be located. The top surface of the base should be 1½" to 2" below the surrounding scenery to allow for realistic banks, and the base should be firmly fastened to the benchwork to hold it flat and level even if the surrounding scenery should settle slightly.

Attach the cardboard scenic support web to the water base, allowing for sloping banks, and cover it with plaster-soaked paper towels. Wipe or scrape away any plaster that finds its way onto the water area. After the plaster is dry, sand the water base to remove splinters, fuzz, or other irregularities.

The first coat of Earth latex paint on the scenery base should also be brushed over the water area to help seal the surface, but the texture sprinkled over the wet paint should only go to the edge of the water. If texture strays onto the water area, remove it after the paint dries by gently scraping the surface and sweeping the particles away with a brush. Then lightly sand the surface to smooth it.

Now seal the water base with a

thick coat of full-strength acrylic matte medium. After this dries it will be impervious to water-base products, and will keep the base from absorbing the paint used to color the bottom. Let the matte medium dry several days before you color the bottom.

Building a poured base. A poured base for flat water is made by building the general shape of the body of water right into the scenic base, then pouring in a thin plaster mix to form the flat bottom. Since the plaster mix is liquid enough to be self-leveling this method is excellent for water areas added after scenery covers most of the benchwork.

The plaster product I use for poured bases is Savogran Wood Putty, a patching compound that contains wood fiber. Mix the powder with about one-third more water than the package directions recommend, and wet the scenery base thoroughly with water before pouring. Check that there are no holes where the wood putty mix could leak out, and pour the soupy mixture into the water area. The wood putty mix should flow into all corners of the water area, and there should be enough of it that it can find its own level. If the putty won't flow, the scenery base is too dry; quickly rewet the base and prod the putty along to get it moving again. Water sprayed on top of the putty will "melt away" any large ripples or uneven areas.

As the wood putty sets, some water will rise to the top, forming a slick which should not be disturbed: Let the water evaporate. After a day or so the putty will dry out, forming an almost perfectly flat surface. This water base will be softer than the surrounding plaster because of the extra water added to the mix, but the softness will not affect the final water surface if you are careful not to mar or scuff the wood putty.

Let the poured base dry several days, then sand away any high spots. Fill holes or low spots with more soupy wood putty, thoroughly pre-wetting the area surrounding the hole so the dry base will not suck all the water out of the soupy mix. Let the putty dry completely, and carefully go over the entire poured base with extra-fine sandpaper to smooth it. After brushing and vacuuming away all dust, seal the surface with full-strength matte medium. Apply the matte medium with a wide brush, trying not to leave any marks.

Using plexiglass. The third method for building flat water is to use plexiglass or glass in one of three ways. The first is to use the glass or plexiglass just as you would plywood or Masonite: that is, paint its top surface so nothing underneath can show through. The second way is to paint the water bottom on the underside of

This two-part epoxy model water appears blue only because it reflects the background color. For that reason, the base for most water areas should be black or greenish-black, not blue.

This two-part epoxy model water appears blue only because it reflects the background color. For that reason, the base for most water areas should be black or greenish-black, not blue.

the glass and treat the top surface as the surface of the water. Yet a third method is to build a detailed lake bottom, place a sheet of transparent glass over it, and again treat the top surface of the glass to look like water.

Construction with glass or plexiglass is similar to using wood for the base. Except for the see-through method, the glass, either painted or

unpainted on the bottom, is set into the rough scenery and a rippled surface added on top of it. With the see-through method a lake bottom is built in three dimensions, painted, and detailed before the glass is placed over it. Bank scenery is brought up to the edge of the glass, painted, and textured before the shiny, rippled water surface is added.

Forming banks. After the matte medium sealing coat on the flat base has dried, bring the surrounding scenery up to the water base to form banks. Group several sizes of rocks along the banks where the base meets the scenery and sprinkle smaller stones over and around them. To smooth out the rough piles of stones and make them look as if wind, water,

Plywood or Masonite
water base

A

Bank texture added

Varnish or gloss
medium

Surface
sealed

Poured plaster water base (solid)

B

Water surface: gloss medium

3-D bottom

Flat glass or plexiglass base

C

This is the scenic support for a river. The cardboard web supports flat pieces of cardboard, forming a rough bottom. After applying plaster-soaked paper towels, thin wood putty was poured into the stream bed to make a perfectly flat and level water base.

and ice deposited them there, sprinkle on sifted sand. Now moisten the banks with wet water spray and sprinkle more fine sand over the bank and down to the edge of the water, forming a gentle transition. Using a soft brush, push all the loose sand and rock on the water surface back into the banks. Gently blow away any particles that remain on the water surface.

Now soak the banks and stone piles with wet water. Check to see that nothing has worked its way onto the water surface, and saturate the banks with matte medium solution. Allow the banks to dry for several days, then prod to make sure all the stones are stuck firmly in place. If some are loose, spray on more matte medium bonding solution.

Painting flat bottoms. Before you start to paint it, visualize how the bottom of your lake or pond should look. Should it have narrow beaches dropping off quickly to deep water? Will there be sandbars where the flow of water slows down? Should the water be clear or muddy green? Try to think how the water would look to a person in a plane above it. From that vantage

To make a sandy base for a shallow stream I sprinkled on coarse sand and pebbles, bonding them in place with matte medium solution. I colored the stream bed with dilute Earth paint after the matte medium dried.

This creek consists of over 20 coats of high-gloss spar varnish brushed over a dark-colored scenery base. Because varnish soaks into the scenery and creeps up the sides of the banks, the banks had to be touched up with earth paint after the water surface was complete.

point, water isn't blue at all, or aquamarine (the color swimming pools are painted), but shades of brown, black, and green. Usually, as the water gets deeper the sandy bank color gradually changes to solid black.

If all that's true, then why does water look blue from our normal, down-to-earth viewpoint? The answer is that water is shiny, and the deep blue or blue-green we see is the color of the sky reflected by the water. The shiny surfaces that we'll apply later to our model water do the same thing, and if we want our water to look blue in photos and to eye-level viewers, we'll have to provide a blue backdrop to furnish the color that the water reflects.

I use only two colors when painting flat bottoms: basic Earth and black. Start on the banks, brushing 1:1 Earth paint over sand areas and working the color out into the water area where shallows would exist. After applying all the Earth color, use Mars Black tube acrylic, Polly S Engine Black, or flat black latex paint to color the "deep" portions of the water. Start at the center of the pond, and work the black up to the earth-colored areas. Where they meet, feather the colors together and make the transition as gradual as you can. If the colors start to dry, a squirt of wet water will allow you to continue blending.

If you have an airbrush, painting the bottom is even easier because you can spray the gradual light-to-dark transitions. Airbrushing requires lump-free paint, so use Polly S thinned with equal parts water. Start by spraying the banks and shallows with Earth, then, without cleaning the airbrush fill the jar with 1:1 Engine Black. Spray this along the edges where the shallows drop off into deeper water, and gradually shift to pure black in the deepest areas of the pond.

Simulate the tops of underwater stones and rocks by mixing a brush

load of the Earth paint with just enough black that the color is a little lighter than the surrounding bottom. Dot this color along the banks close to shore.

After the bottom paint dries, add detail along the banks. Such things as logs, old tires, swamp grass, and pieces of broken pilings can be glued in place with white glue or generous squirts of matte medium. Paint all details before they are set in place.

Building 3-D stream bases. Shallow, fast-running rivers, creeks, and brooks must be built into the scenery base while rough construction is going on. What we need is a shallow trench

lower than the surrounding scenery. Ideally, such a stream bed should run from one place to another, perhaps flowing into a broad, flat-base lake or pond, but I have seen (and built) effective streams that didn't go anywhere at all.

Prepare the brook bottom exactly as you would a pond or riverbank. Position large stones first, then smaller ones, then sprinkle sand over the whole area. If the banks are steep brush on white glue and use the whisking technique from Chapter 5 to blow sand from a folded 3 x 5 file card onto the wet glue.

Make overhanging or undercut

To detail the banks, sprinkle on plaster rocks, small stones, and fine sand. Move the texture materials around with a brush, mist with wet water spray, and bond them in place with a generous application of matte medium bonding solution.

CHAPTER 7

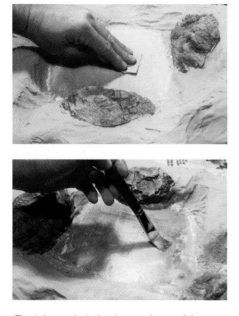

(Top) I sanded the bare plywood bottom of this small pond so it would be as smooth as possible before sealing. (Above) Next came the sealer, a thick coat of full-strength matte medium. I brushed out the matte medium, leaving as few brush marks as possible. It's important that the sealer be allowed to dry completely before proceeding with the painting steps.

This narrow stream bed was built into the scenery base. To make the rapids section the sides and bottom were covered with sand, then stones and boulders were dumped into place and bonded with matte medium. After the polyester resin water was poured and had set the tops of the rocks were repainted with flat Earth color.

banks with a stiff mixture of Sculptamold applied with your fingers, painted with latex Earth paint, and sprinkled with texture. After the Sculptamold dries add more texture under the overhangs using the whisking technique. Soak the stream bed with matte medium bonding solution, and allow it to dry overnight before coloring.

Color the stream bed using the rock colors described in the recipe box in Chapter 4. Start by spraying on the light rock color, allow it to dry, then follow with several light squirts of India ink relief wash. Be careful to keep the stream bed coloring away

from rocks colored earlier; adding more paint could turn them unrealistically dark. Next glue painted detail in place; this can be as simple as a few logs or weeds or as complex as a fallen tree with all the roots exposed. When you are satisfied with the stream bed and all the paint and glue has dried thoroughly, the stream is ready for the application of one of several types of "water."

Water materials: gloss varnish. The water material you add over the base is like the frosting on a cake: It can either make the illusion or break it. The first material I ever used, which still yields excellent results,

was high-gloss varnish. Painted over the water surface or brushed into a stream bed, varnish looks best where flat, calm water is to be modeled. Every brand and type of high-gloss varnish I have tried has worked well as water.

One caution when using varnish or any product which contains petroleum-base thinner: Always test it first on a scrap piece of scenery. If the scenery under the test section starts to soften or to pucker, stop; it's better to try to salvage a small section than a whole pond!

When the base is ready the varnish is applied in many thin coats, let-

To paint the pond bottom, work Earth color down from the banks and brush Mars Black acrylic out from the middle. Gradually blend the colors together where they meet.

Color the bottom so it looks as it would from a plane flying overhead. The bank color extends into the black bottom color to represent shallows, and rocks, gravel, and grass texture are bonded to the banks before adding the glossy water surface.

CHAPTER 7

Making gloss medium water. After finishing the surrounding rocks and painting the water base, prepare the banks by sprinkling them with sand and fine plaster rubble (1). Add larger stones, and bond everything in place with a liberal application of dilute matte medium. The seaweed along the tide line (2) is more fine sand, colored with Burnt Umber thinned with gloss medium. I scrounged a dozen or so boxes, tires, wheels, and boards and glued them in place with white glue (3). Dab a heavy coat of gloss medium on the water base to build up ripples (4). The finished gloss medium water (5) shows the painted-on surface chop.

ting each one dry before adding the next. I add varnish coats each morning and evening for several days until the water builds up to a high-gloss shine, and on occasion I have applied as many as 40 coats to obtain the degree of body and shine I wanted. Color can be added to the varnish before brushing it on; almost any paint will work as long as the thinner base is compatible with the varnish. Remember that a little color goes a long way, and just the hint of green slime or mud-colored silt is most effective.

Due to capillary action you'll find that a lip of varnish creeps up the sides of the banks. After the last coat of varnish has dried thoroughly, these areas must be repainted with a flat, non-water-base paint such as Floquil Railroad Colors. Polly S and other latex-base paints won't stick to the glossy varnish surface.

The last word on using varnish is that you should not try thinning it and pouring it onto the water base. This may look great while it's wet, but as it dries the heavy coat of varnish will

shrink, leaving a puckered, wrinkled mess. Excess thinner will also be absorbed by the surrounding scenery, taking some of the shiny varnish along with it.

Water materials: acrylic gloss medium. We've already used a lot of acrylic matte medium for scenery building, and when we come to building water there's a use for its gloss counterpart. Acrylic gloss medium is a thick, white acrylic varnish with the consistency of whipping cream. Like matte medium it is found in art-supply

CHAPTER 7

stores. It dries to a crystal-clear, high gloss in 20 to 30 minutes, and once dry it is water- and oil-resistant. It has a hard, shiny surface that looks as if it's just been waxed. Because it is an acrylic emulsion it can be mixed with acrylic paints, Polly S, and tinting colors. It has some body, so it can be worked with brushes to represent every kind of water, from calm rippled ponds to fast-moving rapids and waterfalls. Thinning with water decreases its gloss, so always use it full strength for modeling water.

I use gloss medium two different ways to model water. The first is to brush it over a painted flat bottom. Start by painting the deep parts of the flat bottom (plywood, Masonite, or Formica) black. Add earth color as you paint toward the banks, feathering the two colors together to make a gradual transition from deep black to pure earth. Simulate sandbars and other shallow water by spraying thinned earth paint over the black base. When the base color is completely dry, apply gloss medium as described below.

The second method is to brush gloss medium over glass or Plexiglas, where the gloss medium, along with the see-through properties of the glass, provides a look of genuine depth. Brushing gloss medium over old waterways built using some other material is also a way to revive their sparkle and add surface ripples.

To apply gloss medium, use a soft, 1" round brush to scoop about 4 tablespoons into a small jar. Add a little Cobalt Blue tube acrylic, less than 1/8", and mix thoroughly. Work this tinted medium onto the painted water surface, using the brush to form gentle ripples and slow-flowing currents.

Spread the medium up to but not onto the banks. Allow it to dry about 10 minutes to stiffen slightly, then texture the surface with a 3/4" stiff brush to make it look like wind-blown water. Repeatedly dabbing the brush into the thickened gloss medium produces small, random ripples.

Another way to make waves and ripples is to use the airstream from an airbrush or compressor after the gloss medium has been laid on with a brush. Hold the tip of the airbrush 6" to 8" from the surface, directing the airflow to push and "whip" the gloss medium. The airstream also removes small air bubbles lurking just under the surface of the medium.

As the gloss medium dries it shrinks slightly, and the texture becomes more subtle. Once the first coat has dried thoroughly I apply two more blue-tinted coats, allowing each to dry before adding the next. The hint of blue adds a transparent haze that gives the water a touch of mystery and depth.

For the final coat brush on clear,

SCENERY BASE TRENCH FOR BUILDING A STREAM

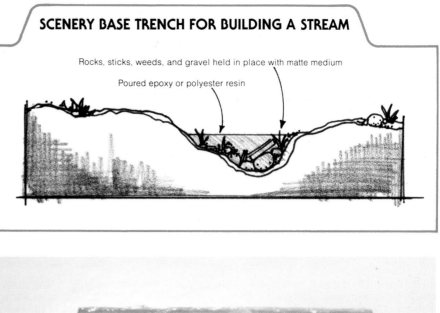

Rocks, sticks, weeds, and gravel held in place with matte medium

Poured epoxy or polyester resin

The bottom of this small plexiglass square was painted with blue and green acrylics, and the top was coated with gloss medium. Some extra gloss medium and a few touches of white acrylic were used to build up the frothy bow waves and wake.

HIGH-GLOSS EPOXY COATINGS FOR CALM WATER

These products are sold in hardware, craft, hobby, and some woodworking shops for such applications as finishing coffee-table and bar tops and making decoupage projects.

EnviroTex

    Environmental Technology Inc.
    P. O. Box 365
    Fields Landing, CA 95537

Behr Super Gloss Build 50
    Behr Process Corp.
    Santa Ana, CA 92702

Ultra-Glo

    Chemco
    San Leandro, CA 94577

(Left) EnviroTex is one of several two-part epoxy coatings which make excellent calm water. These products form hard, high-gloss surfaces that are resistant to alcohol and water (right). The cross section of these epoxy coatings is quite thin, so if the surface is scratched or otherwise damaged the water can be repaired by recoating it with a second layer.

(Left) Polyester casting resins make superb rippled water. Several brands are sold in hobby and craft stores. Most can be tinted with special transparent dyes. (Right) This water consists of two layers of polyester resin. The natural-looking surface ripples develop as the resin hardens. To clean polyester resin surfaces wipe gently with a soft, damp cloth.

TYPICAL POLYESTER RESIN POND

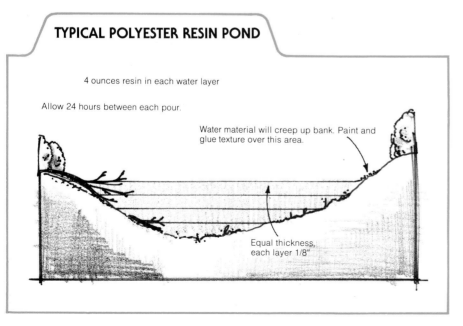

4 ounces resin in each water layer

Allow 24 hours between each pour.

Water material will creep up bank. Paint and glue texture over this area.

Equal thickness, each layer 1/8"

untinted gloss medium. Use a small brush to add extra medium around the bases of pilings to represent swirls and ripples.

Gloss medium makes such good waves that it's possible to make unrealistically high seas. If you do, use a sanding block to remove the wave crests, mop up the sanding dust, and apply a smooth coat of clear medium, brushing it out well in the wave troughs.

Boat wakes can be modeled by piling gloss medium along the bow and behind the stern. Accentuate such features by dry-brushing their tops with Polly S Reefer White, white tube acrylic, or acrylic modeling paste after the medium dries. Seal the surface with another coat of gloss medium. Use this same technique to model fast-flowing water in streams and rapids.

Waves and white water. Acrylic

CHAPTER 7

Pritchard's Pond on my Carrabasset & Dead River Ry. is the largest expanse of polyester resin water I've ever poured. The chief drawback of this water material is the powerful chemical smell given off by the resin as it cures.

(Top right) After pouring the resin, work it to the edges of the water area with a small disposable brush. (Right) Remove air bubbles trapped in or under freshly poured resin by puncturing them with a sharp object such as tweezers.

modeling paste is a thick, white, glossy goo that can be thinned with water. It is compatible with all acrylic products, dries slowly, and can be worked for many hours. I use it to model ocean waves and other rough water. Apply it with a wide brush, pulling the paste into peaks. The modeling paste is stiff, and will hold its shape until it dries.

To model fast-flowing water, brush modeling paste on the prepared stream bed and smooth it with a wet brush to form ripples and eddies. Add small amounts of blue-green acrylic tube paint to the paste to color it, but always start with less than a drop of color in a tablespoon of paste. Allow at least 24 hours for the paste to dry before applying final coloring and gloss medium.

Modeling paste dries pure white, but by mixing it with gloss medium you can achieve a frothy, milky look, excellent for boat wakes. Mix equal parts of gloss medium and modeling

POLYESTER CASTING RESINS FOR RIPPLED WATER

These products are sold in craft and hobby stores for applications such as plastic stained glass projects and small clear castings. Polyester resins have limited shelf life; if you cannot be sure that your dealer has fresh stock, consider purchasing the material direct from the manufacturer.

Castolite-SG
    Castolite Corp.
    P. O. Box 391
    Woodstock, IL 60098

Clear Cast
    American Handicrafts Company
    3250 W. Seminary Drive
    Fort Worth, TX 76133

Polyester Casting Resin
    Natcol
    P. O. Box 229
    Redlands, CA 92373

Chemco Casting Resin
    Chemco
    San Leandro, CA 94577

This pond was made with Clear Cast polyester resin. The gentle surface undulations occur naturally as the resin hardens. Note how the resin creeps up the banks, requiring touch-up.

The water in this pond is three layers of Castolite-SG. The surface of the pond was whipped while the resin hardened to produce the effect of rough, windblown water. Logs, weeds, and other detail were added before each layer.

paste, apply it thick, and don't judge the results until dry. Practice on a scrap section of water before trying this effect on your favorite foreground scene or diorama.

Titanium White tube acrylic mixed with equal parts of gloss medium also makes realistic white water. Use a small brush to stipple this white mixture onto wave tops, around obstacles in the water, and behind fast-moving boats. Study color photos from magazines like *National Geographic* to get the white water effects just right. You won't be able to judge your results right away, so wait until the first application dries before adding more white. A little goes a long way.

Simulate slow-moving, muddy water by adding a little Polly S Mud to the gloss medium. Apply this over your flat base with an artist's palette knife (a butter knife will also do in a pinch). The knife lets you lay the medium on in broad strokes. Muddy water is pretty much opaque, so if you color each gloss medium layer, little coloring of the flat base is required beforehand.

Using gloss medium with Plexiglas. When glass or Plexiglas is to be used as a flat, non-transparent base for gloss medium water, the first step is to apply acrylic modeling paste to build up ripples. Use a stiff-bristled brush to pull the paste up into waves and swells. Paint the paste after it dries, but instead of using black and earth as on a flat pond bottom, use various blues and blue-greens.

The surface of the water serves as a palette to mix the acrylic tube colors. Start by squeezing out 1/4" of Ultrama-

rine Blue and 1/8" of Chromium Oxide Green. Spread the two colors over the water, blending as you go. Keep the overall color light by mixing a little white latex paint into the blues, and add a drop or two of water to keep the paint thin enough to spread. Around the edges, mix in a little earth color to denote shallow water. Allow the paint to dry several days before applying gloss medium.

To achieve a similar effect with more depth, omit the modeling paste. Instead, paint the underside of the Plexiglas with the colors described above, and after the paint dries seal the bottom with a heavy coat of Ultramarine Blue. Then apply gloss medium to the top surface. For see-to-the-bottom water, build and paint a detailed three-dimensional bottom, set the clear Plexiglas in place, and form the banks. Build up ripples and gloss with four coats of gloss medium as described above.

If you're modeling an oceanfront scene where the tide comes and goes, make the shoreline look wet by thinning gloss medium with an equal part of water and brushing this over the lower portions of the banks. This provides a not-quite-wet glisten. Use dabs of full-strength gloss medium as an adhesive for old tires, barrels, and other tide-line details.

To color deep ocean water add 1/4" of Mars Black acrylic tube color to 1/2 cup of gloss medium. Brush the black-tinted gloss medium onto the deep water; don't try to add texture — just brush as smoothly as you can. This is the first layer of deep ocean water. While it is wet paint the second layer.

To create the second deep ocean color add 1/8" each (just a dab) of Raw Sienna and Burnt Umber tube acrylic to 1/2 cup gloss medium. Brush this thoroughly over the sand, rocks, and from the shoreline out to the deep water, blending it into the first coat. There should be no sharp boundaries between the shallow and deep areas — this brown layer adds the look of sand and silt to the shallows.

Now apply more gloss medium as described above, adding waves and ripples. A good way to evaluate how the water will look when dry is to place a light above and behind the water to reflect off the surface toward you.

Water materials: epoxies. Modern chemistry has produced several products that make excellent shiny water surfaces. Handled according to the manufacturers' directions, they are safe to use and yield consistent results. Before I dive into the how-to of simulating water with them, let me issue a strong warning: These chemicals are dangerous, and must be kept out of the reach of children. You must always wear rubber gloves and safety glasses or other eye protection when handling these materials, and after applying them you must be careful not to breathe the fumes. Always use a fan and open plenty of windows to ventilate the area properly.

The easiest products to use are high-gloss epoxies intended for making thick, high-gloss finishes on coffee tables, decoupage projects, and bar tops. The brand I've used most often is EnviroTex, a two-part (clear and amber), self-leveling epoxy available

in craft, hobby, hardware, and woodworking shops. EnviroTex is fairly expensive compared to varnish or gloss medium, but it makes the best mirrorlike calm water I've ever seen. One quart (two one-half pint containers) will cover an area 2' x 2'. Its biggest advantage over other chemical finishes is that it gives off little in the way of offensive smell, an important consideration if you have friends you want to keep and family you want to remain related to.

To use high-gloss epoxy the scenery base must be prepared just as for varnish or gloss medium water. This material works best on flat-bottom lakes or ponds, and because it is made to cure with a thin cross section it should not be applied in a deep basin. The water surface must be level so the epoxy won't run out on the floor.

Check the surface of the water base for dust or texture that might cause the surface to dimple, and if the water extends to the edge of your layout, make a cardboard-and-masking-tape dam to keep the epoxy from dripping on the floor. Next, shine a strong light under the water base, shut off the room lights, and look for pinholes where epoxy might leak through. This is important! If you leave a hole, no matter how small, epoxy will find it and leak out onto the floor. Repair holes with a dab of acrylic modeling paste or caulking applied with your fingertip.

Read the instructions that come with the epoxy, and measure the required amount from each container into paper coffee cups. (Where equal parts are required, draw a line inside each cup the same distance from the bottom.) One ounce of epoxy mixture will cover an area about 6" x 6".

Mix the two parts in a disposable container. Cut one end of a wooden tongue depressor so it is square, and use it to mix the epoxy vigorously for about 2 minutes. This is important, because incomplete mixing will cause soft spots in the completed water.

When the epoxy is thoroughly mixed, pour it onto the base. You have only 15 minutes to complete pouring before the mixture starts to cure. Use the tongue depressor to help move the epoxy, and pour it near but not up to the banks. The material is self-leveling, so it will spread out until it finds its own level. Don't try to whip up the surface to form waves or ripples; they will just flatten out again.

Air bubbles can be removed from the surface by breathing on it (honest) or by gently passing the flame of a butane torch near the surface. (Carbon dioxide reduces the surface tension of the material, allowing the bubbles to escape.) EnviroTex sets in 5 to 7 hours, and it cures completely in 72 hours. Try to keep dirt and dust off the sur-

Malcolm Furlow

Malcolm Furlow made this waterfall by gluing strands of fiberglass aquarium-filter material to the riverbed and working layers of blue-green and pearl-tinted polyester resin over them. He highlighted the rapids with white acrylic before pouring the final coat.

COLORS FOR POLYESTER RESIN WATER

All quantities are for 4 ounces of resin.

Layer 1 (bottom):
 2 drops dark green flat hobby enamel
 2 drops tan flat hobby enamel

Layer 2:
 ½ drop blue resin dye
 2 drops yellow resin dye

Layer 3:
 2 drops blue resin dye

Layer 4 (top):
 Clear, no coloring

The best ocean water I've seen was on Bill Aldrich's HO Shoreline Division of the New Haven. Bill placed the ocean area in the corner of the room and hid most of the horizon with a break-water painted on the backdrop. He sculpted the plaster water base and painted it with acrylics, then he coated the waves with polyester resin.

face of the epoxy until it cures.

Water materials: polyester resins. Polyester resin is by far the most difficult water-making material to use, but used properly, it yields rippled plastic water that has to be touched to be believed.

Polyester resins consist of a thick, honey-like resin to which a small proportion of clear, water-like catalyst is added, drop by drop. An exact number of drops of catalyst is required per ounce of resin.

Extreme caution is required when using polyester resins. Methyl ethyl ketone peroxide, a dangerous chemical, is the catalyst, and you must always wear eye protection while handling it. People with sensitive skin should also wear rubber gloves. Always work in a well-ventilated area. The powerful fumes from curing polyester resin will invade your home and the smell will last for days if not properly exhausted. Long or concentrated exposure to these fumes can make you sick.

The recipe box on page 79 lists brands of polyester resin suitable for making water. The first is Castolite-SG, which is formulated for making plastic stained-glass craft items. It

sets fast and hard in thin cross sections, and has a gently rippled surface. Castolite provides a three-page information sheet on modeling water.

Another brand, Clear Cast, is for casting plastic items with thicker cross sections than are possible with Castolite SG. It pours well and sets with a slightly rippled surface. Dyes are available separately. Some casting resins require an additive to make them cure properly in open air (rather than in an enclosed mold), and this additive is required for making resin water. Check the instructions for the product you choose.

Polyester resins work best when they are poured, not brushed, into a waterway, and preparation of the pond or stream bed is a little different from what we do for varnish or gloss medium. These resins contain strong chemical solvents that are capable of softening or dissolving many plastics, and every scenery material used in and around the water area should be tested beforehand to see if the resin will affect it.

Polyester resin also softens white glue. When this happens, small details can break loose and float where you don't want them. I place most details

directly into the resin with tweezers after pouring, and glue larger items or those that will float with 5-minute epoxy beforehand.

Matte medium is also softened by polyester resin, but if the bottom is not disturbed the softened medium will hold detail and textures until the resin gels. Plaster rocks and cast-metal details are unaffected. Plastic details, on the other hand, will be crazed, warped, or even melted by the combination of solvent action and internal heat generated as the resin cures. Ground foam, dyed sawdust, and lichen seem unaffected, except for a little color bleeding.

Resin application procedures. Details in the water should be complete and the painted base should have several days to dry before you pour the first resin layer. Use an inexpensive plastic measuring cup with one-ounce graduations to measure exact quantities of resin in accordance with the manufacturer's instructions.

Since the depth of each layer of resin is critical to proper curing, you must pour just enough resin, no more and no less, for each layer. Castolite recommends 7 ounces of resin per square foot of water surface, and this

CHAPTER 7

gives you almost the perfect ⅛" depth for each layer, no matter which brand you choose. For example, for a pond 9" x 9" I calculated that 4 ounces of resin would be required to cover the bottom to a depth of ⅛", so for each layer I mixed a 4-ounce batch.

Prepare the scenery base as you would for epoxy water, but substitute 5-minute epoxy thickened with sawdust as a pinhole and gap filler.

After measuring, pour the resin into a disposable mixing container (not plastic!). Following the manufacturer's instructions, add the catalyst, drop by drop. Gently stir the resin with a wooden tongue depressor for 2 or 3 minutes, trying to avoid trapping air bubbles in the mixture. While stirring, frequently scrape the sides of the container to ensure that all the resin is mixed with the catalyst. Add paint or dye to color the resin (see below) while mixing.

Next, slowly pour the resin onto the water base. Work it to the edges with the stirring stick, and prick bubbles with a toothpick. If you are pouring water on a diorama, slowly tip it from side to side to distribute the resin evenly. Any casting resin that accidentally gets on rock surfaces, or other areas where it will spoil realism, can be removed with acetone. Brush the surface and wipe excess acetone away with a rag (acetone will not work after the resin sets).

Heat is critical to properly cure the resin, and in my basement, where the temperature rarely goes above 65 degrees F., additional heat is needed to start the resin on its way to a fast, hard set. To warm the setting resin to at least 70 degrees, I place a 100-watt incandescent bulb 8" above the resin for the first two or three hours after pouring. If the temperature of your railroad room is at least 70 degrees, the lamp will not be needed.

Check the resin after several hours to see if it is setting properly. Gently prod the surface in an inconspicuous spot with a toothpick; if the resin is sticky and the consistency of Jell-O, curing has begun. Leave the surface undisturbed for 24 hours before pouring the second layer, and wait 24 hours between subsequent layers, too.

Coloring resin water. Special dyes, usually sold with the product, are used to color polyester resin. I've used only blue and yellow. The dyes are strong and must be added sparingly — a drop or two in three ounces of resin is plenty. Different tints can be added to various layers as they are poured.

I add three or four drops of flat dark green and tan hobby enamel (see recipe box) such as Humbrol, Pactra, or Testor's to color the first layer of resin. The paint clouds the resin slightly, adding a bit of murky mystery to the bottom. It's as if the viewer were looking through a layer of mud and algae.

To the second resin layer add 1 drop of blue dye and 2 drops of yellow, and in the third layer use 2 drops of blue. The top layer goes on clear. You're free to try other coloring combinations depending upon the type and characteristics of the water you're modeling, but remember that too little color looks far better than too much.

About a week after pouring the final resin layer — after most of the smell has gone away — touch up the banks. Like EnviroTex, polyester resin creeps up the banks, and must be covered with fine sand or painted with Floquil Railroad Colors. The final touch is to glue a few lily pads on top of the water, if appropriate.

Ripples and rough water. Polyester resin can be manipulated while it cures to make ripples and rough water. Wait for the resin to start gelling, then stab and pick up some of the material from the water surface with a round-ended stick. At first the resin will stay up in a peak, then it will sag back and try to level itself. Keep prodding — almost whipping — the resin until it holds the waves and ripples and looks like rough water. Use a hair dryer set on low heat to accelerate setting. If the cured surface does not look like what you had in mind, pour another layer and try again.

A quick way to achieve a rippled effect over cured resin water is to mix 5 drops of catalyst with about ½

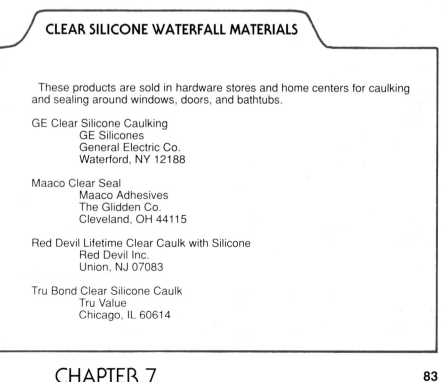

CHAPTER 7

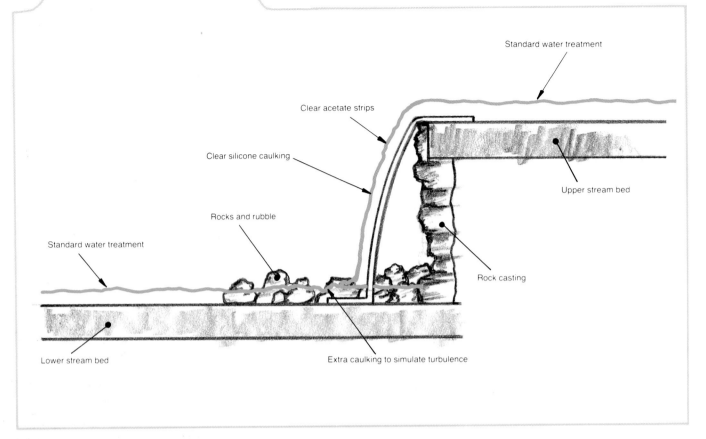

Standard water treatment

Clear acetate strips

Clear silicone caulking

Rocks and rubble

Standard water treatment

Upper stream bed

Rock casting

Lower stream bed

Extra caulking to simulate turbulence

This falling water consists of silicone rubber caulking spread over clear plastic strips. The secret to realism is to make sure that the water falls straight down.

ounce of resin. Mix thoroughly, then brush the mixture onto the water surface. Use an old brush, because it will be ruined when the resin hardens. One-half ounce of resin will cover about four square inches when brushed in this manner.

The resin will start to gel about 10 minutes after it is mixed, so you have to work fast. Set the hair dryer on low

heat and hold it 6" above the brush as you apply the resin. After brushing on all the resin, go back and stipple the surface with the tip of the brush. Dab the bristles into the surface, keeping the brush in motion. The air from the hair dryer will flatten the stippling, but as the resin begins to gel the ripple texture will remain. When the resin begins to stiffen, liberate trapped

bubbles by stabbing them with the tip of the brush.

Now let the water surface cure. When the thin top coat hardens the ripples will remain. Because extra heat will be generated by the additional catalyst in this final coat, the resin should not be allowed near anything that might be damaged by heat. Never use extra catalyst with more than 1/2 ounce of resin; if you do, so much heat will be generated that the resin layer will warp, crack, and pull away from the water base, sometimes taking most of the scenery base with it.

Waterfalls and rapids. Convincing waterfalls are spectacular, and they're not hard to build. The first step is to build the scenery base as described above. Plan carefully: The water must follow a realistic course and fall over a rock face.

To model the falling water I use thin vertical strips of clear acetate, aquarium filter material, or stretched poly fiber fill glued in place with a clear adhesive (5-minute epoxy, gloss medium, or my favorite, clear silicone bathtub sealant).

After the adhesive dries, coat the strips with clear bathtub sealant to give the falling water bulk and shape. Apply the sealant with a fingertip, smoothing it over the thin clear strips. Add several thin layers of sealant, letting each dry before adding the next. The water should fall straight down

George Sellios built this realistic waterfall using a strip of clear plastic held in place with 5-minute epoxy. The plastic was streaked with Polly S Reefer White to model the air trapped in fast-moving water. EnviroTex was poured both top and bottom and brushed over the falls. While the epoxy was wet George added bits of fluffed cotton at the base of the falls.

unless deflected by a tree branch, stump, or rock outcropping.

The silicone rubber gives the fragile strips strength and body. (If your falls don't look right, allow the sealant to dry overnight and cut away any water that does not fall straight down.) Add more sealant until the water looks real. Clear silicone bathtub sealant is messy stuff, so work with disposable gloves and have a couple of rags handy.

After you've created the shape of the falls, brush the last coat of wet silicone lightly up and down with an old paintbrush to add texture. This smooths the rubber, giving it the look of water rushing downward.

Now add white froth to simulate air trapped in the turbulent water. Mix equal parts Titanium White or Polly S Reefer White and gloss medium. Apply this where turbulence would occur, again using up-and-down strokes. After this dries evaluate the results; if you want the falls whiter, add more paint.

When it's dry seal the white turbulence with a heavy application of gloss medium. Add drips and small rivulets using a paintbrush.

When the waterfall is complete, make the water above and below it. Any technique described in this chapter will work. Make sure the water material flows over the falls — most of it will run off, so be prepared to spread it again. Keep doing this until you have pleasing transitions between standing water, rushing water, and the falls.

Puddles and drips. To make small quantities of water such as puddles, inside barrels, or water running from pipes, use 5-minute epoxy. Of the available brands, several set crystal clear, and polyester resin dyes or enamel paint can be added to color them. Mix the epoxy according to the directions and coax or dribble it into place with a toothpick.

Questions and answers

Q: Can epoxy and polyester resin be used over Styrofoam scenery?
A: Yes, in fact, no special precautions are required with epoxies such as EnviroTex. To use polyester resin the Styrofoam must first be sealed to keep the resin from reaching and attacking it. Apply at least 1/4" of plaster or Savogran Wood Putty over the Styrofoam, extending the plaster up to and well over the banks. It is important that there be no holes through which resin might leak, because if it reaches the Styrofoam it eats it away rapidly.
Q: After several months of heavy family traffic in my railroad room the water areas were dusty. After I cleaned them, they were scratched and dull. Can I wax the water to restore the shine?
A: I've heard of people waxing water surfaces with furniture polish or bowling alley wax. I suspect that while this does produce a hard, smooth surface the wax coat may dull the sparkle of the water at least slightly. I prefer to add a coat of gloss medium over the scratched water to renew it.
Q: Why not thin gloss medium with water so it can be flowed onto a smooth base to represent calm water?
A: I tried this several times because I didn't believe the results of my first test. Adding even small amounts of water to gloss medium dulls it considerably, and the more water added, the duller the resulting finish. The best way to model flat, calm water is to use one of the two-part epoxy finishes; high-gloss varnish comes in a close second. I strongly suggest you reserve gloss medium for modeling water where a rippled surface is important, then use it only at full strength.
Q: I've had poor results making gloss medium water. I prepared the base as you suggested, but after the medium dried the gloss surface was not smooth. It was rough, like sandpaper. What went wrong?
A: While I can't say exactly what went wrong, I'd be inclined to use a different brand of gloss medium for my second try. To fix the problem, sand the unsatisfactory areas flat and apply another coat of gloss medium. If the surface still is not smooth, repeat the sanding step and add another thick coat of gloss medium.
Q: How can I model a polluted waterway? I've seen water that was green, brown, and even gray.
A: Use a muddy black rather than solid black to paint the water base. Mix equal parts black or blue (or green, for really polluted water) with latex earth. Feather this color from the center of the pond or stream to the earth color on the banks. This mixture softens the dead black and looks good even if you don't have a sky backdrop to provide blue reflection.

CHAPTER 7

The painted backdrop behind this section of Bob Hayden's layout is far from artistic, but it does hint that there is something beyond.

Backdrops and background scenery

A backdrop behind a model railroad serves at least two purposes. First, it reinforces the illusion created by the three-dimensional scenery, and second, it helps hold the viewer's eye within the scene by hiding out-of-scale distractions around the perimeter of the layout. Even a simple backdrop with hazy blue sky and gentle rolling hills provides enough natural extension of the scenery that the viewer will feel there is more beyond the horizon. By giving the illusion of distance, the backdrop helps place the whole railroad in the setting you've imagined.

The simplest backdrop: flat, blue, and portable. Over the years I've built several flat backdrops to use as photo backgrounds, and building one is good practice for putting up and painting the backdrop for a large layout. I have used 1/4" plywood, 1/4" and 1/8" Masonite, linoleum strips, galvanized sheet metal (rolled flashing comes in 14", 20", and 28" widths), and even 3/8" plaster wallboard. Because portability is important, I now favor lightweight materials, including Styrofoam, Upson Board, and Fome-Cor board.

Extruded Styrofoam insulation makes excellent flat backdrops. The slabs I buy are 1" thick, 2' wide, and 8' long. Styrofoam takes latex paint well if it is primed with several coats of flat white. Upson Board is a pressed paper product used to build store-window displays. It is 1/8" thick, and has a pebbled, cream-colored surface that takes paint without priming. Upson Board comes in 4' x 8' sheets, is relatively light, and can be formed into gentle curves in corners. It can be stapled, glued, or nailed. The best place to find it is at a large lumberyard; if you have trouble locating Upson Board, try calling a display company to see where they buy theirs.

Fome-Cor board is a display and artist's material that consists of a styrene foam center with smooth paper on both sides. It comes in 1/8", 3/16", 1/4", and 1/2" thicknesses, is light, and will not warp. It is available in sheets up to 4' x 8'; smaller sizes are stocked in craft and art stores. Fome-Cor board must be primed before painting.

Continuous backdrops. For a non-portable layout I prefer a backdrop that extends completely around the room. This means making curved corners so the backdrop appears continuous. I've used 1/8" tempered Masonite for this, which works well but requires a robust framework and leaves seams to fill with joint compound.

To bend Masonite around tight curves try spraying it with a wetting agent such as Fantastic liquid cleaner. This makes the Masonite soft and flexible. After the Masonite is in place and allowed to dry, the curved surfaces will be fuzzy from the soaking, so sand and seal them with clear varnish. Repeat the sanding and sealing over the whole length of the backdrop until the surface is smooth.

I fill the seams between panels with spackle, then sand smooth. Even after sealing Masonite absorbs moisture during hot weather and dries out during the winter. The resulting expansion and contraction opens and closes the seams, creating cracks. One solution is to cover the Masonite with a continuous sheet of unbleached,

The trains furnish the action and interest on our layouts, and backdrops should not be so detailed as to detract from them.

perma-pressed muslin, glued on with waterproof vinyl wallpaper paste. The paste is brushed thickly onto the Masonite and the muslin is smoothed into place using a wallpaper brush. When the muslin is dry prime it with several coats of flat white latex paint.

Another useful background material, the one I use on my railroad, is 36"-wide linoleum runner. This may not be stocked in your area, but floor covering dealers will order it for you. Floor runner comes in rolls long enough to go all the way around an average railroad room without a seam. I mount the linoleum with the shiny, finished side against the wall. The back, which becomes the sky, takes paint better than the shiny side, and the texture doesn't show when the backdrop is viewed under normal lighting.

Build the backdrop before you start construction on the layout. If it's already too late for that, move the railroad away from the walls if possible,

and enlist the help of several friends. My layout is in the basement, and before installing the backdrop I stuffed fiberglass insulation in the gaps where the floor joists meet the concrete foundation walls. Once your backdrop is up it's too late to go back and insulate.

I attached 1" x 3" strapping to the basement walls with a Ramset, a device that shoots special hardened nails into concrete with .22 cartridges. The top piece of strapping runs horizontally along the top of the foundation, and another piece is fastened about 30" below it. The distance between these pieces varies depending upon the heights of the ceiling and the layout; keep the bottom support below layout height so no nailheads will show. Nail vertical pieces of strapping between the top and bottom supports every 30" to keep the middle of the linoleum from sagging.

Making curved corners. Corners require planning before nailing up the vertical strapping. You'll need to deter-

mine the approximate radius of the curve, then measure that distance from the corner to position a vertical where the curve will start. On my backdrop the verticals are 2' from the corner. The linoleum backdrop is fastened to these verticals and allowed to take a natural curve through the corner.

Now unroll the linoleum and fasten it in place. This job requires two or three helping hands, more if available, to avoid bending or creasing the backdrop. If your room is large or the runner only comes in short rolls, butt the seams together tightly.

Start at one end of the room and fasten a corner of the linoleum to the top strapping. Have one person unroll the linoleum, another smooth it out, and a third drive the nails. Use $^{1}/_{2}$" or $^{3}/_{4}$" roofing nails, and set the heads slightly below the surface of the linoleum by tapping with the hammer. Heavy industrial staples driven with an electric staple gun also work and are easier if you are short of helpers.

As you reach each corner, form the linoleum into a smooth curve before fastening it to the vertical strapping. Smooth the linoleum as much as you can while nailing it up; the final surface should not be tight as a drum, but as tight as you can get it without stretching or ripping. After several months a few minor sags may develop in the unsupported sections, but these won't be noticeable unless the backdrop is viewed from an extreme angle.

Seams, priming, and painting. Next, fill all seams and cover all nailheads with drywall joint compound. Cover each seam with a 1/8" layer of joint compound extending about 4" on either side.

Then, starting at the top, bed a strip of paper or fiberglass joint tape into the compound by drawing a wide putty knife over the tape. Work from top to bottom, sinking the tape into the joint compound.

After the joint compound is dry, usually overnight, apply a second layer, smoothing and feathering the edges into the backdrop on both sides of each joint. After the second layer dries, sand the seam to a smooth, flat, invisible joint. The joint will require several coats of primer to seal it completely.

Prime the backdrop with flat white latex paint. You can brush, roll, or spray, but apply several thick, even coats. The white primer seals the linoleum, provides tooth for the backdrop colors, and brightens the blue sky color applied over it.

For sky color start with a bright blue that looks good under all types of lighting and on color film. Several are listed in the box on page 94. Buy more paint than you think you'll need; I painted a backdrop 3' high and 76' long with one gallon, and had enough paint left over for several flat sky backdrops. You'll also need flat white, which can be the same paint used to prime the backdrop. Round up a wide paintbrush, rags, and a bucket of clean water. I use an old shower curtain to protect the floor.

Apply the sky blue after the primer has dried for several days. I use a wide brush, but if you own a sprayer you may want to try it; the principles are the same regardless of the application method. If it is a bright, sunny day look out the window and note how the sky color changes as you look up. Overhead the sky is deep blue, but toward the horizon the color gets lighter until it is almost white.

Painting sky and clouds. Paint the sky portion of the backdrop in six-foot sections, overlapping and blending each section. Start at the top, applying the blue with horizontal strokes. Paint the top third blue, then rinse the brush and apply the white,

This backdrop curves around a corner in the distance, then bellies out in a gentle S shape to hide some pipes behind the station. Because it is so close to the station, trees and shrubs were painted on the backdrop, then texture was applied over the paint to add just a little 3-D quality to them.

starting at the bottom. Work the white up the backdrop until it mixes with the bottom of the blue area.

Next, without adding any more paint, blend the white with the blue, working from the middle to the top of the backdrop. Use a light touch, and try to pick the brush off the backdrop surface without leaving brush marks. The sky should look layered, not

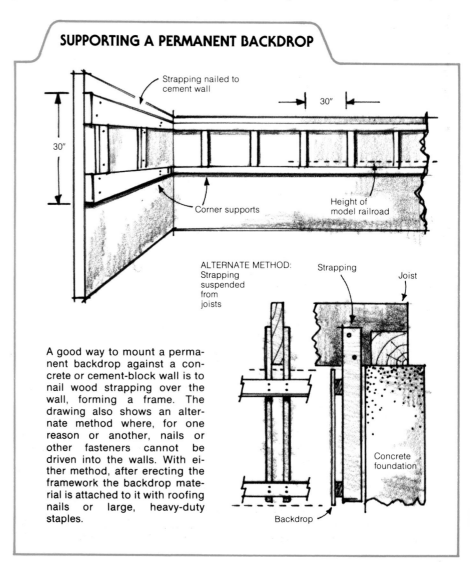

SUPPORTING A PERMANENT BACKDROP

Strapping nailed to cement wall

30"

30"

Corner supports

Height of model railroad

ALTERNATE METHOD: Strapping suspended from joists

Strapping

Joist

Concrete foundation

Backdrop

A good way to mount a permanent backdrop against a concrete or cement-block wall is to nail wood strapping over the wall, forming a frame. The drawing also shows an alternate method where, for one reason or another, nails or other fasteners cannot be driven into the walls. With either method, after erecting the framework the backdrop material is attached to it with roofing nails or large, heavy-duty staples.

CHAPTER 8

These are the three brushes I use for adding hills and trees to painted backdrops. The large one with white bristles is a No. 12 Bright, the middle brush is a No. 7 Round, watercolor brush, and the brush on the right is a No. 16 Tapered Flat.

These hand-painted clouds add life and distance to this scene. Photos were used for reference here, but a slide could also have been projected onto the background.

streaked. If the paint starts to dry while there are areas yet to be blended, moisten the brush with water. Don't be too fussy: As long as the top is blue, the bottom is white, and there are no brush marks, your sky will look great.

Now add clouds to your backdrop — if you want them. Often the layered look we achieved above is enough. The layering produces just a hint of high cirrus clouds. A few modelers argue that they don't have the talent to paint realistic clouds, and worry that they'll spoil an otherwise fine backdrop. This is true if you overdo them. My preference is to paint clouds, but to keep them light enough to add interest to the sky without drawing attention to themselves.

You don't have to be a weatherman to understand how clouds should look — just look out the window. The easiest to paint are high cirrus clouds. These are horizontal, alternating layers of white and blue. Make them while the backdrop is wet by adding a little more white to the brush, brushing in broad horizontal strokes, and not blending the white completely with the blue. (If you painted the backdrop as described above you already have some of these high cirrus clouds.)

Puffy cumulus clouds are easier to paint than they look. Use a stiff, 2" hair-bristle brush (nylon bristles are too soft), and while the backdrop paint is wet, pick up white paint on the tip of the brush and push it into the backdrop in a rapid, pecking motion. This "woodpecker stroke" produces overlapping puffs of white, and the pushing motion will mix the white slightly with the blue. If the clouds look too white repeat the woodpecker stroke without adding any white to the brush. You can keep doing this until the cloud almost disappears. To smooth the clouds and blend them into the backdrop use light horizontal strokes with a clean, large, flat brush.

Clouds can also be created by dabbing the backdrop with sponges dipped in white paint. Use a variety of sponge shapes and a thin layer of white paint in a roller tray. Dab the backdrop with a light touch and keep a rag handy to catch drips.

Now step back and admire your sky. It should be impressive just the way it is, but it needs a few distant hills or mountains to add depth. Let the sky paint and clouds dry for several days before you begin painting them.

Foothills and mountains. If you built a small-scale planning model of your layout, refer to it to determine where you should paint distant hills and mountains on the backdrop. Use a soft lead pencil to mark the locations of background features. Unless your foreground scenery will be spectacular, keep the background hills gentle and rolling, or make the horizon flat. Keep the painted hills slightly lower than the buildings near the backdrop.

After sketching in hill contours with the pencil, add texture to what will become the nearest painted hills. This breaks up the surface of the backdrop and adds a little three-dimensional quality to it. Mix a handful of sawdust or scenic foam in a cup of flat latex paint (the color doesn't matter), and brush this goop onto the backdrop. You can also use ceiling paint texture mixed with any of the distant hill colors, or simply glue the texture to the backdrop by brushing on white glue and blowing sawdust or foam into it.

We'll paint the backdrop hills in layers, starting with the most distant. These will not have any surface texture, and the tops of the hills will only show a subtle sawtooth line of treetops.

Combine 3 cups of flat white latex paint and 1 cup of sky blue in a jar, then add 4" of Mars Black acrylic. Mix well, and label the jar for identification: I call this color "most-distant

gray," and we'll use it as the base for several other colors as well.

Using a flat, 1"-wide nylon brush, apply most-distant gray using your pencil lines as a guide. Stipple the tops of the distant hills with the edge of the brush for a slight sawtooth effect. Work around the backdrop, painting all the most-distant hills.

After the most-distant gray dries, mix and apply distant gray, a greener gray that represents the next closer line of hills. Add 1/2" of Mars Black and 3" of Chromium Oxide Green to 1/3 cup of most-distant gray. Apply this color to form hills with a sawtooth forest top along the upper edge.

The third color, distant green, also represents tree-covered hills. Combine 3 tablespoons of most-distant gray, 9" of Chromium Oxide Green, and 1/2 teaspoon of matte medium. (You may want to add as much as 2 tablespoons of matte medium to keep the mixture workable.) Brush this on the closer hills as before, but make the individual treetops larger and more prominent.

Wait a day or two for all the background colors to dry thoroughly, then spray a light mist of flat white over the hills. This white separates the distant hills from those closer to the foreground. After the white dries apply the closer green color over the textured portion of the backdrop. The tops of these hills should have the most distinct tree shapes.

Making convincing tree shapes. Next paint the backdrop trees that will be just behind the three-dimensional scenery. Use tree green, and make ragged, conical shapes by slapping the vertical edge of a 1" brush lightly against the backdrop.

If you don't like your hand-painted tree shapes, try this: Cut a 1/2"-thick kitchen sponge into quarters, then trim each quarter into pine-tree shapes. The shapes need not be exact; anything tall and triangular is okay. Wrap a piece of masking tape around

CHAPTER 8

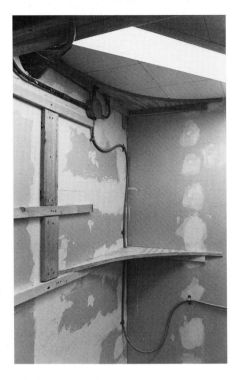

This Upson Board backdrop was mounted on strapping supports with contoured plywood formers behind the corners (left). After finishing the joints, priming, and painting (above), the entire expanse of sky appears perfectly smooth and seamless.

your index finger, sticky side out, pick up a tree sponge on the tape, and moisten it with closer green. Dab the sponge on a rag to remove excess paint, then pat the sponge on the backdrop along the top edge of a hill line. To break up the pattern, change sponges every now and then.

Add shadows under the branches with the tree shadow color. Dip the tip of the brush in the paint and stipple it along the tops of the line of trees and again just below that line. This mixes with the green to produce a dark shadow.

Wash and dry the brush, then mix the tree highlight color. Stipple this onto the tree line, being careful not to cover all of the tree shadows. Work fast so the colors blend right on the backdrop.

Now you should see bright green tree shapes in light and shadow, shapes sufficiently vague that they look like a forest when you stand two or three feet away. Continue, this time using a little more white against the black shadow, and dabbing some trees with straight Green Gold. Don't worry if the paint looks too bright; we'll take care of that in the next step. Paint tree green and individual shadowed tree shapes right over the areas where you applied texture earlier. The stippled paint will be reinforced by the texture beneath it. Now let the backdrop dry for several days.

Open fields and farmland can be painted with grass yellow. Use this color for areas where the backdrop looks like it extends into, or meets, the layout.

Spraying atmospheric haze. I paint only a few clouds on my backdrops because too much backdrop detail can distract the viewer and detract from the railroad. To blend the backdrop colors, I add a second semi-transparent white haze, using an airbrush or spray cans. Spray cans are easy to use and yield broad hazy areas, while an airbrush gives slightly smoother results and allows you to paint around the treetops. Either way, use flat white enamel, spraying it lightly onto the backdrop several inches on either side of the horizon and into the valleys between hills where fog or mist would settle naturally.

Before using spray cans, think about your safety. Aerosol cans put a lot of fine paint particles into the air, and these are both a respiratory and a

Note how the sky color on this portable backdrop gradually changes from strong blue at the top to almost pure white at the bottom. I don't paint clouds on my backdrops simply because I can't do it well enough to make them look convincing.

Here's a blue backdrop after painting the first line of distant hills. The distant hill color is a dead, grayed blue made by mixing flat white latex paint with a little blue and a small dab of black artist's acrylic tube color.

CHAPTER 8

This stippled treetop effect was obtained by using the side of a fairly wide, flat brush. Next, the rough texture on the right side of the picture will later be painted to simulate a closer line of distant tree-covered background hills.

Another section of backdrop after adding the closest line of tree-covered hills and some light-and-dark stippling to represent masses of trees. Each color layer is based on the same formula, with more green added for each line of closer hills.

fire hazard. You'll want to open windows, set up an exhaust fan, and wear a face mask, preferably a respirator. Cover the layout with a drop cloth if it can't be moved out of the way.

Hold the spray can about 12" from the backdrop and spray with sweeping horizontal arm movements, keeping the can moving a constant distance from the backdrop. Watch how the paint hits the surface; it should strike the surface gently and about half the paint should drift away. The idea is to mist out the horizon line, softening it and tying the trees, hills, and sky together.

Be careful; it's easy to apply too much white, and too little is better than too much. If the white paint drifts where it is not wanted, such as into the textured areas of the backdrop, moisten a rag with thinner and wipe it away. If you want extreme control over where the white will go, cut bond paper masks and tape them in place.

The backdrop should not be so interesting or so detailed that it detracts from your layout and trains, but if you want buildings on the backdrop, try using cutouts from photos or magazines. Selecting the pictures is the hardest part, because the perspective must be correct or the effect will be ruined. Cut, trim, and install individual photos using the procedures for printed paper backdrops described below, and after installation mist them with white to blend them into the rest of the backdrop.

Double-backdrop techniques. Two-piece backdrops are popular for museum dioramas and displays, and they are catching on with model railroaders. They consist of a blue sky backdrop as the rear element, and a second backdrop cut to the profile of distant hills or mountains in front of it. Both the backdrops are painted

Robert Hamm built and painted this impressive double backdrop. The painted landscape stands about 2½" in front of the blue sky; both layers were made from galvanized sheet metal flashing.

To mount a printed paper backdrop, start by trimming each section so that no white paper or printed sky will show (1). After positioning each section, lightly mark its horizon outline on the sky (2). Brush rubber cement on the outlined area (3). Do one section at a time, first coating the sky area and then brushing rubber cement on the back of the paper section. When the rubber cement on both is tacky, cover all but a 2″ band at one edge with newspaper (4). Align the printed section and press the edge into place (5). Hold the rest of the backdrop section and slowly slide the newspaper to the left, pressing the backdrop down as you go (6). Remove excess rubber cement by rubbing gently with a gum eraser (7).

using the techniques described above.

An alternative treatment is to make the second, closer backdrop from ragged foam rubber or screen wire cut into mountain shapes. These "foredrop flats" are covered with small bits of lichen and different shades of scenic foam. They give the rear scenery a three-dimensional quality.

Painting with projected slides. Modelers with a talent for painting often project slides of their favorite scenes directly onto the blue backdrop, using the slide as a guide for shapes and colors. All layout lighting should be installed before the projected background is painted, and shadows painted on the backdrop should match those in the foreground.

Start by marking a level horizon line on the backdrop. Mark the line in chalk at slightly below your eye level.

Project the slide on the backdrop, aligning the projected horizon with your chalk line. If the shadows are coming from the wrong direction, reverse the slide in the projector. Use only pictures where the camera was level or tilted slightly downward.

Trace the basic outlines onto the backdrop using light chalk or pencil lines. You can fudge the areas where the slides overlap by moving the pro-

CHAPTER 8

To make dozens of trees along a tree line, cut a kitchen sponge into several small tree shapes. These are used like rubber stamps: Dip the sponges in the backdrop color and pat them on the backdrop.

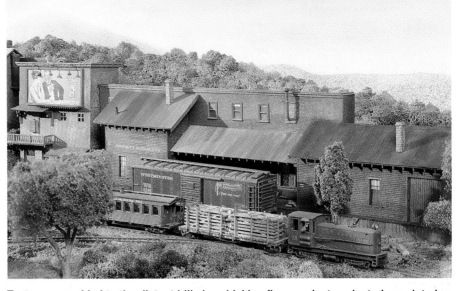

Texture was added to the distant hills by whisking fine sawdust against glue painted on the hill outline. After the glue dried it was colored with "most-distant gray." A flat white overspray tones down the gray and simulates haze.

jector up, down, closer, or farther from the backdrop.

Paint within the boundaries of the lines using the standard backdrop color recipes. Start by painting large blocks of color, working from most distant to closest. You may have to project the slide and redraw the chalk lines between colors.

Slide projection works well if you want to duplicate specific scenes, but the technique requires a degree of talent as well as experience in mixing colors. Also, because you start with detailed colored slides there's a tendency to try to paint all the details. Don't do it unless you're an artist. Instead, stick with basic shapes, outlines, and simple colors — so you can get back to working on the trains!

Installing paper backdrops. Some commercial paper backdrops consist of a landscape printed on white paper which must be cut from the paper backing and mounted on a blue background: others include blue sky. Both types can be mounted permanently on your own seamless sky backdrop.

You'll need a hobby knife, pencil, straightedge, masking tape, gum eraser, lots of old newspapers, and a fresh bottle of rubber cement. Start by selecting the printed scenes, temporarily taping them in place, then step back to judge the effect. Move the pieces until you like what you have, then note where each section goes.

Trim the edges of each printed section with a sharp hobby knife and straightedge (you can use a paper cutter for straight cuts). If you have the type of backdrop that must be cut out,

lay the printed sheet on a flat surface covered with several thicknesses of newspaper and trim away the white paper. Use a new blade in the hobby knife, and cut using short, controlled strokes. Change blades often.

Position the trimmed sections on the backdrop with masking tape. If something doesn't look right, change it now. Draw a light pencil line along the top edge of each printed section. On cutout backdrops this line will follow

the scenic contour; on backdrops with sky included the line will be straight. The pencil line will serve as a guide for applying rubber cement. Remove the printed sections and place them face down on a clean surface.

Now apply a thin coat of rubber cement to the backdrop where the first printed section is to be mounted. Brush cement up to the pencil line and down to the bottom of the backdrop, then coat the back of the first printed

These full-size HO Walthers "Instant Buildings" flats were placed against the backdrop to provide a finished look during construction of the foreground city. Eventually they'll be replaced with low-relief (and underscale) background flats.

All colors are flat latex wall paint or artist's tube acrylics.

Sky Blue:
>Sears No. 125, Royal Blue Medium Bright
>Sears No. 942, Larkspur
>Ward's No. 187-B-3-71, Tahoe
>Tru-Test No. E223, Bluejay
>Tru-Test No. E224, Zenith

Sky White:
>Any flat white latex wall paint

Most-Distant Gray:
>3 cups white
>1 cup sky blue
>4" Mars Black acrylic

Distant Gray:
>1/3 cup Most-Distant Gray
>1/2" Mars Black
>3" Chromium Oxide Green

Distant Green:
>3 tablespoons Most-Distant Gray
>9" Chromium Oxide Green
>1/2 teaspoon full-strength matte medium

Closer Green:
>1 tablespoon Most-Distant Gray
>3" Chromium Oxide Green
>1 tablespoon full-strength matte medium

Tree Green:
>1 teaspoon Most-Distant Gray
>2" Chromium Oxide Green
>2" Green Gold (sometimes hard to find; look for Bocour brand)
>1 teaspoon full-strength matte medium

Tree Shadow:
>9" Chromium Oxide Green
>6" Green Gold
>1" Mars Black
>1 teaspoon full-strength matte medium

Tree Highlight:
>1" Green Gold
>1" Titanium White
>1 teaspoon full-strength matte medium

Grass Yellow:
>2" Green Gold
>2" Chromium Oxide Green
>1 teaspoon full-strength matte medium

White Haze:
>Flat white enamel such as Testor's, Pactra, or Humbrol,
>in aerosol can or applied with an airbrush.

IMPORTANT: Paint colors come and go with home decorating fashions so the latex colors listed above may be unavailable by the time you read this. Sears has a list of their discontinued colors and can cross-index them with current ones; other brands may be able to provide the same service.

section, too. Rubber cement is a contact adhesive, so both surfaces to be joined must be coated and the coating must be almost dry before mating them.

It takes about 10 minutes for the rubber cement to dry (actually, it will be slightly tacky, but that's what we want). Fasten a sheet of newspaper to the backdrop with small pieces of masking tape. The newspaper should hang loosely, covering all of the cemented surface except the last 2" on the extreme right edge. This newspaper is important: It serves as a barrier to keep the printed section from accidentally sticking to the backdrop while you position it.

Hold the first printed section against the newspaper, lining up the right edge with the pencil marks on the backdrop. Lift the left edge of the newspaper and check to see if the printed section lines up there, too. Once the printed section is where you want it, press the right edge into the exposed band of rubber cement on the backdrop. The cemented surfaces will adhere tightly on contact and the printed section cannot be removed without tearing it, so there is no turning back.

Now remove the newspaper a few inches at a time, smoothing the printed backdrop section into place with the flat of your hand as you go. Then burnish the printed section with a soft, clean cloth to ensure good contact and proper adhesion. Mount the second printed section exactly as you did the first, butting its edge against the first section. Don't worry about the seam; as long as you join the sections carefully it will be invisible from a foot or so away.

After mounting all the printed sections, remove rubber cement that squeezed out along the top edge or smeared the front surface. Light rubbing with a gum eraser will pick up and roll away the unwanted cement. Finally, mist flat white paint along the horizon line to tone down the colors and "homogenize" the backdrop.

Structures as background scenery. There's never enough room for buildings on a model railroad, and one of the ways to create the impression of a large city or a vast industrial district is to use low-relief structures as part of the scenery. These flats can be glued to the backdrop, placed against it, or set on the background scenery in front of it. This type of background scenery can (and should) be used on every model railroad.

The scale of background flats is not important as long as they are smaller than your full-size foreground structures. N scale buildings look good behind HO structures, and HO and N buildings look good behind O (HO in the middle distance, N behind). Even flats smaller than N will not look out of place as long as nearby objects are the same scale.

Flats don't necessarily have to be placed only at the extreme rear edge of the layout; I've positioned several flats halfway up the side of a hill. Some were built so only the upper half or third would show, and the lower portion was a plain plastic stand. These can even be added after the scenery is finished by removing lichen, trees, or ground cover and making a flat spot on the plaster shell.

The main consideration when building and placing flats is the angle

CHAPTER 8

This hillside town consists of a few HO buildings backed up by three-quarter structures that progressively get smaller and become N scale flats at the rear.

Viewers of this scene rarely catch on that the white house near the backdrop is printed paper, almost N scale, and only 4" from a full-sized HO structure. The forced perspective creates an illusion of distance.

This before-and-after pair points out how building flats can expand a small area. The water tank in the upper photo is lonely and isolated, with only a lichen-covered hill and the painted backdrop behind it. After adding the building flats in the lower view, the same area includes just enough hint of a town to suggest people and activity. The water tank is less than a foot from the backdrop in this area.

from which they will be viewed. Most of my flats are built for only one viewing angle; from this angle they look like complete buildings, but when viewed from elsewhere they look like what they are, flat building fronts. Hide edges and restrict viewing angles by placing trees, more buildings, and other view blocks on either side of the flats.

It is important to think of flats as part of the background scenery, not as individual models. Much of the detail built into regular structures can simply be left off flats. Doors and windows can be glued to the surface of the structure. Glazing can be glued to the rear of a window casting before it's added to the building. I use clear plastic with curtains painted on the back, and the entire rear of the window is painted black. Loading platforms are made from painted blocks of wood. Details can be anything that's three dimensional and that looks interesting. Much of my detail comes from small odds and ends found in plastic military kits. Add most of the detail to the roof because that's the part of the building that your viewer will see first.

On my HO layout, I've built flats from plastic kit parts. Most are no more than 2" deep and 3" tall. Two or three N structure kits provide enough raw material to produce several flats. New walls and roofs can be built from brick paper glued to cardboard and dusted with gray chalk to tone down

Always keep the final viewing angle in mind as you assemble building flats. It makes no sense to add detail that will never be seen or paint effects that will never be appreciated. This small HO scale flat was built to be viewed only from the front. The rear of the flat shows how parts that would not be seen were left unfinished. The white cardboard on the rear below the clock tower supports the roof and prevents light from leaking through the rear of the structure. This flat is only 2″ wide.

This odd-shaped N scale flat was built from a single plastic kit. Because the main portion of the building extends out at a 45-degree angle, this flat can be viewed from the front and both sides.

the walls and assemble them with white glue. Only the parts of the structure that can be seen on the layout should be added.

Color these mini-buildings with Polly S, felt-tip markers, watercolors, acrylics, or colored pencils. After painting, stain them with a black India ink wash and pick out a few surface highlights by dry-brushing. Dust them lightly with gray pastel chalk after the coloring is complete. The farther the buildings are from the front of

the color. I weather flats to remove the plastic sheen, and add shadows under cornices and overhangs with a dusting of black pastel chalk.

Because the flats are much farther from the viewer than full-size buildings, great liberties can be taken with color and texture. The structures can be glued to small blocks or have a stiff wire inserted in the base to facilitate mounting. They can be glued in place or left loose. Just make sure they are straight and level.

A final trick to make flats look convincing is to place visual dividers between them and the closest full-scale buildings. The dividers can be clumps of trees, stone walls, fences, a stream, hill, or even a lichen hedgerow, and it need only be one or two inches wide to separate the full- and reduced-scale modeling.

Copy-machine modeling. Background flats can even be made using a copy machine to reduce plans from model railroad magazines, architectural journals, and library books. Reduce the plans to about N scale, then glue them to stiff cardboard with spray glue or rubber cement. Cut out

the layout, the grayer I color them.

No shadows on the backdrop! Nothing makes a scene look phony faster than shadows on the backdrop. As you place flats note how they look under your layout lighting. Do they cast shadows? If they do, will the shadows be seen from normal viewing angles? To eliminate shadows, lower the flats, move them away from the backdrop, or mount them at an angle so two corners of the building are against the backdrop.

Several N scale kits were butted together to form a pleasing cluster of building shapes. These will be used behind full-scale HO structures. The N scale structure is painted and ready for placement near the backdrop.

CHAPTER 8

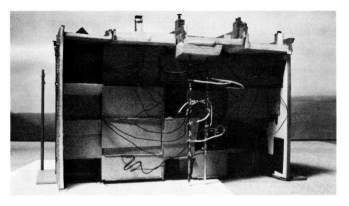

This HO flat was built from a Magnuson Models kit. I wanted to illuminate different combinations of windows for a night scene, and the rear view shows how each room was blocked off with cardboard. The wiring is messy but simple: Two brass rods serve as plus and minus connections for all bulbs.

Questions and answers

Q: What can be done to change the look of commercial printed backdrops? Seeing identical backdrops on half a dozen layouts is distracting and unrealistic just because of the sameness.

A: Not much can be done to change the printed pictures on the backdrops, but you can cut individual buildings or blocks of buildings from the printed sheets and rearrange them. Be careful that you keep the perspective the same.

Most printed backdrops represent summer. To change the season, I once added white Polly S "snow" to window ledges and rooftops, and eliminated summer trees.

Try mounting a printed backdrop on a large sheet of Plexiglas. Cut out several window openings with a sharp hobby knife, and glue small pieces of transparent red, yellow, and blue plastic behind some of them. Then cover the backs of all the window openings with tracing paper. Finally, place a light behind the backdrop to provide a realistic night effect.

Q: I plan to attach part of my layout's scenery to the backdrop. How should I go about it without messing up the backdrop?

A: If you must attach scenery to the backdrop for support, roll the rear edge — the part that touches the backdrop — under, so it cannot be seen

Several things can be done to modify commercial printed backdrops so they don't all look the same. To change this Walthers backdrop, I painted in snow on the tops of the buildings, on window ledges, and along the ground. I also cut out many of the windows so that the backdrop could be illuminated from behind for a night scene.

unless someone stands on a chair and looks straight down at it.

Glue the cardboard web to the backdrop (I use hot-melt glue), then cover the backdrop with newspaper or paper towels to protect it. Apply plaster-covered paper towels just as you would anywhere else, and proceed with the water-soluble method. Try to keep water, paint, and adhesives away from the protective paper. When the scenery is done, remove the paper.

Q: How should I build a freestanding, double-faced backdrop that runs down the center of my layout, dividing one side from the other?

A: The best material for the job is Upson Board or sheet metal. Build a framework of 2 x 2s or 2 x 4s anchored securely to your benchwork, and attach sheets of Upson Board or metal to each side of it. Seal the seams and paint each side just as described for wall-mounted backdrops.

This shallow background hill was built right against the backdrop. I protected the backdrop from plaster and paint spatters

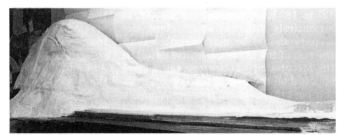

during construction by taping paper towels between it and the cardboard web (right).

Diorama techniques for foreground scenery

So far, I've discussed basic techniques that produce scenery built for broad effect, scenery with realistic colors, believable textures, and varied foliage. The trees, rocks, and grass in this basic scenery look realistic when viewed from a distance of two or three feet, and lots of small details and fine textures can be omitted because they could not be seen and would not add anything to the overall scene.

The foreground of your layout, the 12" to 18" band nearest the viewer, is an entirely different story. Here, the scenery should be more detailed than the rest of the layout, because detail in the foreground implies the same level of detail on the rest of the layout, even if it isn't there. In this chapter and the next one, I'll describe ways to plan and detail foreground areas. By the way, many of the techniques are borrowed from, and applicable to, diorama construction.

Planning foreground space. Even if you carefully planned scenery for your whole railroad as described in Chapter 1, the foreground requires more consideration. You must visualize each foreground area as a scene, and each scene should be separated from other parts of the railroad by natural or man-made boundaries: hills, rows of trees, roads, tracks, and so forth. The boundaries serve as bookends to keep the viewer in the scene; they must be planned to guide the viewer and to prevent his attention from escaping to the backdrop.

After building basic scenic forms and adding rough color and texture in the foreground, you must decide what each area is to be used for. Will it be agricultural, industrial, or residential, or will it be used for some activity such as a logging operation? Will there be structures? After the content of the scene is established, the next step is to consider how you can compose the scene to make it come alive.

Tricks with slopes and structures. One simple foreground scenery trick is to make the scenery rise slightly as it recedes from the front edge of the layout. Viewers won't notice the slight slope in the scenery toward the rear of the scene, but the rise will break up the tabletop look. Sloping terrain seems to expand the space in the scene, because at eye level the viewer can see more of what's in it.

Set the structures in place and move them around to find the best locations. First try all of the conventional places — parallel to the track or at a right angle to the edge of the layout — then shift the structures to spots where a building would "never" be placed. Then put the backs of the buildings to the front of the layout or to the track, and try elevating a building on paint bottles to simulate a

CHAPTER 9

(Above) Perhaps the easiest way to handle the areas at the front edge of your layout is to make the scenery slope upward as it moves toward the backdrop. Because the viewer can easily take in everything in the scene, the slope has the effect of expanding the space. Here, the gentle slope also leads the viewer into the center of interest.

(Left) The foreground areas of any layout require special thought and special scenic techniques to ensure they make the best possible impact on the viewer. This example is the HOn2½ Thatcher's Inlet Ry., a 3′ x 6′ 6″ seacoast-theme layout I built over 10 years ago. Thatcher's Inlet was virtually all foreground, and included exactly the kinds of detail and viewer interest I feel are important for such areas.

taller foundation. What you are looking for is an exciting arrangement for the structures.

After several tries an arrangement will click, the buildings will look right, and your foreground scene will come alive. Leave the structures in place for several days, then come back and look again. If the scene still looks right, you have found the right spots for the buildings. If the arrangement seems correct but the structures are too close together, try moving them apart a little. If the composition is strong, a little extra space between the individual elements won't destroy the effect; if the arrangement is weak, the extra space will quickly make the weakness obvious.

Now look at the areas around the buildings: Is there an obvious, clear-cut theme, or do the buildings need a lot of supporting detail to tell the viewer what the scene means? If supporting detail is needed, try positioning some of the larger items. Then check that the scene still looks right, that the buildings still fit, and that the viewer will see what you want him to.

Active and transition areas. I call foreground areas where buildings have been placed "active" areas, active because the viewer will stop and spend time looking at the buildings, scenery,

THE EFFECT OF FOREGROUND SLOPES

Look up at scene for space expansion.

Look down into scene and space seems smaller.

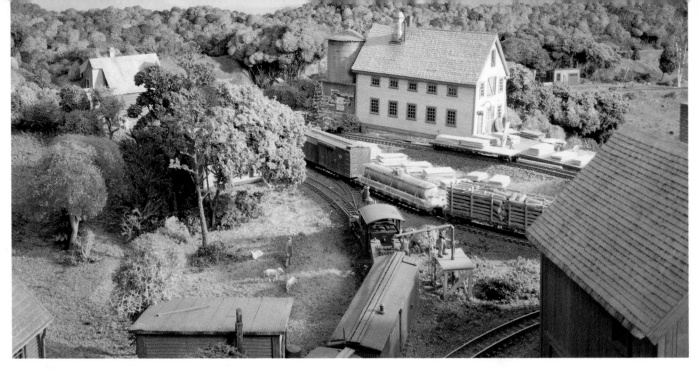

In this example of leading lines, the strongest line, of course, is the railroad track, but note how the roof lines of the buildings on the right and left frame the scene and point toward the large white mill building. It's clearly the center of interest here.

and details. By careful planning you can even control the order in which he sees the elements in the scene.

The spaces between active scenes, the scene dividers or "bookends," are "transition" areas. These areas can be clumps of trees, hedgerows, rock piles, or any other realistic continuation of the basic scenery. Transition areas should be passive, that is, they should not have a lot of eye-catching details, because their role is to provide buffer zones between active foreground areas.

If you plan several active areas in the foreground of your layout your hardest job will be to make each different from all the others. One important method of combatting sameness is to avoid having anything parallel to anything else. Of course, a mainline track and its passing siding must be parallel or pretty close to it, but buildings and other features along the track need not line up with the track or each other.

Leading the viewer through the scene. Next we must structure the scene to make the viewer see what we want him to. Just as a painter divides his canvas into shapes and areas of color to direct the viewer, so can we use leading lines in active foreground areas to guide the viewer through the scene. Leading lines are natural paths the eye uses to take in the scene; on a model railroad the track most often does this, but we can supplement it with roads, waterways, and fences.

What kind of lines will lead? Well, lines that start at a large building and radiate outward work well. For instance, a fence or road that leads from a large building to a second center of interest will be followed almost automatically. Roads or waterways extending into the scene from the front edge of the layout lead well, and if such

lines do not cut through a transition area the viewer's attention will remain in the active area. On the other hand, when a road or a brook connects one scene to another the viewer will go with it.

Gentle S curves within a scene lead the viewer along the curve, and break up space in a pleasing manner. Gentle curves have the advantage of making a scene seem larger than it is; in a flat scene the track itself may be the S curve that breaks up the area. Curving leading lines should not be parallel to the track or the edge of the railroad.

The rule of thirds. If no obvious center of interest suggests itself for an active scene, you can fall back on the rule of thirds. Mentally divide the scene into north-south and east-west thirds, noting where the dividing lines cross. These four points are the natu-

Three ways to use fences as scenic dividers. (Above) A very short fence was used here to keep the viewer's attention from straying beyond the foreground buildings. (Above right) This length of plastic fence hides where the rear edge of the layout meets the backdrop, only 3" away. The lichen tufts were glued in place after the fence was installed. (Right) Here short fences were used to contain the small graveyard and to keep it separate from the surrounding scenery.

CHAPTER 9

This stretch of plain scenery along one wall of my railroad room is a transition area between active scenes. The lack of trees, stumps, and other details in this foreground is intentional: I want viewers to follow the trains through the scene, but when no trains are present I want their attention to be directed to the active areas on each side of the transition.

ral centers of interest. Select one point for the largest element in the scene, and choose another for a smaller structure or cluster of detail. The smaller center of interest will balance the larger one.

Now use a leading line such as a road or fence to lead the viewer from the main center of interest to the secondary one. The rule of thirds keeps you from placing a structure or other center of interest dead in the center of the scene, which would make the scene static and dull.

Another way to ensure that your visitors will take in the details in the foreground of your layout is to use a color triangle. If you place the same bright color in three places in a scene, the viewer will be led from the closest, to the next, then to the last. A simple example is three figures, each with a red shirt. Any brightly colored objects

This active scene is located to the left of the transition area shown in the photo at the top of the page. Here's what I want viewers to see: the covered station, a railroad freight house, and a long, curving storage spur with a foreground junkyard on both sides of it. Once again the track is by far the strongest leading line, but the dirt road into the station also helps move the viewer through the scene.

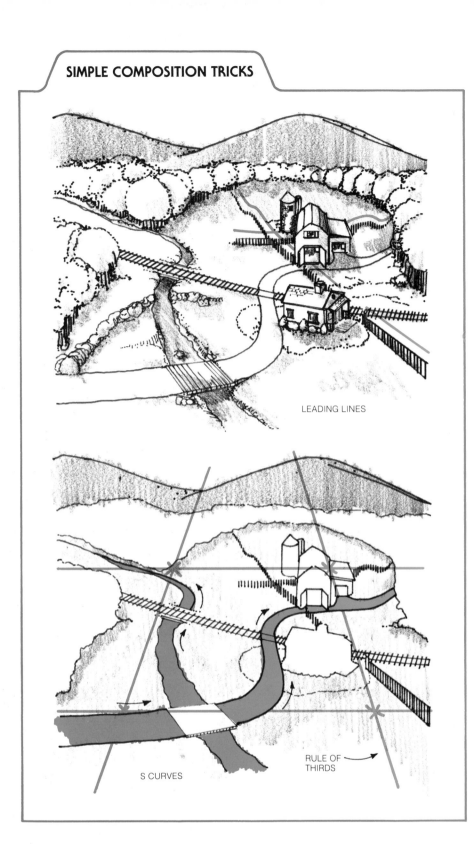

LEADING LINES

S CURVES

RULE OF
THIRDS

will work: oil drums, advertising signs, even scraps of new lumber.

Items with similar shapes can work the same trick, and when repeating shapes are combined with bright colors the eye will jump from one to another like magic.

Fences as scenic elements. Along most railroad rights-of-way fences sep-

arate railroad property from adjacent land. The fences keep kids and cattle from wandering onto the track, and are an important part of lineside scenery. Without them, the landscape appears empty. Fences in the foreground make excellent leading lines to direct the viewer from the edge of the layout to the center of the scene, to point out

The dirt road first leads to the right, then left and into Malcolm Furlow's town of Sheridan. Fences and retaining walls reinforce the leading lines, and the timber cribbing around the turntable pit helps separate that center of interest from the town above it.

Malcolm Furlow

CHAPTER 9

your favorite scratchbuilt building, or to keep an active area separate from an adjacent scene.

Fences radiating from a central point separate an area into many slices, like a pie, and make the total area look larger than it is. Long fences built in perspective (large in the foreground, smaller toward the background) produce the effect of distance in a small area, and short fences can suggest a complete length of fence or enclosure. On a narrow shelf railroad a board fence can even be used to hide the rear edge of the shelf where it meets the backdrop.

Busy or balanced? If we were painting a picture of our active area an art critic might say the picture was too busy, that too many things were happening for anyone to make head or tail out of it, that more than one center of interest is too many. We don't have to follow all the rules for painting, of course, but it's worthwhile to keep this criticism in mind. As each foreground scene nears completion, examine it in terms of how much content is enough.

Can you ever have too much detail? You certainly can, particularly if it means the whole scene looks like a jumbled mess because there are just too many things happening at the same time. Try to strike a balance between austere scenes that lack detail and scenes that are so busy the viewer can't tell where to look. For me, the balance is a busy scene that is not so busy that the viewer is confused; I want the viewer to see all the detail while he moves slowly along the lead-ing lines to the center of interest. If detail is grouped in clusters it will not make the scene as busy as it would if detail were spread evenly over the area.

By the way, you don't have to wait until all your rough scenery is finished before building an active foreground area. By completing even a small foreground you get to try all the scenery-building techniques on a small scale, and you also get the thrill of having one part of the layout done. This can be just the inspiration you need to forge ahead through basic scenery construction so you can get to the fun parts.

Techniques for foreground scenery. To adapt water-soluble scenery materials to foreground scenery you have to think and work on a slightly different scale than you did while building and texturing the broad expanses of your layout. As we've already discussed, each scene becomes important, and all the elements in each scene have to be individual models in their own right.

For starters, instead of simply covering the plaster-soaked paper towels with latex paint, in the foreground we'll want to texture the plaster soil surface in one of several ways. A rock mold turned inside out and pressed into the fresh plaster will give rough, angular texture to bare ground. Or, gently jabbing a large, stiff-bristled paintbrush into the damp plaster will yield a realistic, rough, pebble-like texture.

Sculptamold can be rubbed over the damp plaster scenery base to level it and produce a smooth, hard-packed earth surface. This technique is identical to that used to make Sculptamold roads in Chapter 5.

Foreground soil colors. For close-up viewing, the colors of the soil should be varied. Variety makes foreground scenery more interesting, which helps it hold the viewer's eye longer. The individual soil shades are used only on bare ground; the rest of the foreground will be covered with ground foam and several shades of turf texture.

I use Polly S, Badger Air-Opaque, tube acrylics, and tinting colors for individual soil shades. They can be used as they come from the bottle or mixed to the desired shades. To determine what you need, make a color chip of your basic earth latex. Now mix a color that is lighter (whiter) than the basic earth color. Note the proportions of paint to the amount of water used, and add the formula to the color chip. Make two more earth shades darker than the basic color; mix them by adding different amounts of the black India ink wash to the basic earth color. Add these colors to the chip and keep them for future reference.

If you want to try your hand at mixing your own soil shades, start with your basic latex earth color, diluted 1:1 with water. To lighten it, mix one part 1:1 earth with one part flat white latex.

To make a soil shade slightly darker than your basic earth add $1/8"$ of Burnt Sienna tube acrylic or tinting color to an ounce of 1:1 earth. Mix thoroughly (some tube colors tend to clump in the bottom of the bottle), then check the color on a scrap of scenery or on an out-of-the-way section of your railroad. The dark soil shade should look different from the basic earth color under normal railroad lighting; if not, add more Burnt Sienna, $1/8"$ at a time, or several tablespoons of black wash until it does. (There's no sense in mixing a shade that looks the same as the basic color under railroad room lighting.)

The darker soil shade can be lightened with flat white to make a color slightly grayer than basic earth.

FOREGROUND SOIL COLORS

Where Earth is called for, use the same Earth latex paint you have selected for the rest of the layout, scene, or diorama.

Light soil:
  1 part 1:1 latex Earth
  1 part flat latex white (or Polly S Reefer White)
  Increase the proportion of white slowly until you reach the desired shade.

Dark soil:
  1 ounce 1:1 latex Earth
  $1/8"$ Burnt Sienna artist's tube acrylic

Mud:
  1 ounce 1:1 latex Earth
  $1/8"$ Raw Sienna artist's tube acrylic

Concrete color for foundations:
  4 parts flat white latex (or Polly S Reefer White)
  1 scant part Mars Black artist's tube acrylic
  1 part Raw Sienna artist's tube acrylic
  3 parts full-strength matte medium

Alternate concrete color:
  1 teaspoon Polly S Reefer Gray
  4 drops Polly S Roof Brown

This stone wall was made by piling up pebbles sifted out of builder's sand and soaking the pile with matte medium.

CHAPTER 9

(Soil is often gray around industrial complexes and railroad loading facilities.) For a more mud-like color, try adding 1/8" of Raw Sienna to 1:1 earth; to darken it add black wash. Bottle, label, and make a color chip of everything as you go along so you can repeat the results.

Always add dark to light. This gives you control over the result because you can immediately see if the mix turns too dark.

To use the varied soil colors start by painting the scenery with the basic earth shade. As it starts to dry, use a 1" brush to add highlights with lighter soil colors. Make the soil shades progressively lighter as you work to the high spots on the textured soil surface, then spray with a fine water mist to blend the colors. After the excess water has dried, apply darker soil colors and spray with water to blend.

To add depth to the shadows and show off the texture, lightly spray black India ink relief wash. When the area dries, lightly dry-brush the textured bare soil areas with flat white, but remember that for this soil detail coloring to work, all the different shades must blend and look natural.

Foreground texture and detail. After the bare ground areas have been colored, add texture materials. These can be sprinkled into the wet earth paint, but if the paint has already dried, coat areas where you plan fields and woods with a solution of equal parts white glue and water to which several drops of detergent have been added. Work with an area no larger than one foot square so you can apply the texture before the glue dries. For the initial texture use the material chosen for the rest of the scenery so overall colors will match.

The texture used on the rest of the layout is usually too coarse for foreground use, so you'll need to process

Where will the buildings look best? Will they lead the eye through the scene? One way to answer these questions is to build cardboard structure mock-ups and move them around the scene. You'll know when you find a pleasing arrangement — the shapes will all seem to fit.

your own fine textures or find appropriate commercial products. Fine dyed sawdust is available from Highball Products, along with several grades of scenic rock, ballast, and coal. John's Lab offers grass, earth, and ballast textures suitable for foreground and diorama use. Fine ground foam is available from Woodland Scenics and AMSI, among others.

Apply foreground textures as described in Chapter 5. Sprinkle the material over the dilute white glue; add texture, layer upon layer; mist with wet water; and spray with matte medium bonding solution. As you go, add clutter clusters and embed such natural details as gravel piles, stone walls, pieces of wood, branches, and logs in the texture.

Because each item in the foreground is a model in its own right, each must be built, painted, and placed

for the best possible effect. For example, while weeds on the rest of the layout can be simple tufts of carpet fabric or bits of natural growth, foreground weeds may be as elaborate as tiny twigs covered with fine ground foam. Even rocks become an interesting exercise in detailing; color the castings as described in Chapter 4, then work them over with individual colors of powdered chalk applied with a small brush.

I model New England, where an important foreground detail is boulders. I make them from balls of Sculptamold mixed to a clay-like consistency. Shape the boulders with your fingers, making the largest about 20 scale feet across, then add surface detail by pressing an inverted rock mold against the soft Sculptamold. Carve cracks with a hobby knife.

Paint boulders the same way as

In this waterfront scene the retaining wall, pier, and pilings were painted using the methods described for painting cast details. The dry-brushing highlights the coarse texture of the pilings. Note the variety of weeds used here in the foreground.

I carved cracks in these Sculptamold boulders as they dried, then colored them with basic rock color. After gluing them down I sprinkled texture material around their bases and sprayed it with matte medium bonding solution.

Some types of painted detail are never appreciated properly because they are hidden inside a building. In this foreground area I worked as much indoor detail as possible into an outdoor scene, in this case a general store.

(Above right) After spraying this road with India ink wash, I drew a very wet brush along the road in the direction of travel with long, even strokes. The middle of each traffic lane is darker than the edges, simulating grease and oil drippings.

rock castings. Many boulders in my neck of the woods are darker and greener than surrounding rock faces, so I use the blue rock color (page 34) and extra India ink wash. After they dry I flow a weak wash of gray-green over the "north" face, allowing it to soak into the Sculptamold. After the boulders are set into the scenery, dry-brush the top surfaces to show off the texture. Fine foam or sawdust can be glued to the top and sides to represent vines and lichens.

To enhance this Campbell pine tree for foreground use I lightly misted the air-fern foliage with matte medium and sprinkled on fine blue-green foam.

After adding foreground details, look over each scene for white spots or stray bits of plaster. Touch these up with a small brush and thinned earth paint. The earth color will blend with the surrounding scenery and hide the defect. Tone down shiny areas with a dusting of pastel chalk.

Diorama-quality trees. Deciduous trees in the foreground require extra attention. Often the twig armatures used for background trees can be used, but the trunks require extra detailing and painting. To add three-dimensional bark and root texture, first rough up the lower portion of the trunk with coarse sandpaper. Drill a hole (about No. 60) in the bottom of the trunk and glue in a length of wire, leaving about 3/4" extending below the base of the tree. Stick each tree armature into a block of Styrofoam covered with a piece of thin plastic from a sandwich bag.

Now mix a stiff batch of Durham's Rock Hard Water Putty, acrylic spackle, or two-part epoxy putty. Mix only enough to make a ball the size of a large marble, and make it a little looser than modeling clay. Spread the putty onto the lower portion of the trunk, feathering it into the upper portion of the armature. Pull some of the putty down and away from the tree to form roots. Make the roots thick so they won't crack during handling and carving.

Leave the putty alone until it begins to set. When small pieces flake away when scraped with a pointed

tool, scribe bark texture. Use a light touch, and occasionally remove putty chips with a soft brush. The brush will also smooth out deep bark lines. When the bark texture is complete, allow it to dry overnight.

Start painting the trunk by applying a coat of straight Polly S Roof Brown, Earth, Dirt, or Sahara Sand, depending on the bark color of the tree modeled. After that dries, dry-brush the bark with a lighter Polly S color like Gray, Mud, Earth, or Concrete. This brings out the bark texture and readies the tree for the next step.

Brush India ink wash onto the tree armature with a soft brush; it will sink into the putty and darken the colors and it will also flow into the cracks and depressions.

After the black wash dries, lightly dry-brush the tree again with Polly S Reefer White. At this point the trunk can be left as is, or the coloring can be carried one step further. Choose one of the Flo-Stain line of wood stains, say Walnut, and lightly streak it over the bark. Do not cover all of the tree with the stain; just use a little here and there, always brushing with the grain.

Complete the tree by adding foliage material over the branches. Extra-fine foam can be added over the foliage material to vary the color and texture. Make sure you add enough foliage material to the tree to make it look full; one thing that makes a foreground tree look phony is not having enough "leaves" on the branches. Foreground trees should be the largest on

CHAPTER 9

(Right) These photos show the same cast-plaster retaining wall before and after application of the black relief wash. The wash both brings out detail and enhances natural shadows.

your railroad, so they can contribute to the near-far illusion.

Foreground pine trees. Pine tree kits suitable for foreground use are available from several firms. All include some type of metal or wood armature, and separate foliage material. Campbell pine trees consist of pre-shaped, pre-drilled wooden dowels with air fern (the dyed skeletal remains of a saltwater animal called Sertularia). The air fern must be glued into pre-drilled holes in the trunk, then the tree is trimmed and placed on the railroad. Other brands require similar preparation.

After assembling an air-fern pine, spray the tips of the branches with matte medium bonding solution and sprinkle on fine dark green and blue-green flocking. I like to use this on foreground pine trees because of the needle shapes of the individual bits of nylon. Large foreground pines look best grouped in threes. Sprinkle fine brown foam under the trees to represent needles.

Another type of pine kit, from Woodland Scenics and others, has cast-on branches. The trunk must be painted before assembly. The procedure is the same as for deciduous trees, except that the relief wash is eliminated. By the way, pine trees need not look drab or uniform, and you should vary the texture and color of the foliage on individual trees. Overall, pine foliage should be a little darker than that of deciduous trees, tending toward gray, blue-green, and gray-blue rather than yellow shades.

Track is scenery too! Track in the foreground of your layout deserves the same care in coloring and weathering you give to the rest of the foreground. Uncolored track looks toylike; handled correctly it will blend into the scenery around it.

Start with the ties. Chip and split a few tie ends with a hobby knife, then prime the track with Polly S Roof Brown. Paint the sides of the rails with a mixture of equal parts Polly S Rust and Roof Brown (you'll be surprised how much this improves the look of even Code 100 rail). If the track is already installed and ballasted this is a tedious job, but well worth the effort — one way to save time is to paint only the side of the rail that can

Water putty was added to the base of this plastic tree trunk and carved to simulate bark. After planting the tree in the scenery, foam was glued around the roots.

A lot of modelers forget to paint and weather the track. This commercial plastic track has been treated with the same techniques used to color the other items in the scene.

Some detail items are hard to find a place for. My solution was to build this contractor's yard using detail parts I'd been saving for years. Each item was painted using the three-step process described in the text, and everything in the scene was glued down with white glue so it can be removed if a better use for the detail comes along.

be seen from the normal viewing angle.

Next, heavily dry-brush the tie tops with a mixture of two parts Polly S Earth to one part Reefer White. After this dries, brush random ties with black India ink relief wash, and hit a few others with Flo-Stain Oak and Driftwood.

After the paint dries, clean the rail tops and inside edges with a cloth dampened in thinner. Finish up with a Brite-Boy track cleaner or other mild abrasive.

Building paved roads. I build paved roads using Sculptamold, and the technique is similar to the dirt roads described in Chapter 5. The box on page 109 lists formulas for blacktop and concrete colors. After spreading and smoothing the Sculptamold, add details such as broken edges and pot-

holes with a modeling knife. If the road surface is too rough after it dries, smooth it with sandpaper. Use the same mixes for modeling sidewalks.

Another way to model paved roads is to pour a soupy plaster mixture into a frame or mold, which eliminates the need for spreading and smoothing. Use the formulas in the box that call for Savogran Wood Putty, and pour the mix into built-in-place forms. Moisten the surface where the road will go before pouring, then let the mix set until firm, 15 to 30 minutes.

As the poured road starts to set the surface can be smoothed by skimming a metal straightedge along the tops of the forms. Add cracks and patches, and work scraps of foam or lichen into the cracks to represent weeds. Sand the road surface after adding details, brush away the plaster dust, and proceed with coloring. On a concrete road, scribe expansion joints and cracks into the surface after the wood putty dries, then apply additional coloring and weathering with thin washes of Polly S or ground pastel chalk dust.

Telephone poles and wires. Realistic phone poles probably add more visual appeal to a railroad right-of-way than any other single element. Many good kits are available, but I like to build mine from scratch. I use the 4" wooden dowel handle of industrial cotton-tipped swabs. These are sold in Radio Shack stores for cleaning electronic parts (they also make great disposable paintbrushes).

Cut the cotton tip from the dowel. Add a stripwood crossarm and bits of plastic for insulators. Color the pole with Flo-Stain Maple, and add a V-shaped crossarm brace made from wire.

The hardest part of installing poles is stringing the wire. My elbow or forearm always rips out the work just when I'm ready to stand back and admire it. I learned a trick several years ago that has saved all the telephone wire I've installed. I use Lycra-Spandex Rubber thread for the wires. This is the same stuff that is used in the waistband of your boxer shorts to hold them up. It's soft, flexible, and will stretch all the way to the ground if necessary.

Lycra-Spandex thread comes on spools like regular thread. Color it with various alcohol dyes (mix 2 teaspoons of liquid shoe dye with a pint of rubbing alcohol): dark brown for insulated wire, faded green for bare copper wire. Hold the thread in place with a drop of super glue.

Working with cast details. Hundreds — maybe even thousands — of cast detail parts are available to help bring foreground scenes to life. The most important consideration in using

Extreme side lighting reveals the wealth of texture in this small foreground scene. The dirt road was made by smoothing plaster with my fingers as it set; the wheel ruts were added with an old HO scale automobile. This road originally came out quite glossy, and I had to apply tan chalk dust to kill the objectionable shine.

these items is painting them so all the built-in realism will be visible. I use a three-step painting procedure to color and weather these parts.

Gathering detail items is almost a hobby within a hobby. I store the parts on strips of double-stick tape arranged on one-foot squares of corrugated cardboard. Grouping parts so similar items are together makes finding and painting them easier. Make sure all the parts are clean and free from dirt or grease before coloring them.

Once a cardboard square is full of parts, they can be primed. I use Floquil Primer, a light gray. The easiest method is to spray a light coat of primer, but brush painting is okay if you use a paint such as Polly S which will not harm plastic items. After priming, set the cardboard square aside for several days to let the paint cure thoroughly.

Finish painting and weathering. Briefly, the three steps in painting detail parts are (1) painting base colors over the primer, (2) flowing on a black wash to provide an artificial shadow, and (3) dry-brushing with white to bring the surface highlights forward.

Start by painting base colors with a brush or airbrush. Add about 20 percent white or light gray to each base color so the parts will show up better under weak lighting even after the dark relief wash. Heavy weathering effects such as rust spots, oil streaks, peeling paint, and chemical discolorations should be brushed on when you paint the base coat. Leave the parts on the cardboard square for about a week before proceeding, so the base coat will dry hard.

Next comes the relief wash, which adds shadow to all recessed areas of the parts. Use our standard India ink wash, flowing it onto the parts with a large, soft brush. By brushing in the direction that rain water or wind

PAVED ROAD MIXES

Blacktop mix*:
       ½ teaspoon India ink
       ¾ cup water
       1 heaping cup Sculptamold

Blacktop mix No. 2:
       ¾ teaspoon India ink
       1 drop Cobalt Blue artist's tube acrylic color
       ½ cup water
       1 cup Savogran Wood Putty**

Concrete:
       ½" Mars Black artist's tube acrylic color
       ½ cup water
       1 cup Savogran Wood Putty**

Concrete road paint:
       4 parts flat white latex paint
       1 part Raw Sienna artist's tube acrylic color
       3 parts matte medium

* Add a small quantity (less than ⅛") of Cobalt Blue tube acrylic to this mix if it will be viewed under incandescent lighting.
** Savogran Wood Putty is a plaster-like patching compound available at most hardware stores.

would move surface dirt as the wash dries you can achieve a subtle and realistic weathering effect. An easy way to handle small parts is to dip them in a jar of black wash and place them on paper towels to dry.

After the wash dries you'll see that it has run into all the surface irregularities, leaving a dark but almost transparent layer. On flat surfaces the wash dries quickly, leaving a dirty, grimy look.

Dry-brushing. The third step is dry-brushing each detail item with flat white or other light-colored paint. I use Polly S because it has excellent dry-brushing qualities. This step accents protruding detail, separating it from the dark shadow areas created by the wash. One way to think of it is that dry-brushing adds the natural highlights you would see if the model were placed in bright sunlight.

I have several brushes used exclusively for dry-brushing. They range from a small one with eight or nine bristles to the largest, which is ½" wide. Both round and flat brushes

It's the foreground details, like telephone and telegraph poles, that convince your viewers that the rest of the layout is just as detailed.

A supply of painted and weathered figures and parts comes in handy when it's time to detail foreground scenes. I painted and weathered these castings while I watched TV football (I see about every third play).

CHAPTER 9

work well, and almost any brush suffering from old age will qualify. Feel the bristles and note where they change from soft, near the tip, to stiff, usually about halfway up. That's where to cut the bristles straight across with scissors to make a flat end.

My favorite dry-brushing colors are Polly S Reefer White, Earth, and Reefer Gray. Always dry-brush with a color lighter than the base color; for example, use Reefer White over light colors (beige, yellow, tan), Earth on warm colors (red, orange, brown), and Reefer Gray over cold colors (blue, green, black).

Thin each bottle of paint with several drops of water. Dip the brush into the paint so the tips of the bristles are barely dampened with paint, then stroke the brush back and forth on a paper towel to remove all but the last traces of paint. To test for the right amount, stroke the brush over the palm of your hand. Only the slightest wisp of color should be left behind on your skin.

Hold the brush perpendicular to the part, and, working from top to bottom, gently stroke the brush downward using short patting motions. Paint should be left only on the top edges of raised detail, and there should be no brush marks or streaks. Brush marks mean there is too much paint on the brush, or the paint is too thin.

For a heavier dry-brushing effect scrub the part vigorously with the brush, using both up and down strokes and depositing paint on all surfaces. If you overdo the effect, dip a cotton swab in clean water and scrub away the excess paint.

Dry-brushing, like all weathering effects, works best when it is subtle. On some parts I have dry-brushed with several different colors to achieve effects consistent with the base colors. For example, you can lightly dry-brush bright orange rust over darker rust brown, and dry-brush light gray over dark grease stains.

Subtle dry-brushing can be applied in layers, each successive layer lighter than the last. First dry-brush with a large brush and a color only slightly lighter than the base. Next, apply a lighter shade with a smaller brush, and finish by dry-brushing light gray or white on only the uppermost edges.

Questions and answers

Q: I built a road on my layout using Sculptamold, but when I clean my track with a Bright Boy, the paint on the road scrapes off at the road crossing.
A: It sounds as if the surface of the road is a little too high where it meets

George Sellios' HO Franklin & South Manchester Railroad is a magnificent example of a layout with top-notch foreground detailing. George's techniques are simple, but his results are fantastic!

the track. Scrape or sand the road surface until it is about $1/32$" below rail level, then repaint.
Q: When I built a road on my layout using the water-soluble method, the surface came out glossy. Can this be corrected?
A: First try repainting the road surface with basic earth color. After it dries weather the road with pastel chalks. The chalk will look flatter and more dusty if you sprinkle it on. Don't brush the chalk, as doing so may revive the shine. If this doesn't work, let the road dry for 5 to 10 days, cover all structures, track, and nearby scenery, and spray the road with Testor's Dullcote.

Every so often you'll apply Polly S over plaster or Hydrocal and it will dry with more sheen than you'd like. To further dull the paint try mixing talcum powder with it. You'll have to experiment with the exact proportions: I add several teaspoons of paint to a shallow dish and mix in about $1/2$ teaspoon of talcum powder. If the paint thickens add several drops of water and mix. The talc may change the color of the paint slightly, so try it out on a piece of scrap wood or plaster before using it on your scenery.
Q: Is there any way to increase the

illusion of distance between foreground and background on my shelf railroad?
A: The illusion of distance is best created by changing colors and sizes. Use bright colors in the foreground, gradually shifting to duller ones as the scenery approaches the background. Add increasing amounts of blue-gray foam or sawdust to the texture as you work toward the rear of the railroad. I mix three shades of green foam: medium yellow-green for the foreground, medium green with a little blue-gray for the mid region, and green with more blue-gray for background areas.

A second illusion that always works but is never discovered by casual observers is to place large models near the front of the layout and gradually diminish the size (not necessarily the scale) of the objects as they approach the background. This works for everything, not just structures: Trees, shrubs, and detail items should diminish in overall size as the distance from the viewer increases. Place tall handbuilt trees up front, but use simple weeds dipped in foam as small trees in the rear. Viewers don't catch the ruse because it is only appropriate that things farther away should look smaller.

CHAPTER 9

This is a small "live" area of my layout. The track, road, and grass areas are permanent, but the buildings, trees, and other props were taken from other parts of the layout and set up just for this photo.

Special situations and special effects

This chapter brings together several topics which, for want of a better label, I call "special effects." Included are nonpermanent or "live" scenery, scenic weathering, lightweight scenery techniques, and a few ideas on showing off your railroad for the best overall effect.

"Live" scenery. A live scenery area is part of the foreground of the layout that you decide not to finish, where rough scenery and textures are in place but nothing else is glued down. The track that runs through a live scenery area is the only permanent feature.

This is a handy thing to have. It makes a fine place to show off new models and to experiment with scenic ideas, and it's also a solution to the problem of having a foreground area

that you know should be interesting, but not knowing just what to put there. I once arranged a small factory complex on the live scenery area, then, after I was satisfied with the grouping, transferred it to its permanent location elsewhere on the layout.

Live scenery is a tool for planning active foreground scenes on the rest of your railroad. On my layout the live area changes constantly; I think of it almost as a "horizontal bulletin board."

Styrofoam makes a good base for a live area because it is soft enough that you can plant and replant trees, weeds, and fences in different locations. Build the base as described later in this chapter, paint, and sprinkle on basic texture materials. Leave the finish texture — which would be glued

down elsewhere — loose; the rough texture will keep it in place.

Trees for the live area should have about 1" of wire sticking out of their trunks so they can be pushed into the Styrofoam and stand alone. When the live area is revised, hide the holes with a pinch or two of texture.

Using the live area. To work a building into the live area, decide on the best location and gently brush loose ground foam against the foundation, hiding the gap. Add bits of lichen, weeds, and fences around the building, and make roads and paths by spreading finely sifted dirt. Define the edges of a road with green texture. Make rock faces in molds on your workbench, color them, and prop them in place. I've even made portable Styrofoam hills to use with live areas. When

I use this portable hill in conjunction with my live scenery areas. The hill has a standard cardboard and paper-towel base covered with plaster rock castings, but Styrofoam could also be used to make such a piece of movable scenery.

you decide to revise the scene, remove the structures and details, sweep up the loose texture, then have at it again!

A live area is particularly useful for photography. Photos are easy to set up and easy to light along the front edge of the layout, and it's a simple matter to find a good camera angle. If you have enough different buildings and props, the live area can be photographed, changed, and photographed again — and look like a different spot on the layout in each shot.

Weathering scenery. One of the major types of scenery weathering, the severe bleaching and fading effects of the sun, has already been covered in the section on dry-brushing rock castings (Chapter 4). Another important weathering agent is wind, which picks up dust and dirt and deposits them on everything near the ground. The color of the settled dust should always be the same as your basic earth shade; in fact, one way of modeling the effects of windborne dust and dirt is to overspray most of your railroad with very dilute latex earth.

A good earth overspray is the basic rock color (page 34) diluted with an equal amount of water. Airbrush this lightly over most of your layout, but do not hit waterways or structures. This is a good technique, but it has one serious drawback: It's easy to overdo. The trick is to use just enough paint so the whole railroad takes on a slightly drab tone, and to stop before you've gone too far. Practice first on a piece of dark cardboard, using only enough air pressure and paint to slightly cloud the dark color.

On distant parts of the layout try adding a little blue to the earth color to simulate atmospheric haze. As you spray, keep in mind that the idea is to color the scenery just enough to provide a unity that your viewer can't quite put his finger on.

Using pastel chalks. The subtle colors required for scenery weathering can be achieved easily with pastel chalks. Several brands and types are available in hobby and art stores; all work fine. Buy a small starter set of pastel sticks (later you'll want to select individual sticks of the colors you use most).

The other materials you'll need are talcum powder, coarse sandpaper or a coarse file, a large soft brush, several paper cups, and a spray can of workable matte fixative such as Floquil Flat Finish, Krylon Crystal Clear, or Testor's Dullcote. These should be available at the hobby shop or where you find the pastels.

To make a specific color such as light earth tan, first select two chalk sticks that will get you in the ball park. Since earth has some brown in it, start by rubbing a brown stick against the file or sandpaper. (To contain the mess, I grind chalk in a shoe box cover and decant the powder into paper cups.) Next grind some yellow into the brown, stir with the brush, and check the color. If it needs a little white, add talcum powder to the cup. Stir again and check the color. When you have about the right shade — it doesn't have to be exact — you're ready to apply the chalk.

The application technique I use most is tapping. Pick up a brushload of powder and hold the brush about 5" above the area to be dusted. Tap the metal ferrule of the brush gently, as if you were knocking the ash off a cigar, to sprinkle the powder. The powder should fall gently, almost like rain, from the bristles of the brush. This technique is good for depositing dust along the sides of a road and over low foliage.

You can also apply pastels by brushing and scrubbing. To brush, pick up powder on the brush and gently stroke it against the scenery. Take it easy: If you rub too hard the powder will take on a shine. Excess chalk dust can be blown away. Scrubbing does just what brushing doesn't do: It removes most of the powder. Scrubbing works well on rock faces where you want to work the powder into cracks and crevices.

Two other ways to apply chalk are whisking and patting. Whisking chalk is exactly the same as whisking texture material: Place a little chalk powder on a folded file card, hold it near the scenery, and blow across it as if you were whistling. Whisking deposits a light coat of powder which can be scrubbed into the surface or spread around with a brush. Patting is also just what the name implies: Start with a brush loaded with chalk powder and pat it onto the surface. Patting works well for simulating spills and stains around loading docks.

After all chalk powder is applied, use a light overspray of flat finish or Dullcote to fix it in place. Be careful; too much fixative will darken the powder. The clear flat should barely dampen the chalk powder, which will turn dark at first but become lighter as it dries.

Man-made weathering. Man and his machines change natural colors wherever they go. Trains leave behind deposits of cinders, coal dust, soot, and oil; cars and trucks leave ruts and oil streaks. Dry deposits can be modeled with powdered chalk, and oil stains made by thinning Polly S Grimy Black or Oily Black and brushing the thinned paint between the rails. Use the same technique in yards to simulate soil discolored by years of dirty work.

Rust is everywhere you find iron or steel, and it comes in many colors. Fresh rust is the bright orange color that comes in a bottle of Floquil or Polly S Rust, but as rust ages it becomes reddish, then brown, and finally almost black. With pastel chalks in several rust-earth shades you can simulate rust of all ages. Start with brownish-orange and a little white talcum powder, then experiment. Dab rust anywhere water reaches steel — bridges, scrap piles, signals, and a hundred other places. Remember that water carries rust stains onto nonmetallic surfaces such as masonry bridge abutments, so be sure to model that weathering effect as well.

Chalks are almost a must for foreground roads. Brush coarse chalk powder onto the road surface, working along the direction of the road. Add dark and light streaks to give the road character, apply a few oil stains, then seal the surface with matte fixative. Foreground roads treated in this manner are dead flat with finely detailed surface texture.

Weathering plaster with watercolors. Watercolor is a medium that yields subtle color variations without a lot of effort. The thin, translucent paint adds only add a hint of coloring, and if you make a mistake, a moist brush will erase it.

I prefer tube watercolors (available in art supply and craft shops), but

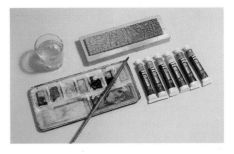

Plaster castings, plastic details, and scenery can be colored using tube-type water colors. I use a child's metal palette to mix and dilute the colors.

CHAPTER 10

Styrofoam scenery support is useful for portable layouts where weight and resilience are important considerations. After the Styrofoam pieces are glued together (above), they can be formed with woodworking tools such as a rasp (above right), or gouged out with a screwdriver (right), or covered with plaster-soaked paper towels.

you can start with a child's watercolor set sold in toy stores. Tube watercolors have the consistency of toothpaste. They are almost pure pigment, without much binder, so they'll stick only to porous surfaces like plaster or Sculptamold.

Select the following colors to start: yellow, red, crimson, light and dark blue, brown, green, and several earth colors including Burnt Sienna. We'll combine these to make realistic brick, rust, and concrete.

Mix the watercolors on a grade-school watercolor palette or any non-porous surface. Squeeze 1/8" of each color onto the palette, and have a shot glass of clean water handy. You'll need several wide, soft brushes, and a folded paper towel to dry them as you paint.

Use watercolor to highlight or add a variation of color to painted plaster surfaces. Use thinned blue to add shadows under rock overhangs and beneath trees in the deep forest. Be careful with this — the color cannot be removed from scenic foam. Add rust stains around signals, bridge footings, and junk piles.

Areas that are constantly damp often have a slight tint of green from moss or algae. These areas include rocks along streams or brooks, waterfront piers, bridge abutments which are always in the shade, and the north side of trees and stumps.

To model this growth, mix 1/8" of green tube watercolor with four or five brushloads of water. Flow the mix onto the appropriate surfaces, being careful not to leave brush marks or sharp edges. The green should just

barely tint the area to which it is applied.

Always evaluate colors after they have dried because they will become less brilliant. If you don't like a color it can be removed with a brush full of clean water and a damp paper towel. Use the paper towel to blot away water and color without disturbing the scenery underneath.

Styrofoam scenery. Styrofoam is a great base for lightweight scenery. It can also be the sole material used to build the benchwork, scenery base, and rocks for dioramas, modules, and portable layouts. It is especially appropriate as a scenery base for portable layouts and modules, and for lift-out sections on permanent layouts.

Extruded Styrofoam comes in large light blue or pink sheets, usually 1" or 2" thick, 2' wide, and 4' or 8' long. It is strong, very light, and resilient enough to withstand considerable handling, even abuse. I once built a display layout from scraps I found at a construction project. It was practically bullet-proof and withstood many a rough trip in the back of my truck.

Another common plastic foam is called "beadboard." This is made by pressing individual beads or "bubbles" of plastic material together to bond them. It's commonly used as insulation in refrigeration equipment, and small molded sections of it are used to pack fragile products and electronic equipment. Because it has little cross-sectional strength, I stack beadboard over a wood or extruded Styrofoam frame.

To build a scenery base with Styrofoam I start by cutting blocks and

stacking them on top of each other to form the rough scenic contours. Use regular woodworking tools, and make the blocks oversize, because the finished contours will be achieved by removing material, not by adding more. Glue the blocks together with white glue or Liquid Nails construction adhesive (sold in caulking-gun tubes for installing paneling), add weights, and let the glue dry overnight. If any of the pieces need to be held in position, insert a long finishing nail through the stack to hold it together.

Special water-base contact cement is available for Styrofoam. It's applied to both surfaces and allowed to dry to a tacky surface. The Styrofoam blocks are mated together for an immediate bond. This adhesive is good for places where the nails won't reach or where there's no room for weights.

After the glue dries and the nails are removed, contour the Styrofoam with a wood rasp, keyhole saw, hacksaw blade, coarse sandpaper, and Stanley Surform tools.

I favor adding a single layer of plaster-soaked paper towels over the foam as a scenic skin, so the contouring need not be exact. Styrofoam is dissolved by all petroleum-base paints and thinners, but the protective layer of plaster-soaked paper towels effectively seals the surface against solvent attack. The water-soluble coloring and texturing methods in this book have no effect on the Styrofoam scenery base, and can be used with or without the plaster skin.

Polyurethane scenery. Several rigid polyurethane products are handy

This scene holds together because there are no strong, bright colors in it. Everything has been weathered with earth tones.

for making lightweight scenery. Foam insulating sealant is a one-part, moisture cure, polyurethane foam dispensed from an aerosol spray can. Similar to sprayed-foam home insulation and the stuff used for flotation in fiberglass or aluminum boats, it contains no formaldehyde and is flame retardant. I've tried several canned products from the hardware store; all exhibit the same characteristics.

Dap Kwik Foam cures tack-free in about 20 minutes and is fully cured in 24 hours. Another brand is Great Stuff, made by Insta-Foam Products, Inc. This is a minimal expanding foam which dries tack-free in about 45 minutes. The big disadvantage to building a lot of scenery with this foam is cost — a relatively expensive 24-ounce can covers only about 2 square feet to a depth of about 2".

Foam insulating sealant is handy for roughing in scenic contours in small areas and making small scenery repairs. I've sprayed it over crumpled newspaper to make low hills and structure foundations and to provide support under sagging cardboard roads. After it sets the newspapers can be removed, leaving a strong, hollow shell. Some practice is needed because the foam expands as it's applied. After it sets it can be cut with a hacksaw blade, hot wire, or hobby knife and shaped into realistic contours.

Note how all the colors in these photos tend toward pastel tones and grays. This subtle homogenizing effect is achieved by adding white, gray, or earth colors to the paint used on every model on the layout, then dulling each color even further

with weathering treatments over the basic paint coat. You can achieve a similar effect by lightly airbrushing existing scenes with thinned Earth paint, but the technique requires restraint: It's altogether too easy to overdo it.

CHAPTER 10

The stains on the ground near this building are Polly S Oily Black applied directly from the bottle, and the coarse sawdust texture under the oil drums was painted brown to represent dead leaves.

These foreground rocks were colored in the usual manner, then dusted with powdered pastel chalks to add depth and interest. I even tried using a little green chalk powder to simulate moss growing in some of the cracks, since this formation is near water.

Mountains in Minutes Polyfoam, a two-part urethane, is sold specifically for making scenery. It takes some getting used to, but produces good results. Equal portions of the two chemicals are mixed and poured onto the scenery base, smoothed, and allowed to expand. The foam hardens in about 5 minutes at 70 degrees, then can be shaped using the same tools as for Styrofoam. Complete instructions are provided by the manufacturer.

Commercial display and model builders apply polyurethane foam with a spray gun. They mound the foam onto a scenery support lined with plastic; after it sets they carve it into hills, rocks, and roads. Large lift-out sections are made by spraying the foam into a hole cut into the layout which has been lined with sheet plastic wrap. The plastic separates the lift-out section from the rest of the scenery and allows easy removal after the foam sets. All scenery construction and detailing is then completed on the lift-out section on the workbench.

Polyfoam is expensive, there's lots of waste, and you don't have nearly the control that you have with plaster. But if weight and durability are the most important considerations, urethane scenery is for you.

Making urethane foam rocks. Perhaps the best use for Polyfoam is making lightweight rock castings for portable layouts. The procedure is the same as for making plaster rocks with one important exception: You must treat the mold with a release agent, and lots of it. I use a heavy spray application of Armor-All or Pledge furniture polish, spraying several coats into the mold and allowing each to dry. This must be done before each casting is made.

Mix equal parts of the polyfoam chemicals and pour them into the treated mold. Swirl the polyfoam around in the mold to cover all surfaces, then allow the foam to expand. The resulting rocks are light, tough, and have reasonably good surface detail. The few small bubbles on the surface of the rock are not noticeable after painting and weathering. The rocks can be carved and shaped, and small surface imperfections can be filled with a bit of Sculptamold on your fingertip.

I've made a few rock castings that were so full of holes that I thought they were useless. (I think the bubbles formed because of moisture left on the surface of the mold by the release

An old shaving brush is handy for applying powdered chalk to broad surfaces such as this dirt road. Brush lightly; too much pressure and the chalk turns shiny.

Here's my pastel weathering equipment: chalk sticks; a file and a coarse sanding block to grind them; two old, very soft brushes; talcum powder; and a tin watercolor tray for mixing the chalk.

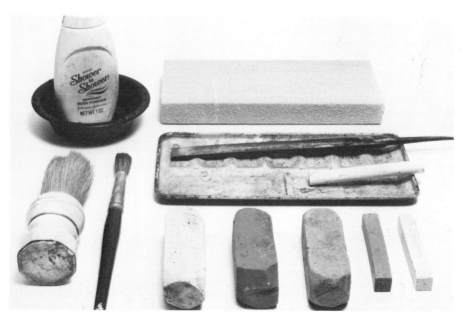

CHAPTER 10

These dramatic rocks on Clarke Dunham's Citibank Station display layout were carved from urethane foam and colored with poster colors.

agent. Be sure the molds are dry before using.) I saved them by making a thin mixture of Durham's Water Putty and brushing it over the surface of the castings. Brush it on thick at first, to fill all the holes. After all the rocks are covered take a stiff-bristled brush and scrub away all the putty on the surface. Wash the brush often in clean water.

Foam rock castings can be molded on the scenery base just like plaster rocks. After filling the mold push it against the scenery and hold it there until after the foam has expanded and cured (about 5 minutes). I place weights along the edges of the mold. If

you don't use weights the expanding foam will lift the mold off of the scenery base, creating a rock casting that looks like a soufflé.

Excess foam can be trimmed with a hobby knife, serrated kitchen knife, or hacksaw blade. Stratified texture can be created by scraping the rock castings with a wire brush, but easy does it! You'll ruin the rocks if you're too energetic.

Mounting and coloring Polyfoam castings. Polyfoam castings made at the workbench can be trimmed and shaped, and the backs scooped out to conform to the scenery contour. When ready to use just fit the castings

One of the first products available for building lightweight scenery was Mountains in Minutes Polyfoam, a two-part expanding polyurethane foam.

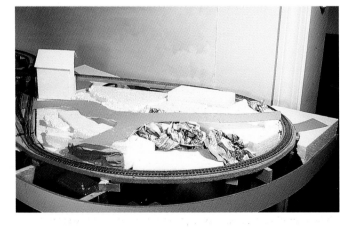

(Left) The support for the polyurethane foam scenery on this portable layout is made of crumpled pieces of newspaper and scraps of Styrofoam beadboard. (Right) Polyurethane insulating foam was sprayed over the supporting base and then allowed to set. A large can of insulating foam will cover about twice the area shown.

CHAPTER 10

together, jigsaw-puzzle style, on the scenery base. Hold them in place with white glue or Liquid Nails. If there are places where the rocks won't stay in place, impale them on a long piece of wire or a finish nail and push it into the scenery until the adhesive sets. Fill gaps with Sculptamold.

Because Polyfoam rocks are not absorbent they must be primed with white or earth-colored latex paint. Follow the techniques described for saving improperly colored rock castings back in Chapter 4.

Rubber rocks. While looking for a rock material that would withstand the punishment of travel on a portable module, I stumbled upon rubber rocks. Easy to make, realistic, and lightweight, they are simply rock molds in reverse.

My experiment started with a product called Flexwax 120. This material is tough and flexible at room temperature, but melts to a honey-like consistency at 120 degrees F. Used by sculptors for making one-time molds such as life masks, it's available from specialty mail-order houses such as Edmund Scientific and Nasco.

I selected several real rocks and lined them up on the workbench, then brushed on a thin coat of Vaseline (Liquid Gold or Pledge furniture polish may also be used). I warmed the Flexwax to 120 degrees, then brushed an even coat over the rock surfaces and followed with more coats to build a mold about 1/4" thick.

While the molds were still pliable and warm to the touch, I carefully removed them from the rock, then trimmed the wax with scissors to remove ragged edges. The scraps were returned to the pot to be used again. I put the molds in my refrigerator to harden.

I removed the molds from the refrigerator and applied a thin coat of latex molding compound (the same stuff we used for making rock molds). After the first coat dried I followed

with two more, and finally with a gauze layer for reinforcement. After the latex dried I removed the wax and returned it to the pot.

Like plaster rock castings, rubber rocks can be painted at the workbench or mounted on the layout and painted there. Apply a bead of Liquid Nails to the rear outer edge of the rock and push it into place. (Be sure to test the adhesive on the back of a scrap of latex before using it on a finished rock — some products will shrivel the latex; most will not.)

I paint rubber rocks with Pactra and Model Master spray enamels. Pactra Flat Light Earth is the base color; over this, aiming down from the top, I mist on Model Master Camouflage Gray. After the base coat dries I finish painting by airbrushing the rock with Badger Air-Opaque colors. These are misted onto the rock to form highlights and shadows.

Ceiling tile rocks. One of the oldest methods for rock strata is stacking broken pieces of fiber ceiling tiles. The result is easy-to-build, believable rocks, which are lightweight, inexpensive, and durable. Several rock faces can be built in less time than it takes to write about it. Painting can make these rocks look like veins of coal, layers of sedimentary shale, or the weather-worn buttes and mesas of the Southwest.

The ceiling tiles are usually 2' by 4', and made from many materials. I like the gray pressed-paper variety. Start by breaking the tile into 3"- or 4"-wide strips, lengthwise. The broken edges, which will become the rock face, should be coarse and ragged. More surface texture can be created by breaking areas with pliers and brushing the face with a wire brush.

Finish shaping the face with a hobby knife. Any of the white ceiling tile surface coating that shows on the rock face should be skived away with a sharp, thin knife. Stack and glue the pieces together on the scenery base.

The excess foam is removed and the scenery shaped using a hacksaw blade. Be prepared to throw away about half of the foam you apply.

Use Sculptamold to fill cracks and gaps and to blend the rocks into the base. After the glue dries a wire brush can be used for additional distressing and to break up strong horizontal lines. Be careful not to remove too much material.

Next, seal the rock face with a heavy application of white or earth latex paint. To smooth away some of the texture and give the rocks an old, weather-beaten look, coat them with a soupy mixture of Durham's Water Putty. Paint the finished rock face using the techniques in Chapter 4.

Lightweight Sculptamold rocks. An easy way to make crumbling, nondescript rocks is with Sculptamold. Mix two parts Sculptamold with one part water to produce a stiff, puttylike mixture. Trowel this onto the scenic base with a butter knife, drawing the knife across the face horizontally to leave a stratified effect. After you've applied all the Sculptamold, use the edge of the knife to smooth away some of the deeper indentations. The workability of Sculptamold can be varied by using more or less water; I like it to slump as it is applied to a vertical surface, so that deep indentations are partially filled in.

Sculptamold can also be cast in latex molds to make lightweight rocks.

Here's another example of a temporary live area. Before I settled on the octagonal novelty station for Taft Lake on my C & D R layout (left), I tried several other stations there, including the one (above) that eventually wound up at Dead River.

Jim Kelly built these convincing rock strata from layers of broken acoustic ceiling tile.

Although these rocks don't have the razor-sharp detail of molded plaster, they look good, especially where weight is a major consideration.

Mix Sculptamold so that it is "juicy," but not soupy (it must have a loose consistency to flow into the details of the mold). Fill the mold, and let it set for about an hour, until the Sculptamold starts to set. Then apply the mold to the scenery base, pushing the edges to seat them as close to the base as possible. When dry remove the mold and wash it immediately to remove traces of dried Sculptamold.

To mold rocks on the workbench, mix Sculptamold to the consistency of peanut butter, then push the mixture into the rock molds with your fingers. Apply it no more than 1/4" thick. Let it set 24 hours and carefully remove the castings. After removing the molds you can bake the Sculptamold rocks in a 200-degree F. oven to dry them.

Color these rocks just as you would plaster. The colors take longer to dry than on plaster, but do not become lighter as they do. The resulting rocks are lightweight and strong.

Showing off your layout. Now let's look at a few things you can do to display your railroad to best advantage. This requires a little showmanship: Viewing your layout should be like going on a ride at Disneyland, where every element in the presentation directs attention to the action.

The first thing viewers should see when they visit your layout is the railroad, without any distracting competition. The railroad should be lighter than the other things in the room so viewers will be drawn to it, and so their attention will remain there. Painting the edges of the railroad a darker shade of earth than you used on the scenery will make the scenery seem lighter. If you favor paneling around the edge of the layout, choose a dark color without texture or anything else that will call attention to it.

I've skirted several layouts with inexpensive burlap held in place with Velcro fasteners. This effectively hides the benchwork and the storage area beneath the railroad, preventing visitors from checking out my collection of junk instead of looking at the railroad above it.

Other things that help show off the railroad are a dark painted or carpeted floor, valances to hide lighting fixtures, and dimmers for the lighting. Important scenes on your layout can be highlighted with small spotlights to draw viewers to them. Be careful that such spotlights cast shadows in only one direction, because double or con-

flicting shadows are unrealistic and a sure giveaway. As mentioned in Chapter 8 there should never be any shadows cast on the backdrop.

Questions and answers

Q: I don't own an airbrush, but would like to give my scenery an all-over dusty look. Any suggestions?
A: Before I tried an airbrush, I toned down scenery with a mixture of one part 1:1 earth latex paint and five parts water. Flow this greatly thinned earth onto grass and ballast; it looks bright when you apply it, but dries to a realistic dusty color. This same thinned paint can be sprayed onto foliage with a pump-type sprayer, but as with airbrushing, be careful not to overdo it!
Q: How should I build movable hills and mountains for my live scenery area?
A: Start with a large block of Styrofoam, shaping it with a saw, knife, wood rasp, or Surform tool. Place rock molds around the edges of the hill, near the base, and cover the rest of the block with Earth and texture.

I add lichen on top of the hill and around the edge; the lichen on the bottom hides the joint between the hill and the rest of the scenery. If you build the hills with different contours front and back they can be turned to make different scenes.

Q: What's the best way to store leftover latex paint and acrylic tube colors?

A: I keep leftover latex paint in clean glass jars with screw lids. Peanut butter jars with plastic lids are the best because the lids can be removed easily. I've tried coffee cans, but they rust after three or four months and discolor the paint.

Pour the paint into the jars, wipe the rims clean, add a tablespoon of water, and screw on the lid. The water will replace any that evaporates. Label each jar with all the information about the paint inside, including dilution, and the storage date. I have used latex paint stored for 5 or 6 years; all it needed was thorough mixing.

Store tube acrylic colors in a large glass jar with a tight-fitting lid. Add a little water to the jar to keep the tubes from drying up. Before sealing the jar, check that the cap of each tube is screwed on completely and that there is no dried paint on the threads. I have had tube acrylics stored this way last for more than 10 years.

Q: I have several places where the track is hard to reach, and I want to add access hatches, but I'm concerned about hiding the edges. What's the best way to do this?

A: Styrofoam is your best bet for the lift-out hatches: It's light, easy to work, and will stand up to handling. Taper the access opening — wider at the top — so the liftout will drop into it snugly.

Try to hide the seams with a natural scenery line. The easiest way is to plan the edge so there is something slightly higher in front of it: a fence, a row of buildings, a tree line, or a hedgerow.

Where the seam cannot be hidden, cover it with a band of commercial

Sculptamold colored with latex earth paint and "slumped" into place makes effective crumbling rocks. Little carving is required.

grass mat held in place with Velcro strips. Add a few small pieces of lichen to hide visible gaps, and don't lose sleep over any edges that can't be seen from normal viewing angles.

Q: I tried spreading two-part foam over a scenery base but it stuck to the stick and made a mess. Any suggestions?

A: The "pros" use a long thin icicle as the spreading tool. The ice won't stick to the foam and the cold retards the foaming action.

Make ice wands in the freezer using a trough of tin foil molded around a broom handle. To use, peel away the foil and wrap a towel around one end for a handle.

Q: How can I make dark-brown Polyfoam scenery instead of the light brown color?

A: Add earth-colored tempera pigments (these are finely ground, water-soluble paints usually used in grade-school art classes) to the urethane "B" component. Stir in the pigment thoroughly, then mix with equal parts of the "A" component.

CHAPTER 10

Modeling the changing seasons

Model railroads usually portray summer. We build scenery with green trees, yellow-green grass, and blue water under a blue sky — perhaps because summer is the season we'd most like to be reminded of. But the changing seasons add color and variety to scenery. Fall foliage on the hillsides and snow on the higher elevations will add touches of interest and brightness to your layout for surprisingly little extra work.

The first task is easy: Pick a season. There's a complete spectrum,

from late summer, with its dying grass, yellowing aspens, and reddish-brown oak leaves; to autumn, when the first frost turns the grasses straw yellow and the leaves turn from green to yellow to deep red; to winter, when the north wind blows and Mother Nature colors herself brown, with snow in the air and on the ground. The choice is up to you, but don't discount the idea of modeling two or more seasons on different parts of your layout.

Realistic fall colors. There's no secret to modeling fall, but there is one

rule: Use a variety of colors. Mix reds, yellows, oranges, and browns, and be sure to include summertime green as well. The green provides the perfect counterpoint to the brilliant hues, making them seem all the brighter.

Sprinkle green trees with an assortment of yellows and reds to show the onset of fall. Make a few trees solid brown, with a fleck or two of dark red to indicate that they've completed their color change. Use the tree-making techniques described in Chapter 6, substituting fall sawdust, foam, and

CHAPTER 11

Real railroads operate year-round, so why should all our scenery depict summertime? A few layouts have been set in autumn, and one or two included snow scenes, but modeling the starkness of winter remains largely a new frontier in scenery building.

(Below) MODEL RAILROADER's N scale Burlington Northern is ablaze with fall colors, as is Bob Hayden's HOn2½ C&DR Ry. (above). Modeling fall is easy; you only have to change the vegetation colors you use.

flock colors. A wide variety of colorful foliage foams is available. Don't forget to add bare trees made from sagebrush twigs, dried weeds, and cast armatures, with fallen leaves on the ground below them.

While driving across the country in late autumn I was impressed by the variety of grass colors. It ranges from bright straw-yellow through yellow-brown to dead, greenish-yellow. The most pronounced color was a straw-gold found in meadows and along railroad lines.

Fall grass and weed textures can be made at home or purchased. Woodland Scenics makes several shades of yellow-brown turf and field grass. Timber Products has fall foliage, ground cover, and weeds in realistic dead grass and leaf shades. AMSI's Flex-Turf, which consists of ground foam texture on a cloth backing, is available in Hillside Tan, appropriate for fall ground cover.

MODEL RAILROADER photo: A. L. Schmidt

A variety of colors is the key to modeling realistic fall foliage. It's important to mix green trees and pine trees with the fall trees for believability.

A rainbow of fall scenic foam colors is available from several scenery manufacturers.

Beautiful foreground fall trees can be made by adding red or orange scenic foam over twigs or commercial tree armatures like this sumac tip. Don't forget the bits of colored foam under the tree to represent fallen leaves.

The leaf colors are just beginning to turn on this section of Bob Hayden's layout. Note how the green provides a counterpoint to the brilliant autumn hues.

Modeling winter. I'm from New England, and I'm fond of winter. Nothing compares with the stillness of a cold morning after a snowfall. The air smells fresh and clean, sounds are muffled, and the snow forms a white blanket over the countryside.

Bringing winter to a model railroad presents formidable challenges, the greatest of which is making realistic snow. We need a white substance that is easy to apply, won't yellow, and sparkles. Substances that sparkle and are in scale are rare indeed; in fact, I've had to compromise: Most of the materials I've used to simulate snow provide a good overall effect without the sparkle.

So you won't have to repeat my experiments, the materials I've used for snow include plaster (both wet and dry), flour, cornstarch, talcum powder, salt, sugar, and baking soda. Although all worked well for one-shot photos (the salt looked great, because it *does* sparkle), none, except plaster, should be used for permanent scenes.

Winter scenes require advanced planning. You can't just stage a snowstorm on an already-scenicked layout, because if snow materials are applied over green texture the dye will bleed through to the surface, tinting the snow a sick green. Existing scenery must be sealed with a coat of full-strength matte medium, white paint, or both.

In one respect building winter scenery is less work than modeling summer. If you start from scratch, the base for a permanent snow scene need only be completed as far as the plaster-covered paper towel stage. Smooth the wet plaster, then model patches of

CHAPTER 11

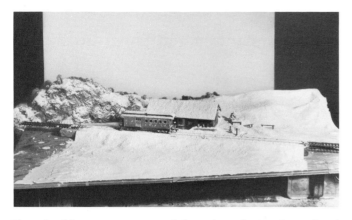

To make this temporary scene I dusted on plaster, then misted it with water. The resulting snow looked more like sandpaper than freshly fallen snow, so I added a coat of loose plaster to make the convincing snow shown in the color photo.

bare ground by gluing sawdust or foam in place. Before applying snow, paint the patches with Polly S Earth grayed with equal parts of Engine Black and Reefer White.

Acrylic snow. One of my snow scenes is built on a Sculptamold base. I started by troweling loose Sculptamold over the scenic shell, building up snowdrifts and piles of plowed snow. I sprayed the Sculptamold with water and smoothed the surface.

After a couple of false starts I came up with a snow formula based on Titanium White acrylic. It provides a hard, semigloss white surface that is flexible and easy to clean. It can be used over any white scenery base.

Combine the ingredients listed in the recipe box and brush the mixture over a plaster or Sculptamold base. The snow mix can be troweled on thick to make windblown drifts and piled up to look like freshly shoveled snow. To fix areas of the snow surface that don't look right, spray them with wet water and smooth them with a palette knife or Popsicle stick. Another way to smooth the surface is with the airstream from an airbrush hose. Move the hose in a circular pattern — in addition, the air will remove air bubbles trapped near the surface.

On trackwork, carefully brush the snow mixture over the ties, and clean rail tops and flangeways immediately after application. The snow will skin over and set overnight, then dry completely in about three days with only a little shrinkage. Don't touch it while it's drying! If you do, you'll ruin the smooth surface.

Marble dust snow. Marble dust is a relatively new snow material. I've conducted several experiments with it, starting with a standard white scenery base.

The dust is an extremely fine, flourlike white powder, so fine it can't be applied using a standard shaker jar. Instead, use a coffee can with a piece of nylon stocking stretched over

the top. (See Chapter 5 for a photo.) Wear a respirator or filter mask to keep dust out of your lungs.

Sprinkle the marble dust as evenly as possible, holding the can on its side as you shake it. Application is slow, but you can precisely control where the dust falls. I sprinkled marble dust to form small drifts of newly fallen snow, then evaluated my results. The snow looked white, not the vibrant, sparkling white of freshly fallen snow, but the appearance of sifted flour.

Then I ran into trouble. Our standard water-soluble bonding technique of wet water followed by matte medium spray won't work with marble dust. It repels even wet water, which simply balls up, and spraying hard just blows the dust away. It was back

to the drawing board (and the vacuum cleaner).

My second marble dust snow-making attempt started by following the instructions provided by one manufacturer. I mixed marble dust with dilute matte medium (1 part matte medium, 3 parts water) to form a stiff paste, then applied this over the scenery base. I worked the snow with a wet Popsicle stick and plastic bag. This worked, but it was hard to get the snow surface smooth.

I got better results by mixing marble dust with full-strength gloss medium and applying it like paint. In some places three or four applications were required to build up the desired depth. As the mixture started to dry I smoothed the snow with a wet finger until I liked the contours. To complete

MODEL RAILROADER: Jim Hediger

Brian Holtz used molding plaster snow at Winter Park on his HO D&RGW layout. He sprinkled the plaster in place, then misted water on to bond it.

ACRYLIC SNOW

Combine equal parts of the following:

    Acrylic gel (full strength) or gloss medium
    Acrylic modeling paste
    Titanium White artist's tube acrylic

Mix thoroughly and apply with a brush. Leftover mix will keep in a tightly sealed container. Allow extra time for this mixture to dry. Don't test it with your finger; instead use a toothpick, and poke it in an inconspicuous place.

COMMERCIAL SNOW TEXTURES

Marble dust:

    Builders in Scale
    P.O. Box 441432
    Aurora, CO 80044

    AMSI No. A8L 900 snow
    AMSI Scale Model Supplies
    P.O. Box 750638
    Petaluma, CA 94975

Snow crystals (plastic glitter):

    Vintage Reproductions
    Box 7098
    Colorado Springs, CO 80933

Powdered foam plastic:

    Noch No. 875 snow
    Noch GmbH
    D-7988 Wagen im Allgau
    Germany

    Raritan Valley Scenic Accents
    P.O. Box 754
    Neshanic Station, NJ 08853-0754

    Parts Depot No. WW10 snowflakes
    VLS
    Lone Star Industrial Park
    811 Lone Star Drive
    O'Fallon, MO 63366

A few of the new products for making snow. Shown are three grades of fine plastic glitter, and two brands of marble dust.

the effect and add a little sparkle I squirted a few puffs of Vintage Reproductions snow crystals. These fine, glitter-like plastic powders come in pump bellows dispensers. They're best for adding highlights and iridescent sparkle to snow made with other materials

The results with this method looked good and were predictable, and the gloss medium held everything in place. You can't get the same powdery look as by sprinkling on the marble dust dry, but the results are controllable and permanent.

My best results with marble dust were obtained by first puddling matte medium onto the scenery base with an eyedropper, then sprinkling the dry powder into it. White glue, diluted 1:1 with water, also works as the adhesive. When the glue dries, vacuum away the excess dust, then apply more glue, more dust, and repeat until you have contours that you like. Finish by vacuuming up stray marble dust to keep it out of locomotive mechanisms and off the track.

Foam plastic snow. The newest snow material I've found is finely shredded plastic foam. I don't know what this material was originally intended for, but it makes good snow — and it's easier to apply than marble dust because it can be bonded with standard water-soluble techniques. Although the plastic powder is light, with care you can mist and bond it without scattering it everywhere. Like the other materials it must be used over a white base. Add sparkle with one of the Vintage Reproductions glitter materials.

Snow on structures. I've built several snow-covered structures, and the techniques that work best are also the simplest. Use the acrylic snow formula, adding a few drops of water to keep it brushable. Start by painting snow onto all raised surfaces using a small, round-pointed brush, then coat the roof and cover the tops of all protruding details. Make large drifts with Sculptamold and brush on snow mix after it sets.

On window sills, door ledges, and other protruding surfaces where build-

The snow in this winter scene is a mixture of gloss medium, acrylic modeling paste, and Titanium White artist's tube acrylic, the formula in the recipe box. This snow can be brushed on, troweled on, and even heaped up to represent piles of windblown snow. It's my favorite material for permanent snow scenes.

CHAPTER 11

An early winter snow storm has dusted Summit on Bob Hayden's layout, producing a bright spot and an instant center of interest. The snow here was made by sprinkling Noch plastic snow over existing green scenery.

ing up depth is not important, you can use Titanium White acrylic straight from the tube.

After the acrylic snow dries it can't be removed. Unless the building is protected from the snow mixture with a layer of plastic wrap or rubber cement, or the snow is made removable, your model can't be changed back to summer.

Realistic ice and icicles. To make ice, mix equal parts of Vintage Reproductions snow crystals, marble dust, and full-strength gloss medium. Brush this along the edges of waterways and around boulders and banks, where the water moves slowly and ice forms first. Try adding a drop of blue acrylic color to the mixture to add depth.

Model the ice that forms as water oozes from cracks and fissures in rock faces by generously applying this mixture. Brush downward to obtain a waterfall effect. Puddles can be painted onto flat scenery with this mixture. Add several drops of blue-green acrylic color to simulate trapped air bubbles.

An important winter finishing touch is icicles hanging from eaves, gutters, signs, and spouts. I use acrylic gloss gel medium for modeling ice. Available at art supply stores, gloss gel has the same properties as gloss medium but is thicker, about the consistency of marshmallow topping. It can be brushed or troweled onto any surface; when wet it looks like soft white meringue, but it dries to a clear, glass-like surface. Gel holds its shape, is soft and flexible, and won't run or sag when applied to vertical surfaces.

Clear nylon toothbrush bristles make excellent icicles. Cut the bristles to random lengths, then pick up individual bristles with tweezers and dip

WINTER BACKDROP COLORS

All colors are flat latex wall paint or artist's tube acrylics.

Most-Distant Gray:
        3 cups white
        1 cup sky blue (see Chapter 8)
        4" Mars Black acrylic

Winter hills:
        1 cup Most-Distant Gray
        1 cup white
        1/4" Mars Black

Winter pines:
        1 tablespoon Most-Distant Gray
        1/4" Mars Black
        2" Hooker's Green

Bare trees:
        1 tablespoon Most-Distant Gray
        1/4" Mars Black
        2" Burnt Umber

This plastic water tank has been "winterized." The ice on the side of the tank is gloss medium with a touch of acrylic green added for color. The snow over the doors and windows is painted using my acrylic snow formula, and the icicles are toothbrush bristles covered with acrylic gloss gel.

Painting a winter backdrop is more of a challenge than its summer counterpart because you use only a few colors. The nearest trees on this backdrop are just dabs of grayed Burnt Umber placed along the ridge lines.

each in gloss gel. Place each icicle against the building overhang, using the gel as glue. Work the blob of gel with a small brush, making sure each icicle hangs straight down. After the icicles dry, brush more gel over each to give it a long, tapered look. If you want, flow gel into gutters and down the side of the building to represent water that has backed up and frozen.

Mass-produce icicles by spreading white glue on a piece of plastic sandwich bag taped to a flat surface. Dribble the glue back and forth over the plastic in thin ribbons. After it dries carefully peel the glue off the plastic and cut wedge-shaped icicles with a sharp hobby knife (the shape helps keep the icicles from curling). Glue the icicles to the model with white glue and coat with gloss medium.

A dramatic application for ice is on the side of a wood water tank. Water seeps between the tank staves on winter nights, and when it hits the cold air it freezes. More seepage and freezing forms a large buildup of ice down the side of the tank.

Model this giant icicle by brushing gloss gel down the side of the tank. Minerals in the water can tint the ice in a rainbow of spectacular colors, which you can model by adding small amounts of tube acrylic colors to the gloss gel, along with a little Titanium White. Build the ice up, layer by layer, until you have the desired colors and thickness.

Winter trees. Another challenge in modeling winter is building convincing leafless trees. Suitable growths from nature are hard to find because most branch structures are not fine enough. (Evergreen trees, of course, can be used as they come from the box.)

Good bare trees can be made from strands of twisted wire with carved water-putty trunks. Dried sumac tips and sagebrush twigs make outstanding foreground trees.

To add snow to the branches, stick each tree in a block of Styrofoam so it will stand upright. Spray with matte medium and sprinkle the branches with marble dust. After this sets, re-wet with matte medium and apply another coat. Seal the marble dust in place with a fine mist of matte medium. Treat pine trees the same way.

Winter weeds and shrubs need only be colored gray, brown, or tan; they can be small twigs or carpet fiber. Add a touch of brown or Burnt Sienna to warm the dead grass color. Model puddles and ice patches with 5-minute epoxy or use the water-modeling techniques in Chapter 7.

Winter backdrops. Painting a winter backdrop is yet another challenge, mostly because deciduous trees are bare, and painting them takes practice. The base for a snow-covered winter scene is the same "most-distant gray" color we used for summer hills in Chapter 7. Use it straight from the bottle for the farthest snow-covered hills.

The next closer color, "winter hills," is lightened most-distant gray, and each closer color is made from the last one by adding more white to it. Carry this almost to pure white with just a touch of gray-blue next to the three-dimensional scenery.

Paint tree lines using a stiff 1" brush. Before applying the winter pines color, define the ridge lines of distant hills with 1" masking tape. Dab in the rough tree shapes, with the

bottoms of the trees just touching the top edge of the tape, then remove the tape.

Make bare trees by lightly pushing the tip of the 1" brush against the backdrop. Deciduous trees should have a see-through quality not found in the pines. To highlight them, mix a little white into the bare-tree color and lightly dab it onto the treetops. Mist the completed backdrop with white to soften and blend the colors.

Cold lighting. To show off your snow scene to best advantage it should be illuminated differently from the rest of the layout. Use a flat, shadowless white light source over the scene, such as a two-tube fluorescent fixture with a frosted plastic diffuser.

To cast blue light into the shadows add a small blue floodlight 6' to 8' from the scene. These floodlights are sold in hardware stores for decorative illumination. Move the blue floodlight until there's just a hint of color in shadow areas. You may have to fashion simple light baffles from sheet aluminum so blue light falls only on the snow scene.

Questions and answers

Q: I sprinkled plaster over a section of my layout to model winter. I sprayed water on it to bond it in place, but this left a pockmarked look. How can I make the snow smooth again?
A: Brush the plaster with the acrylic snow mixture. It will both smooth and seal the surface. If there are spots you can't reach with a brush, soak them with wet water and sprinkle on more plaster. It will absorb the water and set where it fell, without the dimpled look.

CHAPTER 11

Repairing and rejuvenating scenery

Your model railroad takes a beating even when you're not working on it. Dust, lint, and cobwebs settle on horizontal surfaces, colors fade, and details are knocked loose. This chapter is about ways to prevent some of this damage, and techniques to spruce up tired scenery.

One way to refurbish your layout, of course, would be to start over, replacing trees, buildings, and scenic texture wholesale to give the layout a fresh look. If you choose this approach, simply turn to the front of this book and start reading! If not, stay here and read on.

Let's start by looking at what causes the damage.

Enemy No. 1: Dust. Dust is the worst enemy of a model railroad, as everyone who has spent hours cleaning track will attest. Before we discuss ways to remove dust, let's talk about

Brown scenic foam (above) is the first indication that your scenery needs to be refurbished. The change is subtle and gradual. After cleaning and recoloring (left) the same area is fresh and almost new.

Cleaning day! Start by removing large debris with a soft brush (1). This will reveal loose details, which can be picked off before they go roaring into the vaccum cleaner. Remove dust and loose dirt using a brush nozzle on the vacuum cleaner (2). Wash waterways and roads with soap and water (3). Gently scrub the surface, then mop up the water with a soft cloth. Tight areas around details and under bridges are cleaned with wet cotton swabs (4). Use plenty of them — they get dirty fast!

ways to prevent some of it from reaching the layout in the first place.

My railroad was started without giving any thought to preparing the room, and I've paid for that lack of forethought many times over. Like most, the layout just kind of happened, then grew and grew. By the time I noticed how dirty the layout was getting, it was too late to put up a ceiling and seal the cement floor.

If you're between layouts, or haven't started building, now is the time to think about dust and dirt — and to do something about them. If you're building in a basement, garage, or other unfinished space, seal the cement floor with several thick coats of paint. This will hold down the cement dust and make the floor easier to clean.

The area over the layout is even more important than the floor. It should be insulated, then finished with sheetrock, tile, or another dust-proof ceiling material. I learned this the hard way. Before I put up a ceiling I watched a continuous snowfall of dirt filtering down onto my layout as my children played on the floor above.

One modeler I visited put up a separate ceiling for his layout. It was suspended below the room ceiling, and held the layout lighting. He attached sheet-plastic side curtains to the outer edges of the layout ceiling, and rolled the curtains down to keep dust off the layout between work and operating sessions.

A similar approach is to add removable corner posts to the layout and drape sheet plastic over them when the layout is not being used. Others have used Velcro to attach cloth side curtains between ceiling and layout.

Enemy No. 2: Ultraviolet light. Like most modelers I have fluorescent work lights over my layout. They are easy to install, produce little heat, and are economical to operate. Their biggest drawback is that they produce ultraviolet light, which, just like ultraviolet light from the sun, causes fading.

The fading is proportional to how much the lights are on, and the first item on the layout to lose its color is scenic foam. After several months of exposure to fluorescent light bright green foam turns gradually to yellow-brown. The effect is most pronounced in photographs: Ektachrome slide film sees the foam as a dull green-brown, even if it's a pleasing green to your eye.

One way to minimize fading is to wrap fluorescent tubes in UV filter material. Most clear plastics will filter UV, so the low-cost solution is to wrap a sheet of clear plastic around each tube and tape it in place. Museum-quality UV bulb jackets are available from Solar Screen (see address list, page 2). These slip over each tube and are fastened with clear tape. They are also available in colors for special effects.

Why not forsake fluorescents altogether, and use incandescent lighting instead? The light they provide is warmer, but incandescents are inefficient: It can take dozens of 50-watt bulbs to light a medium-sized layout. The bulbs are expensive to install and operate, and they produce a lot of heat, which may or may not be a blessing, depending on the temperature of

CHAPTER 12

The two-part epoxy water below this dam was badly scratched from years of dust. I cleaned it, then resurfaced the water with acrylic gloss medium.

your layout room. I use incandescent fixtures only for accent lighting.

Cleaning and touch-up. In the end, dust is unavoidable. To remove it, vacuum the layout regularly, preferably with an industrial-strength shop vacuum, and give it a complete cleaning at least twice a year.

Start by removing all loose items — locomotives, rolling stock, structures, and details like automobiles — from the layout. Take these out of the layout room (preferably outdoors) and clean them where the dust won't just wind up back on the railroad.

Then wheel out the vacuum cleaner. Keep the hose nozzle away from live scenery areas, and don't touch the nozzle to water, or you'll scratch it. Hold the nozzle 2" to 3" above the scenery, and tape a piece of nylon stocking over the end to keep figures and loose details from being sucked into the bag. Use a large soft brush or brush-type nozzle to loosen dust and dirt. The bristles may loosen some of the scenic foam and loose details too, so be careful.

After vacuuming, check for spots where bare plaster shows or the texture has been removed. Touch up these areas with a dab of latex paint and a pinch of texture.

Cleaning water. Waterways are first to show the effects of dust and dirt. Use a soft cloth to remove loose

surface dirt. The cloth won't revive the shine and sparkle — to bring it back you'll either have to wash the surface, or if very dirty, wash and resurface it.

To wash the water, mix dish detergent and warm water and apply it with a wide, soft brush. Once the detergent solution loosens the surface crud, wipe it away with a clean soft cloth. You'll be surprised how much dirt you'll find on the cloth.

It may take several cleanings before all the grime is removed. Use cotton swabs to clean around rocks, pilings, and other details. After the water surface dries, vacuum it again to remove loose texture particles and lint. Water surfaces can be waxed after cleaning (just like your car), to renew the shine.

Repairing scratched water. Sometimes cleaning and polishing won't do the trick. On my layout several water areas were badly scuffed from gritty dust and an occasional visit from the family cat. Once glossy and sparkling, the two-part epoxy surface was matte and dull. Gloss medium is an excellent choice for revitalizing "tired" water surfaces. I cleaned the water thoroughly, then applied a layer of gloss medium. Waves, ripples, and other details can be duplicated as on the original surface, or added where they didn't exist before.

Repair badly damaged water with

Old lichen can be revived and recolored while it is in place on the layout with a solution of glycerine, alcohol, and colored inks in a spray bottle (top). Keep the spray from unwanted areas with a cardboard mask. (Above) The treated lichen is brighter and greener and looks fresh and clean once again.

another application of the original surface material. Polyester resin water calls for another layer of resin, epoxy for epoxy, and so forth.

Dust collects everywhere, but it is most noticeable on two surfaces: roofs and roads. Treat both with the techniques used for cleaning water. Vacuum the surface, being careful not to knock off detail, then gently wash with a soft brush and warm, sudsy water. Dry it with a soft cloth, soft brush, or cotton swabs.

Reviving dead lichen. Lichen will eventually dry out, no matter how well it was processed. Dry lichen is so brittle that you can't touch it without it crumbling to powder, so it can't be removed from the layout and reprocessed. One approach is to spray it with a solution of glycerine and water, which works — slowly. Most of the glycerine isn't absorbed by the lichen; instead, it runs off and soaks into the surrounding texture.

Ethylene glycol (auto antifreeze) supposedly has some of the same chemical characteristics as glycerine, so I tried it on lichen, but the fix was only temporary. The antifreeze made the lichen soft, but it dried out again after about three months.

After lots of experimenting I formulated a spray that revives and recolors lichen in one shot. Combine 1½ cups glycerine, 1½ cups rubbing alcohol, and about 2 tablespoons of coloring. (I opted for a liquid coloring agent, fearing that anything solid would clog the spray nozzle.)

The two coloring agents that work are acetate ink and Badger Air-Opaque colors. The ink is available in stationery stores — it's for drawing on clear acetate — and the Air-Opaque colors can be found in hobby shops. Both are highly concentrated, so use the formula in the recipe box as a starting point and adjust it to suit your needs. I add 1 tablespoon green and 1 tablespoon yellow to 1 pint of the alcohol-and-glycerine solution.

Spray the solution on the lichen with a pump-type bottle. The results are instant: The lichen is colored and softened in about a minute, and the color seems to be permanent. Dry lichen not on the layout can be revived by soaking it in the solution, then drying it on newspaper overnight.

I have lichen on my layout that's more than 20 years old. It's been reprocessed or revived several times and is still soft, bright, and clean. Heck, it may last longer than I do!

Saving mildewed lichen. My basement, where the first Carrabasset & Dead River layout was built, is about 200 yards from the Atlantic Ocean. It gets damp, particularly in summertime. This provides a perfect environment for a variety of fluffy white mildew that I found literally taking over the railroad one summer.

Sunlight and fresh air would have solved the problem, but it's hard to pipe sunlight down into the basement. The answer turned out to be a large dehumidifier, which holds down the dampness, circulates the air, and prevents mildew from growing. But I

Recolor faded grass and and tree foliage with rubbing alcohol and ink, or Badger's Air-Opaque colors. It can be applied with a brush, airbrush, or pump sprayer.

didn't know that when the problem occurred, and I had to do something right away, or be faced with replacing an awful lot of expensive lichen.

Thankfully, the answer came in a spray can. I treated the lichen with a fine spray of Lysol disinfectant, which made quick work of the fungus, with little mess.

Before and after. (Left) This small scene shows about ten years of neglect. The water is dirty, the grass is faded, and the building needs a good cleaning. (Right) What a difference clean water and bright grass make. The small pine trees were sprayed with Floquil Pullman Green, and the building and details were revived with a liberal application of the black India-ink wash.

Recolor trees in place using spray paint and a cardboard mask. The cardboard is folded in the middle and has a notch that fits around the tree trunk. This keeps overspray away from grass, structures, and backdrop.

Freshen up details with an India-ink wash. After the black dries the details can be dry-brushed with Polly S Reefer White.

After removing everything from the layout that I could, I vacuumed thoroughly, mostly because the layout needed a good cleaning anyway. Using rags and scrap cardboard to shield structures and other permanent details, I gave the lichen a once-over with the Lysol spray. While the lichen was wet with spray I gently wiped the tops with a soft cloth, removing most of the growth. The disinfectant dries quickly, and leaves the layout smelling pretty good, too. The last step was to clean the track.

I had to use this treatment twice (until I figured out that I needed a dehumidifier), but it had no ill effects on the lichen or surrounding scenery. The lichen was treated in 1976 and remains green and pliable today.

Recoloring tired scenery. Most of the scenery on my layout has been recolored at one time or another. I did this so photos would not show the effects of age and fading. Start by adding at least a little fresh scenic foam. Wet the scenery, sprinkle on the foam, re-wet, and bond the foam in place with dilute matte medium applied with an eyedropper.

After the matte medium dries, color the foam with a spray made from rubbing alcohol and dye. Add 2 tablespoons of green acetate ink or Air-Opaque green to a pint of rubbing alcohol. Another spray can be made from 1 part Polly S Grass Green thinned with 4 parts water and several drops of detergent. After recoloring, add more fresh foam and bond it in place with matte medium.

Badger Air-Opaque colors can be used to recolor tree foliage, rocks, bare earth, and roads. I've obtained the best results using an airbrush. The trick is to recolor everything in batches: Mix a rock color and spray all the rocks, mix a tree foliage color and spray all the foliage, and so on. The colors I found most useful are Green, Lime Green, Yellow Green, Warm Yellow, and Yellow.

Air-Opaque colors are ideal for reviving faded trees. Mix several variations of green, then spray the bottoms of trees with the darker colors and the tops with the yellow tints. (If you don't have an airbrush you can use these colors with a pump-type spray bottle.) Make a cardboard mask by cutting a slot in an L-shaped sheet of cardboard to catch the overspray. Slide the slot around the trunk of the tree so that color will strike only the foliage.

Mix Air-Opaque color 1:1 with water right in the airbrush cup, then go at it. The Badger paints dry flat about 15 minutes after application, and while they'll adhere to most porous surfaces, they won't stick to shiny surfaces like water.

Repainting detail in place. We finish, as you might expect, with the small details. These gather dust like everything else, and the easiest way to revive their colors is a light application of black India-ink wash. This both washes away dirt and restores depth to the shadows. After the black wash dries, dry-brush a few highlights with white acrylic or Polly S paint, then put the vacuum cleaner away and enjoy your clean and revitalized layout!

10/96

Index

Boldface number entries refer to formula or technique boxes.